A

Remarkable Journey

EXPERIENCES FROM THE LIFE
AND
MINISTRY
OF

Richard Berry Whitaker

A
Remarkable
Journey
EXPERIENCES FROM THE LIFE
AND
MINISTRY
OF
Richard Berry Whitaker

ISBN-13:978-1478271048
ISBN-10:1478271043
© 2013 2nd Edition
Cover Photo: Mūsa Bridge, Bauska Latvia
Type-Editing & Cover Design by:
Michael Barlow (contact@michaelbarlow.info)
Additional Editing by Judith Naegle (judithnaegle55@hotmail.com)

CONTENTS

The Early Years

A Street Soldier

CONTENTS

A Long, Dark Tunnel

The Power of Discernment

Tithing

A Sacred Responsibility

In the Presence of Prophets

Serving in the Kingdom

Angels of Darkness

The Ministering of Angels

Beyond the Veil

Missionary Experiences

President's Interviews

Personal Revelation

Rebecca Ann Whitaker

Memorial Services

Whitakerism's

THE EARLY YEARS

On Stage

Some believe that I am all work and no play. That is not true. If I had not entered the world of law enforcement, I probably would have pursued a career in music or in the entertainment industry, not only because of my family background, but also because of my experience in radio, motion pictures and television. Let's go back to my early days on radio. And I mean early days.

It was 1948. I was four and one half years old and Art Linkletter had a new radio program called "House Party." I was in Kindergarten and attending Monlux Grammar School in North Hollywood, California. My first teacher was a pretty young blond, at least as I can remember, named Mrs. See. One day, the producers of the radio show came to our school and asked for one student from each grade to be on the show. My teacher chose me.

When the big day came, we were picked up by a chauffeur driven black limousine and taken to the CBS Radio Studios in Hollywood, California. Inside the studio, we were escorted onto the stage where I sat on the far left end. In front of us sat the audience.

Art Linkletter started with the oldest kids and asked them the questions for which he became famous. Then came my turn.

"Richard, what do you want to be when you grow up?"

"I want to be a horse doctor."

Whatever else was said, I cannot recollect, but I clearly remember a few of the gifts we each received. Does anyone remember the old style army flashlight that had a lens attached at a right angle? Well, we each received that type of flashlight, except that ours were made of a special glow in the dark material. Now that I think of it, it was probably either radio-active or contained a whopping amount of lead!

We also received some 78 rpm records, and then they took us to lunch at the Brown Derby. Not bad for a kid who just started grammar school.

Like so many other little children, the first day of school found me not feeling quite sure about the whole experience, so rather than going it alone, I took my large, red metal, fire truck. It was as big as I was and required that I cradle it with both arms wrapped securely around it.

All went well until Roger Zombek, the kid who lived behind us, made fun of me because I brought my fire engine to school. Was I going to sit and take that? No! So when Mrs. See wasn't looking, "little" Richard Berry packed up his fire truck and walked out of the room, out the school gate and trudged up the street, my blond hair blowing in the wind and my fire truck held snuggly in front of my chest.

When Mrs. See realized she was missing one of her troops, the panic began, and all the while, "little" Richard Berry was making his way up Bellaire Avenue toward home. How my mother didn't see me when she sped to the school I never would know, but on I walked until I reached my street. I crossed Bellaire Avenue, walked to our house and sat down on the front porch. It seemed like forever, but soon my mom drove up. The look on her face when she saw me was one of great relief. Thus ended my first day in the educational process.

I also danced on television. I know, that is hard to believe, but it is true. It was 1956. I was still in grammar school, but had moved on to the sixth grade. Elvis and rock and roll had just started to sweep the country. American Bandstand, the show that Dick Clark made famous out of Philadelphia had not yet hit the West Coast airwaves, but in Los Angeles we did have "The Al Jarvis Make Believe Ballroom" television show.

A number of us sent for tickets thinking it would be fun to attend. Now the kicker was that you had to ask for two tickets, and if you received two tickets, they expected you to ask someone to be your dance partner.

When my tickets arrived, I was shocked. Not to be outdone by the other guys, I asked Diane Williams if she would like to go. She said yes, so at the tender age of twelve, I had my first date.

My dad drove Diane and me down to the ABC Television Studios where the live show was televised. When we arrived at the studio, they gave each couple a number and when your number was called, you were spotlighted. I remember that the dance step was the "Bop." It was basically the old heel toe, heel toe dance step. A few weeks before the show, I rode my bicycle to the Victory Boulevard Recreation Center where I paid fifty cents a dance lesson in hopes of being ready for the big day.

The show started and we were seated in bleachers. When they called our number, Diane and I jumped up, stepped on to the dance floor and gave it our best shot. Boy was I rockin', or so I thought.

Television cameras rolled as we Bopped our way across the television airwaves and I into ballroom oblivion.

In reality, I was horrible. So bad in fact, that the guy who won, a kid named Steven Hertzberg, made a point of telling me how really bad I was.

The show ended, Hertzberg and his partner won, and I haven't danced since. And whatever happened to Diane is anybody's guess.

In later years I worked as an extra in a number of television and motion pictures. Once I earned my Screen Actors Guild card, I acted in television, acting in *A-Team*, *Falcon Crest, Knott's Landing* and in three motion pictures; *Lethal Weapon, The Hidden* and *Internal Affairs*. Although I was asked to work in other films, illness precluded me from doing so and that career ended.

My Short Lived Baseball Career

The year was 1955. The world of Little League was just coming to North Hollywood, California. As kids, we learned that a Little League field would be built on the corner of Oxnard and Fulton. This wasn't far from our home at 12618 Miranda Street, so on the Saturday designated for signups, all the boys on our street rode their bikes over to the field, stood in line and registered for the next week's tryouts. The results of the tryouts would then place us in the Majors or Minors.

All the guys from my street were there. Bill Strong (in later years he was called by his birth name of William B. Patterson), myself, the Reibe brothers, Loren and Gary, Bobby Diamond, who was a child television actor and who starred in the television series *Fury*, Howard Levy, Scott Miller, Evan Binn and Harold Stutz. The ages on the street ranged from eight to twelve. Strong and Binn were the oldest while Howard Levy and Scott Miller were the youngest. I was eleven and fell in the middle.

When the day for tryouts came, they were held on the baseball field at Los Angeles Valley College. Upon our arrival, we were separated into positions. Since I wanted to be a catcher, I stepped into that line. The coaches put us through our paces and by the end of the day, I had beaten out all the others who wanted the position. I was placed on a major league team called the Optimists and told I would be the starting catcher.

Also trying out were others with whom I attended grammar school and who I had known for the past six years; Gene Teich, Barry Stone and Chris Manneff. All were good athletes and could have had promising careers in sports. One died of drugs, another killed himself, and Chris, who had the opportunity to play major league baseball, didn't make the cut. He ended up driving a truck for the movie industry and died at the age of fifty-two from a massive heart attack. Marty Bloom was also in the group. Marty and I have now known each other and kept in touch for the past sixty-two years.

Although I was small, I did pretty well my first and second year, but when the time came for everyone to move on to a Pony Colt League, a league that played on Sunday, my parents said no. I was heartbroken because I had the ability and the desire, and I told them I would not play on Sunday, but they still refused to let me sign up. I found their decision funny in that they were not active in church, but being obedient, I did not go to tryouts and that ended my baseball career.

I have thought about that decision by my parents many times, and although I resented the fact that I wasn't allowed to go on, there is no doubt that their decision was correct. The Sabbath is not for sports, picnics, play or travel to sun at the beach or hike in the mountains. It is the Lord's Day; a day of rest and a day to provide service.

Lost in the Grand Canyon

April 1, 1958, I was fourteen years old and on a trip to the Grand Canyon with the Aaronic Priesthood from the Van Nuys First Ward, San Fernando California Stake. Twenty young men and eight leaders made the trip.

When we arrived at the rim of the canyon, we put our camping gear onto pack burros and began the walk to the canyon floor. After reaching the bottom of the canyon we hiked to a camping area, pitched camp and readied ourselves for the evening activities. At fourteen, I was one of the youngest and smallest in the group.

Night fell and after a camp fire, we retired to our sleeping bags. This was the first camping trip I had taken where sex, not scouting was the topic of discussion. The primary contributor was a kid about a year older than me. As he talked, I thought that he either had a very vivid imagination or had experienced things I had never even heard about. Unfortunately for him, I believe that he had experienced the activities, for as the years passed, he became involved in the drug culture at Santa Monica Beach, and at the age of thirty-six was shot to death by a hired gun who served as an enforcer. The irony of the story is that while I went to church with the deceased, I went to high school with the shooter.

Now back to the Grand Canyon.

Although we spent a cold night at the bottom, I didn't realize how much colder I would become before the experience ended.

The next morning the pack animals were late in arriving so seven of us decided to head out and start to the rim believing that the others would follow. The ages of the seven ranged from fourteen to seventeen, I being the youngest of the group.

Thinking that we could make it to the rim in about four hours and seeing that we had started out under a bright, sunny sky, most of us wore only light clothing. I was wearing a sweat shirt with a cotton T-shirt underneath. Additionally, we had no water.

We began our trek by following a well-marked path. We walked for about an hour when we came to a fork in the trail. The group was undecided on which way to go, so the older boys voted and they choose the left fork. That was a mistake.

Full of confidence, we walked, and walked and walked. Soon the sun was directly overhead and the surroundings were unfamiliar; we now knew that we were lost, very lost and extremely thirsty.

Again we stopped and discussed the severity of our situation, and again, the older boys made the decision to continue on. I remember the contention with the decision, but the older boys pulled more weight and therefore their word was final.

Being the smallest, I fell behind. No one ever checked to see if I was still with the group. So not only was I hot, tired and thirsty, I was now alone.

As I walked over the boulders at the bottom of the canyon, I found a hollowed out rock that contained water. Unfortunately, it also was the final resting place for a dead frog. I passed on the water and continued my journey.

After hours of walking over difficult terrain, I came to the steep wall of the canyon. It went straight up about two thousand feet and had a switchback trail that led to the top. At the bottom of the canyon wall, I caught up with the group. Another decision: Turn back or begin our assent to the top.

The older guys decided to climb, so after we navigated through the large boulders strewn across the canyon floor, we faced the switchbacks.

Walking single file, we climbed up the narrow path towards the top. When I looked down, all I saw was the shear drop that would be the fate of anyone should they slip. Slowly, we climbed. Up, and up and up. Eventually we reached the top. I remember looking back down into the canyon. It was a beautiful view only marred by the fact that none of us had any idea where we were.

As we stood on the rim the sun began to set and dark storm clouds gathered directly overhead. The small trail that had taken us to the rim suddenly merged into a single lane dirt road. It was now dark. We passed an abandoned wooden shack and pressed on.

No one spoke. Our steps were heavy, and it became an effort to put one foot in front of the other. With the darkness the temperature dropped. We had no stars, no moon, only darkness and an impending storm. It was now bitter cold and the wind was blowing. On we walked.

Then it began to rain.

The narrow road turned to mud and the rain turned to snow. Fear gripped us, and then panic set in. Shivering and cold, we silently walked into the blackness.

With our vision obscured by the snow, we stopped and laid our only blanket in a muddy ravine to give us some protection from the wet ground. As we lay in the darkness, sobs penetrated the night. We were freezing and we knew it. Although the youngest, the last thing I was going to do was cry and whimper in front of the others. So while some talked and others whimpered and cried, I prayed.

"I think we should try and get back to the old shack on the rim," said one of the older boys.

"You're crazy," I said. "You'll get lost in this snow storm or fall off the rim."

A heated conversation ensued. Finally, all decided that it would be best to remain where we were until morning. I prayed that we would last that long.

With our clothing wet, the cold became unbearable. Closer and closer we huddled and then as a group we prayed. The storm was unrelenting. Snow covered the landscape and seven huddled bodies. More prayers were offered, more tears shed and as the time slowly passed, my one thought was that I had to stay awake.

Don't fall asleep Richard, I told myself. *If you do, you'll freeze to death.*

Soon, all conversation ended and the only sound I heard was the howling of the storm.

As the night wore on and the ferocity of the storm increased, I again heard whimpering and crying. This was coupled with another request that we start back to the rim. Those who wanted to leave were again talked out of the foolish idea. So, we waited. And I continued to pray.

As dawn broke, the storm abated. Slowly, we dug our way out of the mud and brushed off the snow. We were all alive, but exhausted. At the first rays of light the older boys got up and silently began to walk back towards the rim. One by one they left. Soon, I was not only alone, but I had the responsibility of dragging the heavy wool Navy blanket. Slowly I got up, pulled the blanket out of the mud and started back towards the rim.

We had now been lost for twenty-four hours. *Someone must be looking for us,* I thought.

Through the snow I walked dragging the heavy mud coated blanket. I was tired, thirsty and cold. Snow covered the landscape, but was quickly melting. From the branches of the trees and bushes, I scrapped small amounts of snow in an effort to glean drops of water. And as I walked, I continued to pray.

After about four hours of walking and dragging the blanket, I stopped. I was exhausted and unable to continue. I was discouraged, frightened and alone in the middle of nowhere. As I stood on the muddy dirt road in the vast wilderness above the rim, I dropped to my knees and sobbed.

I called out for the other boys but no one answered. I heard only my echo resonating off the distant canyon walls.

In anguish and in deep despair I cried out, "Mother, oh mother, help me, oh please help me!"

Kneeling in the mud, I bowed my head and poured out my heart to my Father in Heaven. When I ended my pleading, I immediately felt a very warm, calming influence come over my entire body.

Then a still small voice whispered, *Go to sleep Richard, you will be fine.* So that is what I did.

Utterly exhausted, I lay down in the mud on the side of the road and slept. How long I was asleep I do not know, but upon awakening, I was confident that all would be fine.

Leaving the blanket on the side of the road, I started towards the rim and the small wooden structure we had passed the day before. With renewed energy, I trudged through the thick mud knowing that I was not alone and that unseen others surrounded me.

I was not aware of the time but knew that it was well into the afternoon when I finally reached the shack. As I approached, I saw that there was no movement in or around the building. Disappointed and fearing that I would have to spend another night in the cold, I walked slowly up to the shack and opened the door. To my surprise, three of the other boys were sitting inside with a man who was a member of the search party sent out to find us. My first question was, "Do you have any water?"

"No," he answered, "but we will get you some when we get you back with the others."

"Where are the other boys?" I asked.

"They started back down into the canyon with the other search party members earlier this morning."

For the first time in the entire ordeal I became angry. The older boys, upon reaching the shack had decided not to wait until I caught up, but had decided to start down the switchbacks and leave me behind. That was a decision I never forgot.

I was the last of the seven to be found. They said that the search planes passed over me a number of times but never saw me, nor did I ever hear them.

Huddled in the shack, we waited until a truck arrived to reunite us with the rest of the group and our leaders.

In all, we were lost in the Grand Canyon for thirty-two hours. We walked nearly thirty-six miles, including climbing the wall of the canyon via treacherous switch backs. The temperature the night we spent in the snow registered eighteen degrees, which did not include the wind chill factor which we were told took the temperature closer to two degrees.

I have never forgotten the fear that I experienced as I stood alone on that muddy road, nor have I ever forgotten the power of prayer, the calming influence of the Spirit and the knowledge that angels attended me throughout that ordeal.

Protecting My Brother

As a youth, I was quiet, reserved, and didn't have a fist fight until I was in the sixth grade when a kid named Dennis Lussier stopped me outside the gate at Monlux Elementary School and picked a fight. I won.

I didn't have another fight until I was sixteen. It all began when an older kid named Harold Stutz began picking on my younger brother Greg during a street football game. I wasn't there, but when Greg came home crying, my dad looked at me and said, "He's your brother; it's your responsibility to defend him."

With that comment, I walked out of the house and down the street. I asked Stutz why he was picking on Greg. When he stepped forward with clenched fists, I caught him with a left hook to the cheek and a quick right cross to the chin. He went down like a sack of potatoes and the fight ended. The sad thing about that incident was that from that time forward Stutz never walked down the street to play in any of our football or baseball games; he became a recluse.

While I attended high school, Greg again ran into a conflict with the friend of a kid from New York who moved onto the street. I guess by their standards they were tough. Not by mine. After the kid pushed Greg around, I confronted him in the Boy's locker-room and told him to leave my brother alone. He put his head down and bull-rushed me while he flayed his fists like a lawn mower. That was a mistake.

I took two steps back, and drop kicked him in the face, spreading his nose and dropping him to the ground. Whimpering, he said he had had enough. Although I was just getting started, I turned and walked away.

Crossing the Veil a Soldier

While my career on the Los Angeles Police Department began by me being immersed in the violence of the streets of South Central Los Angeles, my ability to make life and death decisions commenced before I put on a badge and strapped on a gun.

On two occasions before I joined the police department, I was shot at and responded in a way that would be considered by some to be overly aggressive. However, as far as I was concerned, I was reacting to the threat of death and doing all within my power to stay alive.

It was 1961 and I was seventeen. On occasion, some of my high school friends and I would drive to the mountains near Soledad Canyon, California, and go shooting. We normally took our .22 caliber rifles, and when I bought a new Winchester 30/30 lever action rifle, I also took this with me.

One day we had finished our shooting in the bottom of a deep canyon and were starting our climb back up the mountain to our cars. As we climbed to the halfway point on the mountain, we suddenly heard gunshots directly below us. Thinking that it was just some other shooters plinking at cans or ground squirrels, we continued our upward climb. Then another shot. This bullet kicked up dirt about ten feet to my left. We turned and yelled at them thinking that we had not been seen, or if seen, they were mistaking us for animals rather than humans. We were wrong.

Suddenly, a third bullet struck just below me. When I realized that the next shot could hit one of us, I spun toward our assailants, snapped the lever of my Winchester and threw a round into the chamber.

As I looked down into the valley, I could see three small figures. One had a rifle in his hands and was taking aim at us to fire another round. Without hesitating, I brought the rifle to my shoulder, aimed at the three assailants and fired. I realized that the distance was probably out of my range, but I was hoping that I would get close enough to deter another shot and send them running. I squeezed the trigger and the rifle recoiled sharply. Boom! The sound echoed through the mountains. Quickly, I slammed another round into the chamber and fired. Boom! I saw the dust kick up near where the shooter stood. As the third round slammed into the ground, three bodies flew in three different directions.

Once I was convinced that we were out of harm's way, we continued our climb without further annoyance from the attackers below.

About six months after the incident in Soledad Canyon, another shooting incident occurred.

While in my senior year of high school, I dated a young lady named Cathy Young. Her father was a real estate broker and one of his many holdings was a ranch located about seventy-five miles north of the San Fernando Valley.

As Mr. Young developed the ranch, he decided he wanted to fence in about ten acres that surrounded the house, so he asked Bob Byron, one of my high school friends and I to build a wooden fence that would surround his home and land. The task required digging each post hole by hand, cutting the wood for the fence, mixing the concrete in wheel barrows and then wheeling the concrete around the ten acres via dirt roads. We then poured the concrete around the post ensuring that everything was squared and level. It was quite a job for two eighteen year old young men, but we did it and enjoyed the work. Mr. Young paid us each $5.00 an hour.

The fence stood four feet high and had three boards across the side and one laid flat across the top. When the entire ten acres was fenced, we painted our masterpiece by hand. As one can guess, many, many weekends were spent working from dawn to dusk on that project.

One day after we had finished the project, Bob and I decided to take his small .22 caliber rifle and go shooting in the vast desert that surrounded the ranch. Although we fenced in ten acres, Mr. Young owned many more acres and it was these that we often explored.

Anxious to do a little shooting, we got into Bob's Volkswagen Bug and drove to the outskirts of the property where we parked and began to walk the many hills, valleys and gullies. As we stepped into one clearing, we saw a figure about three hundred yards in the distance. We called to the man, but our calls were not well received.

Suddenly, and without warning, we heard the report of a high powered rifle and instantly realized that the bullet was aimed at us! We hit the sand and buried ourselves as deep as we could.

I will never forget the thunderous cracking the bullet made as it split the branches of the Yucca trees separating us from our assailant. As we peered up, we saw the sand splatter as the bullet dug its self deep into the ground about twenty feet in front of us.

Believing that we had not been adequately seen or heard, we stood and wildly began to wave our arms and yell thinking that once the shooter realized we were people rather than some type of animal, the assault would end. We were wrong. It didn't.

As we yelled and waved our arms wildly, another shot rang out and a second round pierced the Yucca trees. We hit the ground again and could hear the bullet as it ripped through the trees, snapping the large branches until it slammed its self into the soft sand no more than twenty feet in front of where we were.

Not waiting for a third shot, I grabbed Bob's rifle, stood up and aimed at the assailant in the distance. Squeezing the trigger, I fired my first two shots. The assailant then fired his next round. Again his report was far louder than the dull ping of my rifle. This time his slug slammed into the ground within ten feet of us.

Still standing, I carefully aimed at the distant figure and snapped off the last seven rounds in hope of putting the assailant on the ground, thus allowing us to get to the car and escape the assault.

From a distance, both the assailant and I could see each other. As I cut loose with the last round, Bob and I spun and sprinted for the car. Our feet dug heavily into the soft sand, but we were intent on getting to the car before another round was fired. Reaching the Volkswagen, we jumped in and within seconds, Bob had the car in gear and we were moving back to the ranch. We arrived as the sun set and neither of us could believe what had just happened. Why the assault? I never found out, but we were both grateful for our escape.

Our Wedding Day

Cheryle and I met while we worked at the May Company Department Store in North Hollywood, California. Our first date was January 4, 1964.

Although we went to the same high school and only lived one street from each other, our paths did not cross until we both had graduated and were working.

We were married on January 18, 1965 in my parent's home by Bishop David S. Emory. Cheryle was not a member of the church and I was inactive. She was nineteen and I was twenty. We were both students at Los Angeles Valley Junior College. I was living with the Bob Byron, Sr. family and Bob Byron Jr., was my best man. Cheryle had no girl friends at the ceremony, so my mother's half sister, Betty Lou Berry stood in as her Maid of Honor.

We purchased our white gold wedding bands for $38.00 at May Company and bought our small white sheet wedding cake for two dollars and fifty cents from the Alpha Beta market. Those who attended were both sets of parents, my brother Greg, Uncle Berlin Whitaker, Aunt Rose Whitaker, Grandma Clara Whitaker, Bob Byron, my grandfather, Charles Louis Berry , his wife, Lyle, Betty Lou Berry; and Bishop Emory.

Cheryle wore a tan colored two piece suit and I wore a dark suit. The ceremony was short, with dear Bishop Emory calling Cheryle, Shirley on a number of occasions. We tape recorded the ceremony, but that tape was lost many years ago.

We had little money. I was working at May Company and Von's market earning $1.10 an hour while awaiting entrance into the Los Angeles Police Department Academy, and Cheryle wasn't making much more working at May Company as a sales clerk. What little money we had was spent on the marriage license, blood tests, the wedding rings or was being saved for our first apartment. Since my relationship with my father was strained, he offered no assistance or kind words of support; however, two weeks after the wedding, Cheryle's parents gave us five hundred dollars which was appreciated and much needed.

Our reception lasted ten minutes. We had no honeymoon. Being broke, following the ceremony, I took Cheryle back to her home where she lived for the next two weeks until we had earned enough money to pay our first month's rent.

Our rent was eighty dollars a month for a small one bedroom with one bathroom and a small kitchen. The apartment was located next to the Van Nuys wash and across the street from Ulysses S. Grant High School.

We are both certain that no one expected us to make the marriage work and at times, I wondered myself as I know

Cheryle did. But as I reflect back those many years, of all the friends we had and all those fancy weddings we attended, we are one of only two couples still married, and the only couple that can look at their seven children and twenty-one grandchildren and be eternally grateful for the "Refiners Fire."

Our lives have been different from those we knew so many years ago. Drugs, alcohol, infidelity and cancer have taken their toll on our friends and schoolmates of years past.

As to my friends I met in grammar school and went all the way through high school with, many died young, some by drugs, some in Vietnam, some at their own hands and others from serious illness. They were young men and women who were far brighter than I, far more gifted and talented, but lacked one great character trait I brought from the preexistence: tenacity, the ability and desire to keep on fighting even when the odds were, or appeared to be, insurmountable and overwhelming.

I also know that I brought with me a "fire in my gut and passion in my soul" to do the Lord's work. Granted, it took a few years of inactivity to realize this, but once I committed to keep the commandments and serve, I have honored that commitment.

I am grateful that Cheryle chased me until she caught me, and she is the first to admit that is what happened. When she first saw me at May Company, she said to one of her girlfriends, "I am going to marry Richard Whitaker," and that is what she did.

She is truly an angel and were it not for her, I would not be who I am today. And I am thankful that our children, for the most part, take after their mother.

Our Children Will Be Raised in the Mormon Church

We have all heard of the "Lost Sheep" program. It is not something new, but just a reaffirmation of the Savior's teachings. As I look at this program, I cannot help but think back to when I was one of those "Lost Sheep" of which the Savior referred.

During my early teenage years, what church activity I realized was because of my initiative, not because of any parental support. Later, when the time came for important decisions, I made some poor choices. So at the age of seventeen, since I was not comfortable associating with members of the church, I became inactive.

I always knew that the Church had something to offer and believed it to be true, but I did not have the testimony needed to maintain my activity. My inactivity came gradually, but it came. I never said anything about the Church to Cheryle until we were to be married. At that time I told her that I wanted our children to be raised in the Mormon Church.

"What is that?" she asked.

"You'll find out when the time comes," I answered.

She did not know anything about the Church so without hesitation, she agreed.

After the birth of Shannyn and Cindy, I felt it time to have the girls blessed. The blessings were performed by Bishop Emery. When the girls were blessed, I did not feel worthy to enter the chapel so I sat in the foyer and listened as the blessings were given.

Time passed and after I joined the police department, we moved to an apartment on Victory Blvd. in Van Nuys, California. Not long after moving in we had a visit from our Home Teacher. I was still inactive, working University Patrol and attending school, so when Brother Jim Crawley arrived, I excused myself, went into the bedroom, shut the door and studied.

He was a diligent man who later was called to be Bishop and unfortunately died in his early forty's. I have no doubt that he has received all the great blessings he earned on this earth.

Although I did not return to activity while Brother Crawley was our Home Teacher, his diligence helped pave the way for that future event.

Ask and ye Shall Receive

I entered the Los Angeles Police Academy on October 25, 1965, five months after my twenty-first birthday. I enjoyed the action and the violence of the streets. The shootings and fights all seemed to be exactly what I was looking for, or so I thought. In all the violent confrontations, I never lost; not a fight nor a gun battle. At the time, I took the credit for my mental and physical prowess, but soon learned how wrong I was.

Nightly, I faced the bloodshed of South Central Los Angeles. Citizens killed citizens and others were slain by the police. While I was assigned to car 7Adam42 in Wilshire Division, in a three week period of time, my two partners and I were involved in the shooting of five suspects.

I was trained by some of the toughest police officers to have worked the streets of Los Angeles. They were men in their early twenties and most had military backgrounds. Their training kept me alive, and while working with them I always knew that someone had my back.

Yet, as I excelled, I wasn't totally happy. Although I loved the job with its excitement and nightly adrenaline rushes, I knew something was missing.

With a young wife and two young daughters, I knew that I needed religion, and although born and raised a member of

The Church of Jesus Christ of Latter-day Saints, I did not have a testimony of its truthfulness. So in the summer of 1968, following some remarkable experiences in which my life was spared, I took a thirty day vacation with the intent of finding out if the Gospel of Jesus Christ was true. If true, I would make the necessary changes in my life. If not, I would continue my search.

My parents lived about two miles from our small home in North Hollywood, California and my old bedroom was vacant. After I secured permission to take a month of vacation time, I told Cheryle I was going to go to their home and study each day. And that is what I did. For thirty days, sixteen hours a day, I sat in a small bedroom and read.

I started with books written by American spiritualists. I remember finding some doctrines that seemed true and familiar, but nothing really struck a responsive chord. I then read books on Eastern religions; Zen, Tao, Buddhism, and the works of Confucius; but they also left me wanting more. I read books on Catholicism, Lutheranism and Calvinism. Still nothing. I had only about ten days left when I opened and read the Old Testament and New Testament. Finally, responsive chords were struck, but I felt that there were still some books left unopened.

I picked up the Doctrine and Covenants, read it and then the Pearl of Great Price. My time was running out and I still wasn't sure. Then I picked up a copy of the Book of Mormon I received my first day of Seminary. In Seminary, I lasted three days. I couldn't push myself to get up at 4:15 a.m. every school morning and walk two miles to a bus stop to take a bus to the stake center eight miles away. So, the book was still new.

I started to read.

Sixteen hours stretched to eighteen. I couldn't put The Book of Mormon down. Suddenly, I found I was at my last vacation day. While reading in Moroni, I came to that wonderful promise found in Moroni 10: 3-5. I never had heard of it before, but something prompted me to go to my knees and put the promise to the test. I took my Book of Mormon, opened it to the promise and placed in on the small bed in the corner of the bedroom. I began to plead with the Lord wanting to know if Joseph Smith was a prophet of God and if the Book of Mormon was true. Tears flowed and I continued to pray. Soon, I was surrounded by a feeling of warmth that permeated my entire being. The feeling was overwhelming and tears soon became uncontrollable sobs. How long I remained on my knees spiritually removed from that room, I don't know. But when I finally regained my composure and arose, the warmth had been replaced by physical and emotional exhaustion and I knew exactly what I needed to do to begin the process of repentance.

For the next five months, I spent much of my time asking for forgiveness for thoughts, speech and actions not in keeping with the commandments of God. The process of repentance hurt physically, spiritually and emotionally.

Then one day, the Spirit fell upon me and whispered, *Richard, the process is over and it has been accepted.*

That was forty-four years ago.

Life has not been easy with a stroke at thirty-six and the loss of a career; severe medical trials for eleven years; the loss of a nineteen year old daughter in a traffic accident; cancer striking my eternal companion and my daily headaches compounded by constant severe migraine headaches. But through it all, I have never doubted nor forgotten the feelings that wonderful day in that small bedroom when the Spirit of the Lord bore solemn witness to the depths of my soul that the Book of Mormon was a second witness to the divinity of Jesus Christ and that Joseph Smith was, and continues to be a Prophet of God.

Would I change any of the experiences of the past? No. Would I want to repeat them? No. I have learned to live in the present and look to the future. The past is just that, the past. And from it I have learned a great deal.

To each of you I bear a solemn testimony that this is the work of God. We need to struggle; we need to experience opposition in all things. But even in the darkest moments, we are not alone, for a loving Father in Heaven sent His Beloved Son to this earth to atone for and experience all that was required to allow us to repent and return to Father's presence. How grateful I am for a Savior who would endure so much for me.

Western Union

It was 1968 and we were living in our new home at 5628 Bellingham Ave. in North Hollywood California. We had not been in the house long when we discovered that one of our neighbors was a photographer.

Occasionally, if we were in our backyard, we would see a topless female walk past the fence, but usually they kept to themselves and were very careful in what they did and the noise they made. For this I was grateful.

Our bedroom faced the street and after a short time, I had memorized the sounds of the neighborhood. On occasion, even while asleep, if I heard a sound that was unfamiliar, I immediately was awakened.

Early one morning at 2:30 a.m., a Volkswagen Bug pulled up in front of our house and parked. I immediately was awakened by the rumbling car.

Then the car door opened and closed.

I climbed out of bed, parted the drapes and watched as a figure dressed in dark clothing approach our house. In his left hand he held a flashlight. Slowly a beam of light danced across the lawn and across our window. Then it moved to the front porch. In moments, I had thrown on a pair of Levi's and grabbed my M-1 30 caliber carbine. I slammed a loaded thirty round clip into the magazine and headed for our side back door.

Silently, I opened the door and slipped outside and around the garage toward the front yard. When I reached the corner of the garage, I peeked around the side and watched as the figure continued to check out the front of our house.

Apparently not finding what he came for, he stepped off the porch and began to walk in my direction. Since I still was hidden in the shadows, he did not know I was watching his every move.

When he came to within six feet of where I stood, he stopped and again turned toward the house.

With his back to me, I quietly stepped forward, slammed a live round into the chamber, placed the cold steel barrel to the side of his head and said, "Police officer, freeze or you're dead!"

As soon as the words left my mouth, the hand holding the flashlight began to dance wildly in the darkness putting on a wild light show as the beam bounced up and down and from side to side.

Stuttering, the visibly shaken man, his flashlight dancing and his other hand waving a piece of paper stuttered the words, "We...We...Western....U...U....Union!!"

"Get on your knees," I commanded.

Before the final word left my lips, he was on the ground, shaking violently.

With the barrel of my rifle still pushed flush to his head, I reached down and grabbed the piece of paper.

In the moonlight, I read, "Western Union Telegram."

I pulled the carbine away from his head and told him to get on his feet.

On shaking legs he stood and in speech that was higher than normal, he told me that he was using the flashlight to find the right address in order to deliver the telegram.

After I explained to him how close he came to being shot, I told him to find the address, make the delivery and not come back again this late at night.

I went back inside and watched through the window until the VW drove off.

I forgot about the incident until two months later when my neighbor called to me from across the short chain link fence that separated our front yards.

"Mister Whitaker," he called out, "Would you have any idea where this came from?"

Leaning over the fence, he handed me a soiled and crumpled Western Union Telegram.

"I found it crumpled up in my bushes. It is addressed to me and it is dated two months ago."

"I wouldn't have the slightest idea," I said as I slowly turned, a mischievous grin crossing my face.

As I think back on this situation, I can't remember why I didn't just tell him the truth. It's one of my inconsequential regrets.

An Almond Tree Waterer

The house at 5628 Bellingham Ave, North Hollywood, California was built for my grandparents, Orson and Clara Whitaker by their sons. In 1968, Cheryle and I bought it for $20,000 and it became our first home. Shannyn was three years old and Cindy two.

I had been on the police department about three years and had not yet returned to activity in the Church.

We moved into our home and were unaware that we had been assigned Home Teachers from the North Hollywood First Ward Elder's Quorum. After just a few weeks, we received a visit from our Home Teachers. Brother Earl Glauser and Brother Hal Kofoed invited us to attend church and promised that if the North Hollywood I Ward was not the friendliest ward in the Church, we did not need to return. We debated for some weeks, but after some interesting experiences at work, we decided that it was time to give it a try. At a later date, both Cheryle and I discussed the visit by Brother Glauser and Brother Kofoed. We were convinced that Uncle Berlin, who had once been the Bishop of this ward, had made a telephone call. Following that, the priesthood stepped in.

Everyone was great and it was during this time that I met Bishop Bob McKinney, President Jim Pratt, Keith Barton and many others who would influence me from that time forward.

It is also interesting that these brethren had been friends of the Whitaker family for many years. Dean Moser and Ted Everett also came into the picture during this time.

One night Bishop McKinney invited Cheryle and I over to his home for a visit. During the discussion the topic of tithing was brought up and I admitted to the Bishop that I did not pay it. He told us that tithing was not based on finances, but faith. He asked if we could start by committing to pay twenty-five dollars a month. Although this was not a full tithing, it was a start and we agreed.

The first month we paid our twenty-five dollars, the next month fifty and by the third month we were paying a full tithing. This has always been a great testimony to me not only of tithing, but also the way an inspired Bishop addressed the situation knowing full well that once faith was exercised, the principle would be implemented.

My first calling in the ward was what I refer to as an "Almond Tree Waterer," in that it was designed to test my level of commitment and obedience. Although the task was not invented for me, it did test my resolve.

The assignment was to see me spend ten hours a day for nearly two weeks on a scaffold looking up at the North Hollywood Ward Cultural Hall ceiling and removing acoustical tiles with a hammer and chisel. It was a dirty, tedious job. Both Ted Everett and I spent those two vacation weeks doing this while Cheryle made our Pepsi runs. Not only did I pass this first test, but Ted and I developed an eternal friendship.

Never Write Anyone Off

While I served as a young Elders Quorum president, I found myself on one occasion with President James D. Pratt at a meeting when the former Bishop of my teenage years walked up, and not recognizing me, began to carry on a conversation with President Pratt.

It was this Bishop who had a major disagreement with my parents when I became lost in the Grand Canyon, and after that, his relationship with the family was strained. Following the Grand Canyon incident, the Bishop never paid me much attention because I was not considered to be one of his elite youth.

When the Bishop approached, President Pratt stopped, turned to me, then turned back to the Bishop and said, "Bishop, let me introduce President Whitaker of the Third Quorum of Elders. President Whitaker is the finest Elders Quorum President in the Burbank Stake and possibly the Church."

The Bishop's mouth hit the ground. He couldn't believe what he just heard. I extended my hand and knowing that the point had been made, walked away.

Never write anyone off, never, ever!

That Bishop wrote me off. A Scout leader wrote me off. A Dean of Education at California State University

Northridge wrote me off when he told me, "Mr. Whitaker, you are not academic material and it is my recommendation that you get an Associate Arts Degree if you can and forget about any more college."

When all was said and done, I proved to one Bishop that he had made a judgment error; a Scout leader that he was incorrect in the long run because of the strides made while I assisted my eldest son Richard in his advance to the rank of Eagle at the age of thirteen, and the educator when I went on to Brigham Young University and the University of Southern California to graduate with advanced degrees and honors.

Yes, be careful of your words and actions. Always, rely on the Spirit. In doing this you will not err.

A STREET SOLDIER

A Bold Telephone Call

I entered the Los Angeles Police Academy on October 25, 1965. Our regimen was far different from what is now experienced. At that time the daily format was fashioned after the Marine Corps boot camp at Camp Pendleton, California. It included the same verbal and physical abuse that would accompany any boot camp during a time of war and a period of violent civil unrest.

As the violence on the nation's streets increased, so did the harsh toughness of the instructors assigned to the academy staff; especially since William H. Parker was the Chief of Police and it was his management style to rule the Department with an iron fist, a philosophy that permeated even into the academy.

As we approached the end of our three months in the academy, the time quickly advanced when we would be given our first regular division assignment.

At that time it was common practice for all recruits to be assigned either to Jail Division in Parker Center for their first six months, or to Pedestrian and Intersection Control (P.I.C.) where they would stand in the middle of a busy downtown intersection eight hours a day wearing white gloves and white hat directing traffic. Neither assignment thrilled me, nor were they the reason I became a cop. As far as I was concerned, directing traffic, which I did for two weeks during Christmas 1965, writing tickets or booking arrestees wasn't my game.

Most of the recruits in my academy class believed that it was the "will of God" and it was "set in stone" that they worked the jail or traffic as their first assignment. I believed differently.

One day as I sat in the Academy restaurant, I found out two interesting facts. The first was that the commanding officer of the Hollywood Division was a Captain named Whitaker. The second was the name of the commanding officer at Personnel Division, which was the division responsible for all police officer assignments in the city. With that information, I struck upon a very bold and gutsy plan.

The day after I put all the pieces together, I decided to make my move. Following lunch, I walked over to the public telephone booth located directly adjacent to the flagpole. I dropped a dime into the phone, dialed the city operator and asked for, "Personnel Division, Captain Sansing's office please."

Within moments, Captain Sansing's secretary answered.

"Personnel Division, this is Captain Sansing's office, may I help you?"

"Yes, I responded, "This is Whitaker up at the Academy; I'd like to talk to the Captain."

"One moment please, Captain."

Suddenly the line was picked up.

"This is Captain Sansing, may I help you?"

"Captain, this is Whitaker up at the Academy, how are you?"

"Great, Captain, what can I do for you?"

Beads of sweat formed on my forehead and my hands grew clammy.

"Well, there's a recruit going through the current academy class named Whitaker who graduates in a couple of weeks. I'd appreciate it if you would send him to one of the south-end divisions."

"No problem. Anything else?" asked Sansing.

"That'll do it, thanks."

"Give my best to the family," Sansing said cheerfully.

"I will, and you do the same."

In three minutes, it was over. Now the wait. When the assignment sheets were posted, I was elated.

Because of that telephone call, I was one of only a few members of my class of ninety-eight assigned to a patrol division in South Central Los Angeles. All the others were assigned to jail positions or traffic assignments.

Unauthorized Ammunition

During the mid-sixties, cops on the streets of Los Angeles were only authorized to carry .38 caliber, 158 grain ammunition. To get caught with anything else, even if you had a magnum capacity weapon, could result in disciplinary action.

To get around the rule and put some stopping power behind the weak 158 grain bullets, we hollowed out the soft lead of the bullets making them a hollow point. Not exactly a scientific approach to the problem, but it increased our confidence in the bullet and gave it some knockdown power.

Usually we changed the ammunition in our weapons after we left roll call, but one night I forgot to remove the hollow point ammunition from the previous night and it was still in my service revolver when we were told that we were going to have a formal weapons inspection.

The Wilshire Division Morning Watch lined up in the parking lot and the orders for a full weapons inspection were given. I slid my service revolver from the holster with my right hand, cranked open the cylinder and in a very exacting manner dumped the six rounds of ammunition into my cupped left hand. I then stood at attention as Lieutenant Rudy De Leon and two sergeants started the inspection. Down the line they walked. Lieutenant De Leon stepped in front of me, snatched my weapon, inspected and returned it.

As he stepped to the side, a sergeant picked up one of my bullets. He looked it over, looked at me and dropped it in my hand. Glancing down I realized that I had failed to remove the hollow points and replace them with authorized rounds.

Well, I thought. *If they want me, they have me.*

When the inspection was over and we were dismissed, I heard, "Whitaker, I want to talk to you." It was the sergeant who had found the hollow point.

In a soft tone, he looked me in the eyes and said, "Whitaker, don't ever stand inspection with that ammunition again."

That was it; nothing more. I was grateful for a sergeant who appreciated a good street cop.

Those Old Doors Have Been Known to Fly Open

It was November 1966. The Wilshire Division Morning Watch was walking from roll call into the parking lot when the silence of the night was broken by a radio call that froze the watch.

"All units in the vicinity and 7Adam56, officer needs help, shots fired, officer down, Pico Boulevard across from Sears. 7Adam56, handle your call Code 3. Any other Wilshire unit in the vicinity, identify and handle Code 2."

In seconds, chaos erupted in the parking lot. Sergeant Dick Stevens, one of the Night Watch supervisors ran by me yelling, "Whitaker, let's go!"

With two other officers, I sprinted to a black and white which had been commandeered by Stevens. Tires squealed as the car screamed through the parking lot toward the street. Stevens, seeing that our access had been blocked by a police car parked in front of the driveway, snapped the steering wheel to the left, sending the car careening through the arches at the front of the station. Then, with red lights flashing and the siren wailing, we flew down the sidewalk at sixty miles an hour.

Over curbs and around mail boxes we flew until we were able to slide through a driveway and onto Pico Boulevard.

Since we were only about a minute from the scene, in no time I saw the flashing rear amber lights of the police unit belonging to Keith Dupuis and his partner.

Parked in front of the police car was a new Ford Thunderbird. The front car doors on both vehicles stood open.

We slid to a stop, and as I jumped from the car, I saw one suspect on the ground next to the driver's door of the Thunderbird. Dupuis was also on the ground about ten feet behind the downed gunman. It appeared that the driver suspect had been shot. I saw a second suspect on the sidewalk and Dupuis' partner standing over him. In seconds, the first ambulance, or G-Wagon as they were called, pulled up to the scene.

Dupuis did not move. When I looked at his face, I saw that he had been shot in the mouth. He appeared to be dead.

Stevens and I handcuffed both suspects as Dupuis was loaded into the G-Wagon. In less than thirty seconds, he was on his way to Central Receiving Hospital. Stevens directed me to ride in a second G-Wagon with the shooter who, ironically, also was being transported to Central Receiving.

The G-Wagons in the 1960's were far different from the ambulances of today. They were stationed not at hospitals, but at the individual police stations, and the attendants were not the well trained paramedics or emergency personnel of today. They usually were some guy who possibly had been a medic in the military and had signed on with the city to work the unit. They contained no medical equipment, and looked similar to the old side paneled Helms Bakery trucks. Inside, two wooden benches were attached to the sides and in the center was room for a stretcher. Their sole purpose was transportation.

After I climbed into the G-Wagon with the suspect, the ambulance attendant climbed in and slammed the two rear doors. As we pulled off, the driver did not activate the red lights or siren. He drove slowly ensuring that no traffic laws were violated and as much time as possible was taken before we reached the hospital. Cautiously, he drove down Pico Boulevard and then north on Western Avenue toward the Hollywood Freeway; all this with the suspect handcuffed and strapped down to the wooden plank that served as a stretcher. Once we were on the freeway, the driver slammed the accelerator to the floor and the old truck jumped into the night. When we were at top speed, the ambulance attendant spoke for the first time.

"These old doors don't really lock well and at times they've been known to fly open. The first bump we hit could see them fly open and since the stretcher isn't well secured, we might lose this guy on the freeway. Your call, Whitaker. It would save court costs."

Although the thought of disposing of a cop killer on the Hollywood Freeway was not only unique, but also tempting, I looked at the attendant and said, "Not this trip."

Within twenty minutes we pulled into the parking lot at Central Receiving Hospital. LAPD brass, cops and medical personnel packed the place. As we rolled the suspect into the hospital, I looked into the first operating room where a team of doctors worked feverishly to save Dupuis. And although he was alive when he arrived, he would die a week later, never regaining consciousness.

Later I learned that when Dupuis and his partner drove from Wilshire Station, they observed the Thunderbird driving slowly down Pico Boulevard. The passenger officer ran the license number and it came back a stolen from back East.

Dupuis activated the red lights and the Thunderbird pulled over. The passenger officer approached the passenger side of the suspect's vehicle while Dupuis did the same on the driver's side. As the driver exited the Thunderbird, he slid out sideways not allowing Dupuis to see his waistband or his hands. Then, he spun. In his right hand he held a small .32 automatic. In a single motion he brought the small gun level with Dupuis' face and fired. Before Dupuis could react, the bullet struck him in the mouth.

Dupuis' partner fired six times at the shooter, striking him once in the leg and sending him to the ground. With the impact of the bullet, the suspect lost his grip on the gun.

Then the passenger officer turned to the other suspect who was brandishing a long bladed knife. This suspect was ordered to the ground. He complied, not knowing that Dupuis' partner was out of ammunition.

Both suspects were ex-cons. After stealing the Thunderbird, they spent hours during their drive to Los Angeles stopping and practicing what they would do if they were stopped by the police. Over and over they stopped and set up wooden targets, each time drawing a silhouette of a cop. Then they took turns and practiced spinning and firing. When the time came, their aim was deadly. Eventually, both suspects were convicted of First Degree Murder and sentenced to death. However, their sentences were later commuted to life without the possibility of parole.

A Coward Dressed in Blue

After three months on Wilshire Day Watch, I was rotated to the PM Watch and assigned to unit 7Adam56. My partner's name was Bill. He was an interesting guy. Everything was spit and polish, a throwback to his days in the Marine Corps. Nothing was ever out of place. If we had known about the Obsessive Compulsive Disorder in 1966, Bill would have been the poster child.

It was about 10:00 p.m. on a Friday night when we received the radio call, "7Adam56, 415 (loud) party, 5th Avenue and Country Club Drive."

When we arrived at the location, Bill parked the car at the corner and we immediately found ourselves surrounded by a large group of drunken party goers.

As I exited the passenger side of the black and white, I dropped the radio mike out the window so I could grab it should things get ugly. No sooner had I stepped from the car that I became the focus of attention.

The hostile crowd surrounded me and when I looked for my partner, he was gone!

I was alone.

The anger in the crowd increased as they moved closer and closer. At first I thought that I just had not seen Bill. *He had to be close by* I thought.

My eyes swept the area. He simply wasn't there. Talking fast, I kept the crowd at bay, I reached for the mike, and requested assistance.

Then I saw him.

He stood hiding behind a telephone pole about three hundred feet down the street, smoking a cigarette. The bright ash from the tip was barely visible from behind the pole while the gray smoke rose slowly into the cold night air.

Soon sirens pierced the night. Help was on its way. When the first police car careened around the corner with its red lights flashing and siren blaring, Bill, with all the confidence that his Marine Corps background could muster, stepped out from behind the telephone pole and arrogantly walked toward the crowd. He stood erect, spit and polish with the cigarette dangling from his mouth as if overlooking a battle in which he had been the victorious commander. When the first responding unit screeched to a stop, Bill stepped into the crowd and with a command presence General George Patton would have admired, began to give orders. As the crowd dispersed, a sergeant walked over to Bill.

"Well done Bill. Nice job of defusing a potentially dangerous situation."

Removing the cigarette from his mouth, he dropped it to the ground and put the butt out with the toe of his shoe.

"Thanks, *Sarge*," he responded. "All part of eight."

Later, I told Bill what I thought of him, and my assessment of him as a street cop. My anger only made him smile.

On another occasion while we worked together, he observed a car making an illegal right-hand turn. He quickly pulled in behind the violator and hit the red lights. The driver pulled to the curb and turned off the engine.

While Bill walked to the driver's door, I, unobserved, placed my service revolver behind my right leg and took up a position on the right side of the car just to the rear of the passenger door. In this position, I could watch the driver while standing in his blind spot.

When I approached the car, I remembered that a car of this description was wanted for armed robbery and the occupant was considered to be armed and dangerous.

While I tried to get Bill's attention, I was unable. He was too busy promoting public relations with the driver while ignoring his own safety.

I watched as he asked the driver for his driver's license and vehicle registration. Slowly, the man reached across the front seat and pushed the button opening the glove box.

As the glove compartment opened, I shined my flashlight beam into the box. As I did, the suspect reached into the box. Inches from his hand was a blue steel revolver. Before his hand could grab the weapon, I threw open the passenger door and drilled the barrel of my gun into his ear.

Bill froze, as did the suspect. I retrieved the loaded weapon and we arrested the suspect for armed robbery and carrying a concealed weapon.

Bill was a misdemeanor cop in a felony world.

I transferred to Morning Watch and later learned that Bill's career had spiraled out of control after he was stopped for Driving under the Influence of Alcohol. Eventually, he divorced his wife and left his family.

While still on the Department, he was caught stealing prescription drugs from the homes of victims where he and his partners would go to take a crime report. As the partner took the report, Bill would search the bathrooms for the drugs. His downfall came when he stole some medication for a young man who was epileptic and they were able to place him as the last person in the house who was not a family member. This happened just after the last dose was administered and before the next was due. When the family looked for the medication, it was gone.

Internal Affairs searched his apartment and discovered that he had gone from the Marine spit and polish to living on a lice covered mattress in an apartment which was strewn with empty stolen prescription bottles. To make matters worse, he had been living with one of the division record clerks whose picture was pasted on the walls in a varied array of pornographic photographs. Disgraced, he left the job and died of alcoholism at an early age.

Charlie and His Broken Jaw

It was March 10, 1967, 2:10 a.m. and I was working a black and white in Wilshire Division. My partner was Ron Petroski. This night would be the only time we worked together and it would prove to be eventful.

I had been on the job about eighteen months and already had a reputation for being an aggressive street cop and one who loved physical confrontation. In other words, I loved to fight.

We were working the Morning Watch when we received a radio call, "7Adam42, 459 Silent (burglary alarm), The House of Good Spirits, 2805 West Pico. 7Adam42 handle the call Code 2."

Petroski was driving, and I rode shotgun. As we approached the location, Petroski cut the headlights and shut off the engine. Slowly, we glided to a stop adjacent to the liquor store. Getting out of the car, I hugged the wall and moved quietly to the side of the front window where I glanced into the interior of the darkened store. On the other side of the counter I saw a figure rifling the cash register.

I signaled Petroski that we had a suspect inside. He started the Plymouth and hit the gas! When the Plymouth raced past the front store window, the suspect bolted for the rear door.

In seconds, Petroski had rounded the corner and slid the car to a stop deep within the rear alley. As he jumped from the black and white, the suspect ran out the back of the store. Petroski took aim and fired. He missed.

Hearing the shot, I kicked the glass out of the front door and ran to the rear of the store.

As I threw the door open, I saw Petroski standing twenty feet to my left. He pointed to the darkened rear of the narrow parking area and yelled, "He jumped into the old white van."

With my service revolver in my right hand, I stepped to the van and threw open the door. The suspect was crouched just inside.

Seeing both of his hands and determining that he did not have a weapon, I ordered him out of the truck and holstered my gun. With Petroski covering me, I stepped forward and grabbed the front of his shirt with my left hand. When I did this, he lunged at me. Instantly, I caught him solidly in the side of the jaw with a sharp right hook. I felt the jaw snap to the side and his body go limp. The blow knocked him unconscious which allowed me to throw him face first onto the ground where he was handcuffed.

The owner of the liquor store was called, and while another unit waited for him to arrive, Petroski and I transported the suspect to Wilshire Station and booked him on the burglary charge.

I forgot about the incident until three days later when one of the G-Wagon attendants pulled me aside.

"Hey, Whitaker. You remember the guy named Chung you booked on the burglary from the liquor store?"

"Yep," I replied.

"Let me tell you a funny story about that incident," the attendant said.

"After you booked the guy, all he did was complain about his jaw. He said it was broken. We looked at it and there were no abrasions, contusions or swelling, so we told him he was fine."

I could only smile.

"A day passed and he asked to see us again, and after complaining about his jaw, told us he couldn't open his mouth and hadn't eaten in two days. So we decided to take him to Central Receiving Hospital."

"So what did they find?" I asked.

"I couldn't believe it. You broke not only his jaw, but fractured the left mandible in a number of places! What did you hit him with?"

"A short right hook."

"Whitaker, I'd hate to see it when you really clocked someone!"

Man's Best Friend and a Woman's Also

It was the summer of 1967 and I was assigned to the Morning Watch in Wilshire Division. For about six months, two bandits had victimized the senior citizens who lived in the area of Beverly Blvd. and La Cienega. The victims were white, Jewish and affluent.

At about one in the morning, we received a radio call, "3Adam9, See the woman, shots fired, man down." We then were given the address.

"3Adam9, handle the call Code 2."

"3Adam9, roger," my partner responded.

Code 2 meant, no red lights and siren, but proceed with all haste; and since we were on the opposite side of the division, that was going to take some doing. Luckily traffic was light and the traffic lights were in our favor.

We entered the darkened residential neighborhood and watched the G-Wagon pull up to the south curb. I pulled in behind them and parked.

When I looked to my left, I saw a male Negro, mid-twenties, lying on the sidewalk. It appeared that he was dead.

He was dressed in a long tan raincoat, and in his right hand he held a small, sawed-off, single shot .22 caliber rifle.

71

His right index finger was still wrapped around the trigger and was quivering; a sign that death had occurred violently and not long before our arrival.

On the ground next to him was a small hat referred to on the street as a "stingy brim." His face was covered with blood and a pool of the life giving substance rapidly was forming around his head and slowly snaking its way down the sidewalk and into the gutter. Also standing on the sidewalk not far from the dead man was a woman who appeared to be about sixty-five years of age. Seated at her side was a very large, agitated dog.

While the G-Wagon crew examined the lifeless suspect, I walked over to one of the patrol officers who had arrived at the scene shortly before we pulled up. When I approached, he handed me a small, blue steel .38 caliber revolver.

"This is what the old lady used to blow the dude away," he said. "She's a pretty good shot. Three shots, two hits; and both in the head."

"Not bad," I said.

I asked the woman to have a seat in our patrol car. Opening the door, she tied the dog to the door handle. When I asked her what happened, she shared the following story.

"I live alone in my home that is just down the block. I've lived in the neighborhood for about forty years. Each year it gets worse and worse, but I don't have anywhere else to go, and I am comfortable here, so I stay. I was comfortable until about three weeks ago."

"What happened then?" I asked.

"Every night I take my dog for a walk before I go to bed. Three weeks ago, we went for our walk and returned home. I wasn't in the house ten minutes when there was a knock at the front door. Without thinking, I opened the door and standing on the porch were two colored men. One was wearing a long tan raincoat and had a funny looking hat on his head. I thought the raincoat odd since it was summer, but as I started to say something, the man in the raincoat pulled a rifle from under his coat and then he and his companion pushed me back into my house."

"Was the dog in the house?" I asked.

"Yes, and although he was agitated, he didn't do anything since it appeared that I had invited them in. They then tied me up and robbed me of everything, my money, my jewelry and my silver. With some effort, I was able to untie myself and call the police. I made a police report, but nothing happened with the case until tonight."

"And what happened tonight?" I asked.

"Well, Officer......"

"Whitaker."

"Well, Officer Whitaker, like I said, every night I take my dog for a walk before going to bed, and I wasn't going to let two hoodlums stop me from doing that. So, each night after the robbery when I went out with the dog, I put my husband's small gun in my house coat."

"And where is your husband?"

"He died three years ago. It was his gun the other officer took from me. I've owned it for years and it's registered to Martin, my late husband."

The dog barked. Lovingly, the woman reached out the window and patted him on the head, and then she continued.

"Tonight I put on my housecoat and put the gun in the right front pocket. I wasn't going to walk far, just let the dog out for a couple of minutes. I put him on his leash, and we left the house. I looked up and down the street and not seeing anyone, I felt safe. We weren't out ten minutes when I looked down the sidewalk and coming in my direction were the same two hoodlums who had robbed me before. And Officer Whitaker, they were wearing the same clothing, including the tan raincoat and that stupid little hat."

"Then what happened?" I asked.

"Well, I didn't really have time to do anything. They walked up to me very fast, and the man in the raincoat didn't say a word. He just brought out that small rifle from under his coat, just like he did on my porch; but this time it was different."

"How so?" I asked.

"My dog recognized him. So when he started to raise the rifle, the dog lunged. And as he lunged, I already had my hand on my gun and was bringing it out of the pocket.

"Then everything went very fast. When the dog lunged, I was knocked off my feet and I started to fall backward. Then the hoodlum with the rifle pulled the trigger. I heard his shot as I started to pull the trigger on my gun, but I couldn't aim at anything. I just pulled the trigger three times. I shot while I was in the air before I hit the ground."

"We could use you on the Department," I said. She smiled and continued.

"When I landed, the wind was knocked out of me. I didn't really know what happened to the two men, but as soon as I regained my breath, I lifted my head and looked around. The man with the gun was on the ground, and not moving. The other man was running down the street. My dog was barking, and I was amazed that I still had hold of his leash in my left hand and the gun gripped tightly in my right.

That's when the neighbors ran out and they called the police."

In the world of a street cop, it was a good shooting. The woman fired three times while she was prone in the air and before she hit the ground. Two shots struck the suspect in the face. The third missed.

Street justice was rapidly administered.

The suspect's stray shot never was found.

We drove the woman to the station which gave her time to calm down. Because it was used in a homicide, the gun was booked as evidence.

And what was the final outcome? The suspect was identified as the perpetrator of a number of other robberies in the area where the elderly were victims. The District Attorney's Office ruled the shooting as Justifiable Homicide, the woman was given her gun back and the City of Los Angeles presented her a Citizens Award. The second suspect was later identified, tried, convicted and sent to prison.

And so it was. Because of a dog that remembered and a quick draw by a senior citizen who had the determination to live, a number of crimes were solved and I am confident the lives of other elderly members of that community were spared.

The Egg and I Restaurant

My first experience on the Los Angeles Police Department with armed robbery suspects occurred in 1966 when I was assigned to Wilshire Division. I had about nine months on the Department and was assigned to the Mid-Watch. We had roll call at 6:00 p.m., hit the streets at 6:45 and went end-of-watch at 3:00 a.m.

It was near end-of-watch, and I was the passenger officer in unit 7Adam2 working with Buzz Camp. This was our first time working together, and since he was the senior officer, he drove.

We were assigned to the northwest section of the division which included Beverly Blvd. and the wealthy part of the Wilshire District. The area had costly homes and also numerous upscale restaurants and businesses.

As we drove slowly down the darkened side streets, our radio crackled and came alive with the call, "All Wilshire units in the vicinity and 7Adam2. Possible 211 (robbery) suspects hiding in the alley at the rear of the Egg and I Restaurant. 7Adam2, handle the call Code 2. Any other Wilshire units available to assist identify to Control and respond."

Picking up the radio mike, I acknowledged the call, "7Adam2, roger."

Camp snapped the steering wheel, spun the car around and slammed the accelerator to the floorboard. As the Plymouth's large carburetor opened full bore, the black and white made a violent jump spewing a throaty growl as we sped in the direction of the restaurant.

When we were about a block away, Buzz let up on the accelerator. The car glided quietly down the street and around the corner. When he turned into the alley, he cut the ignition and we coasted to within twenty feet of the rear door and trash collection area.

As we rolled into the alley, he put his high beams on illuminating the alley and the trash dumpster that sat in the far corner against the west wall. The lights were something not normally done when you wanted to confront bad guys in a stealthy manner, but this action probably saved my life.

Farther up the alley we rolled. About ten feet from the rear door of the restaurant, Buzz stopped the car. To my right was the door and above it was a solitary flood light. In front of me and to my left were the trash bins. One butted out into the alley, while the other was piled high with trash and surrounded by old discarded cardboard boxes.

Sitting in the car, I asked myself one question. *If I were a bandit, where would I hide?* The answer, *behind the trash bins and under the boxes.*

I opened the car door, placed my flashlight in my left hand and drew my service revolver with my right.

"Cover me, partner," I yelled to Camp who had stepped out the driver's door and had drawn a bead on the area of the trash bins.

With weapon drawn, I cautiously approached. There was an eerie silence as I thrust the barrel of the revolver behind the bin and pushed the first box to the side. As I shoved my flashlight in from the left side, I drew back the hammer on my .38 and shoved it in behind the stacked boxes on the right. Suddenly, I saw two large brown eyes looking into the light; then another set, and then I saw the small .32 revolver in the hand of the first suspect. He started to raise the gun and then hesitated. I quickly jumped out of the line of fire yelling, "Partner, they've got a gun!" Then just as quickly, I stepped out of any line of fire from my partner.

"Drop the gun on the ground and raise your hands straight up in the air or you're both dead!" I shouted.

Apparently they believed me, for next I heard what appeared to be the gun hit the concrete, and then watched as four hands pushed their way slowly through the empty cardboard boxes.

As I kept my weapon on the suspects, Camp stepped forward. Slowly and with hands held high, each was ordered to step out and prone himself on the concrete with arms and legs extended. They did this without a word. Camp searched for additional weapons as I provided cover.

"Don't even think of moving, gentlemen," I said. "Because if you do, I'll blow your head off." Both remained motionless while Buzz conducted his search and then handcuffed the bandits.

Later interrogation revealed that the suspects had planned on robbing the employees of the Egg and I Restaurant after it closed for the night. It also revealed another interesting fact. When interviewed, the suspect with the gun stated: "I was going to shoot you, but I couldn't see your partner. And then I looked up and saw your gun pointed at my head. You're lucky you're alive, Mr. Policeman!"

As I reflected on the incident, I was keenly aware that it was our deployment, following rules of safety, exhibiting an attitude of controlling the situation, but most of all being protected by heaven.

Tear Gas Empties Wilshire Station

It was the summer of 1967, and with the Watts Riots over and the mini-riots continuing, the Department decided that it might be a good idea to issue all patrol officers small canisters of tear gas spray. It was an idea that was soon to backfire, and we of the Wilshire Morning Watch didn't help matters much.

After being issued our small canister, it didn't take long for John Marzullo to decide to try it out. Marzullo was a partner with another cop named Buck Wright, however, it wasn't Wright that Marzullo solicited to be a part in the prank; it was Whitaker.

We left Morning Watch roll call about midnight. It was mid-week and all was quiet except for a drunk that was booked earlier that evening by the Mid-Watch. The sounds of his screaming and yelling not only filtered through the old brick station, but also made their way out into the parking lot through the barred jail window that was about ten feet above the parking lot.

Carl Porter and I walked out as the drunk's wailing pierced the night. Carl popped the trunk of our black and white and we threw our gear in the back. As I stepped around to the passenger door, I heard someone yell, "Hey Whitaker, come here, I need your help."

Looking behind me, I saw Marzullo standing just below the barred jail window.

"Let me get on your shoulders, I'll silence that idiot," John said.

As I walked over to the side of the building, Marzullo removed a tear gas canister from his jacket pocket. With little effort, I put my head down and while staring at the ground, lifted him onto my shoulders. The wailing from the jail cell intensified.

Suddenly, I heard the sharp spray of aerosol as the entire canister was emptied into the drunk's cell through the bars. Suddenly, all was quiet.

Laughing, Marzullo yelled for me to get him down.

"Took care of that problem," he said as a grin crossed his face. We then walked briskly over to our cars and continued to ready ourselves for the night.

Not two minutes passed when the station doors flew open and the building started to empty. The first to bolt out the side door was the Morning Watch Lieutenant, followed closely by the sergeants and then the entire desk crew and all jail personnel. All were coughing horribly and crying.

"We're under attack," yelled one sergeant as tears filled his eyes and streamed down his cheeks, "the station has been hit with tear gas. Set up a command post. Call the Chief!"

"Somehow they got it into the air conditioning unit," yelled another supervisor. "Everyone take cover!" he shouted.

"It must have been black militants," coughed the Lieutenant.

Silently, our entire Morning Watch stood next to their cars. Looking at each other, we could not contain it. The laughter began. Then while still laughing, each partnership got into their car, drove out of the parking lot and hit the street.

About fifteen minutes passed when Porter and I received a radio call ordering our unit to return to the station. As we pulled in, a sergeant walked over to our car and said, "Whitaker, the Lieutenant wants you in his office." Porter glanced in my direction and didn't say a word.

I walked into the station and saw Marzullo sitting in the hallway. It appeared that I was first.

The Lieutenant's office was very sterile. A large wooden desk sat in the middle of the room. Hardback wooden chairs were placed around the room for meetings. The seat of honor was placed directly in front of the desk providing the great inquisitor a clear view of his subject.

"Have a seat, Whitaker," the Lieutenant said. He pointed to the chair directly in front of him. Sitting down, I quickly found that there was no comfortable way to sit in this type of chair. Comfort wasn't why you were there.

I waited. Time passed. Not a word. You could have heard a pin drop. It seemed like an eternity before the Lieutenant spoke.

"Whitaker, someone sprayed tear gas through an outside jail window into a jail cell tonight. It seems that they wanted to silence a drunk, but the drunk passed out before the gas could take effect and it ended up going into the air conditioning ducts gassing every officer in the station. I was told you might know who did it?"

"I didn't **see** anyone spray any tear gas through a window, Lieutenant."

His tone now changed. If the Lieutenant had been playing the good guy in the "good guy - bad guy" scenario, he now turned his collar and took on the other role.

"Are you aware that if I find out you had something to do with this, I can recommend a twenty-one day suspension?"

"If you say so, sir. But again, I didn't spray anything into the station, Lieutenant, nor did I **see** anyone put anything through a window and spray it."

More silence.

"Whitaker, your reputation in this division is that of a tough street cop considering the short amount of time you have on the job. I don't want those other seasoned Morning Watch officers to corrupt you. You have a future on this department."

"Thank you sir, but again, I didn't **see** anyone spray tear gas into the station."

I sat in the chair motionless while the Lieutenant did his best to give me the old evil eye thinking that would intimidate me. He didn't know me.

"You're dismissed, but remember, I'll do my best to get you those twenty-one days if I find out you gassed the station or had anything to do with it!"

"Yes sir."

Marzullo sat in the hallway waiting. It was evident that they thought that if anyone was going to cop out and break, it would be the new kid on the watch. They were wrong.

"Marzullo, you're next," commanded the voice from the office. As I walked by John, I winked, smiled and shook my head from side to side. I then went back to work.

Later as Marzullo and I talked, the same technique was tried on him and with the same results, except for a twist.

The Lieutenant told John to have a seat. Time passed. After ruffling through some papers as if organizing his case, the Lieutenant looked up and with a serious look on his face said: "John, Whitaker copped out on you. He told me all about it."

Marzullo was expressionless.

I'm going to recommend twenty-one days for him. You come clean and your time will be less. You've got a career to think about...a family...promotions..."

"Come clean about what, Lieutenant?" asked Marzullo.

"Marzullo, don't play games with me. One of you sprayed a can of tear gas into the station tonight, and I want to know who it was!"

"I don't know anything about it, Lieutenant. Nothing. And about Whitaker copping out on me, well, he'd be lying if he said he **saw** me do anything that stupid."

The Lieutenants face reddened. He slammed his fist onto the top of the desk. "Marzullo, the Chief expects me to find out who did this, and I am going to do just that. I'll get you and Whitaker if you were involved. Trust me. I'll get you both!"

"Yes sir. Will there be anything else, Lieutenant?"

In a shrill and irate voice, Marzullo was dismissed.

As he walked out into the parking lot, he caught my eye. All it took was a smile and a wink.

In time, the matter became the joke of the station, and although the rumor abounded that the Morning Watch had something to do with the gassing of the station, the Lieutenant conducted no further interrogations.

I always found it interesting that the brass never conducted an inspection of the tear gas canisters to check them for content, however, the next week they affixed evidence stickers across the top of each canister to seal it and aid in identification if one was used.

Carlton K. Porter

Although I had some very interesting experiences working the various watches in Wilshire Division, my real education began when I transferred to unit 7Adam42 on the Morning Watch.

Officer Carlton K. Porter was my partner and he taught me the tactics and instilled in me a tough mentality that kept me alive during the entire time I worked the streets in South Central Los Angeles.

I remember Carl vividly. He had a reputation as a mean, tough street cop. Basically, he didn't like anyone. He didn't like the public; he didn't have much good to say about his supervisors and he felt most policemen, especially those not working Morning Watch, were worthless.

He had striking blond hair which he combed down to the side: a very pale complexion that accentuated the pox marks and scars of a bad skin from adolescence and cold, piercing blue eyes. He rarely smiled, and always wore a black leather jacket and black leather sap gloves. When he drove, his left hand was on the steering wheel while he kept his right hand, his gun hand, resting on his right leg with his weapon draped over his thigh never far from his reach. He chain smoked and always had a pack of Marlboro cigarettes stuffed above the sun visor.

Carl's weapon of choice was a six inch Colt .38 caliber revolver, and in his rear uniform leg pocket, he carried a 187 Newton sap, named after the LAPD Division where it was first used. The number 187 referenced the California Penal Code for murder. The sap was nearly ten inches long and about one inch thick. It was weighted with lead shot which surrounded a steel bar. All of this was wrapped in a tight black leather skin. Attached to the handle was a black leather strap that allowed the owner to wrap the strap around his wrist when the weapon was in use. The Newton sap had the distinction of being able to knock a suspect unconscious with one blow and never rip or tear the skin; hence, no blood.

To be accepted into Porter's inner circle required one to first prove himself. Fear was not acceptable, and if one showed cowardice, his life could be in jeopardy.

I had not been on the watch a week when I was assigned to work with Porter. It was not long afterwards that one of the other cops on the watch asked me if I had heard about what happened to Porter's last partner.

"No, what?" I asked.

I then was told the following story.

As Porter and his probationary partner drove down Pico Boulevard early one morning, Porter saw two men standing in front of a liquor store. They became nervous when they saw the police car, so Porter decided to stop. He pulled over to the curb and got out of the car. Slowly, and with some reluctance, his partner also got out.

It didn't take the two bad guys long to realize that although Porter had a partner, he was working alone.

When Porter approached the suspects and asked for some identification, they jumped him. The fight was brutal. Porter yelled for his partner to help, but the probationer refused. He stood frozen next to the car and watched.

Fighting for his life, Porter continued to yell for some help from his partner, but the guy stood silent and refused to move. With brutal determination, and a quick right cross, Porter nailed one suspect sending him to the ground. Then he dropped his full weight on the guy's head with his knee. The neck snapped with a crack and the body went limp. Before Porter got to his feet, the second suspect caught him in the side of the head with his foot. The blow threw Porter onto the pavement.

Lying on his back, Porter looked into the man's hate filled eyes. As the suspect kicked for Porter's head, Carl rolled and like a cat was on his feet. The suspect kicked wildly, a move that threw him off balance. Porter stepped back, turned the man sideways and snapped his arm around the suspect's neck in a Carotid Choke Hold.

As the man tried to spin out of the hold, Porter lifted him off the ground and tightened his right arm around the neck, cutting off all blood to the brain. The man's eyes bulged and saliva ran down the side of his mouth. He tried to scream but nothing came out. The more he kicked, the stronger the hold. Soon it was over. Porter held the man's body above the ground while his toes danced in a feeble attempt to make contact with something solid. Then, as quickly as it began, it was over. The limp body hung above the sidewalk held in the vice like grip.

Porter dropped the limp body next to his unconscious companion. His eyes then looked in the direction of the police car and the coward who was wearing the same uniform and badge as he. The man had not moved. He stood frozen against the car.

With his uniform shirt ripped and his face covered in blood, he walked over to the car. Hatred flared from his eyes like fiery darts. Standing in front of his partner, he glared, and then he turned slightly. The probationer relaxed, but as he did, Porter spun and caught him in the stomach with a sickening blow to the diaphragm.

With a gasp, the man doubled over. Porter brought his right fist up in a wicked uppercut that caught the cop on the chin knocking him out and sending him to the ground in a heap not far from the two unconscious suspects. Porter reached down, slipped the cop's gun from its still snapped holster and put it in his waistband. Looking around, he saw that the front of the liquor store was guarded by sliding steel gates.

"That'll do," he muttered.

Reaching down, he lifted his partner's handcuffs from their pouch. He snapped one cuff to his partner's wrist, dragged him over to the grating, and cuffed him to the metal. He then removed his own cuffs. Opening them, he slipped one cuff onto the left wrist of the first suspect, weaved the right arm of the second suspect through the grating and then cuffed both suspect's together. He then walked over to his partner and removed his handcuff and callbox keys from the ring on his Sam Browne.

"You won't need these," he muttered.

Walking away, a sinister grin crossed his lips.

"You three dirt bags deserve each other."

Porter walked over to the police car and climbed in. His breathing was labored and the blood around his mouth had started to dry.

"I've got to give up the cigarettes, they're slowing me down," he said as he wiped away the blood from his mouth with the back of his hand.

Picking up the radio mike, he took a deep breath. "7Adam42, show this unit out to Wilshire Station."

"7Adam42 roger," responded the operator.

Slowly, he turned the black and white in the direction of the station. His mind was foggy and his body ached. Yet only one question entered his mind.

"Why didn't the kid help me?"

The more he thought about it the angrier he got. Soon the gas pedal of the Plymouth was pushed down to the floorboard sending the black and white screaming down Pico Boulevard toward the old station. Porter's hands choked the steering wheel. His knuckles went white.

"You rotten little coward! All you had to do was jump in!"

As he approached the station, Porter snapped the steering wheel, and drove the wrong way into the parking lot. He slid the car into the first parking space, snapped off the ignition, threw open the door and stormed up the station steps into the Watch Commanders office. His hair was strewn all over his head and his face was covered with blood.

"Porter, what happened to you?" asked Lieutenant Rudy De Leon as he looked up from his desk.

"Send a unit over to Pico and 3rd Avenue. You'll find my partner and two suspects cuffed in front of Joe's Liquor. Oh, that coward you gave me as a partner won't need this anymore!"

Porter threw the unloaded revolver on the desk along with the six rounds of ammunition. With that, he turned and walked out of the office.

The two suspects were still down on the sidewalk when a black and white rolled up. Stopping, they glanced around and saw Porter's partner still in a daze, his eyes glazed over and his head bobbing from side to side as he nervously pled with the two suspects not to hurt him.

The suspects were booked for battery on a police officer. The probationer was fired.

"So, Whitaker, that's the background on your new partner. You've taken that probationer's place. Good luck!"

4th Avenue and Pico

It was Thursday morning, July 20, 1967. It was hot and the radio waves in Wilshire Division were quiet. My partner was Werner Kremples.

At 2:20 a.m. we received a radio call and were assigned to handle a family dispute. My attitude was to waste as little time on these calls as possible, while Werner wanted to solve the unsolvable. So while he talked to the combatants, I walked around the apartment and opened drawers and kitchen cabinets knowing that within minutes the fighting parties would soon forget their squabble and want to know what I was looking for. It worked perfectly. Soon they forgot about each other and directed their insults towards me.

With that change of direction, I decided it was time to leave. I told Werner we were wasting our time, and if they wanted to fight, let them, we were leaving. As we left, Werner turned to me and said, "You're cold Whitaker, just plain cold." Once back in the car, neither of us spoke.

With Werner driving, we left the scene and drove down Pico Avenue toward 4th Avenue. When he got to 4th Avenue, he made a quick right hand turn and then a left into a dark alley that ran parallel to Pico. After we entered the alley, he shut off the engine and we coasted into the darkness.

Slowly, the black and white rolled over the uneven dirt road. About half way down the alley we came to the rear of an old service station which was located on our left hand side. The station had a rear washing bay that was shaped like two letter "U's" placed upside down. As we approached the rear of this structure, we both looked to our left into the gas station.

Beyond the rear washing bays we saw a center island that housed a small office. The gas pumps were located on the right side of the center island. As we looked through the darkness into the office area, we saw a male Negro standing in the office door with what appeared to be a large gun in his right hand. In front of him stood the gas station attendant. My eyes then glanced into the darkness just beyond the washing bays where I saw a lookout stationed between the office and the bays.

"Do you see what I see?" Werner asked.

"It's a 211 (robbery) in progress," I whispered. "Unlock the shotgun."

As Werner opened the shotgun rack located just below the front seat, he whispered, "Put out a Help Call."

I slipped the hand mike from the radio, and whispered, "7Adam42 requesting assistance at 4th Avenue and Pico. We have a 211 in progress."

I slid the mike back into the holder, turned off the radio and slipped the Ithaca twelve gauge shotgun from the rack.

Noiselessly, we stepped out of the car and moved toward the suspects. In my mind I thought, *Be with me Lord my God.* With the shotgun at port arms, I moved toward the lookout while Werner approached the office.

As we approached, the gunman in the office door struck the attendant with the gun knocking him to the ground. Once the attendant was on the floor, the suspect began to beat him viciously about the head and face which made a sound much like the thumping on a ripe watermelon.

When I stepped from the darkness into the shadows, I slammed the wooden slide of the Ithaca back which sent a .12 gauge magnum double aught buck round into the chamber. That sound caused the lookout to spin in my direction. He hesitated only a moment before turning to his left. Then he bolted for the street. As he darted across the rear of the darkened station, so did I. This was my mistake. Running, I fired my first round. It missed. Still running, I fired the next two. Again, misses.

Although the first three rounds missed the suspect, they did make solid hits with the gas pumps, plate glass windows across the street and the windshields of parked cars. When the suspect neared the curb at the far side of the street, I stopped, leveled the shotgun and squeezed the trigger. A hit!

I watched him be picked up and thrown about ten feet through the air and slammed face first against the curb.

With an empty shotgun, I turned my attention to Werner and his shots that were piercing the air.

Earlier, when I stepped out of the darkness to confront the lookout, Werner approached the suspect who was pistol whipping the attendant. Hearing my first round slammed into the chamber, the suspect in the office stopped beating the attendant, jumped from the office door and ran into the night. Werner fired at the fleeing bandit with his .38 revolver, but missed the elusive suspect. When his service revolver was empty, he drew his small back-up gun and was about to commence firing when the suspect ran directly in front of me and into my line of fire.

Throwing the empty shotgun into my left hand, I drew my revolver and chased the gunman down the middle of Pico Boulevard. When I closed the distance between us to about fifteen feet, I fired my first round. He jerked, turned and fired. I will never forget the flame shooting from his gun and the sound of the bullet as it whistled past my head. Again and again I fired, watching him jerk each time he was hit, but he didn't fall, nor did he stop turning and firing in my direction.

Down the middle of the street we ran; he, fleeing for his life, and me in pursuit while trying to stay out of his line of fire. After I fired my six rounds, my gun was empty. I slowed up and watched as the wounded suspect ran around a corner and into the darkness. With two empty weapons, I dropped the shotgun, jumped behind a telephone pole, ejected the spent casings from the cylinder and started to reload. In those days, we didn't have the fancy reloading devices they later used. Our method of reloading during a gun battle was no different from that used on the streets of Dodge City or Tombstone during the days of the Wild West. You placed one bullet at a time into the empty chamber.

Unsnapping the leather pouches that carried my extra ammunition, I hurriedly dropped the rounds into my shaking hand which sent half of the twelve rounds into the street. I managed to slam six into the chamber, snap it shut and then head into the darkness after the suspect.

By now sirens pierced the air, coming from all over South Central Los Angeles as they responded to our call for assistance. I cautiously slipped into the darkness and when I was unable to locate the suspect, I returned to Pico Boulevard.

While I walked down Pico toward the gas station, I was approached by John Marzullo. He stopped me and extended his hand.

"These are yours," he said.

He then dropped my six expended .38 caliber casings into my hand as well as the live rounds I had dropped while reloading. "I thought you might want these, especially if your ammo wasn't authorized." The ammunition was authorized, but I appreciated the fact that he was looking out for me.

The shooting lasted about three minutes. In all, Werner fired six rounds from his service revolver, and I fired six rounds from my service revolver and four rounds from the shotgun. The suspect fired three rounds from his pistol. The suspect I shot with the shotgun was hit with nine of the twelve double aught buck pellets. His partner made his way to a hospital where he was treated for gunshot wounds to both legs and later was arrested.

30th and Vermont

I was newly transferred to University Division and assigned to the Morning Watch. My partner was an old timer named Matt Cunningham. Cunningham had forty years on the job and was born, raised and worked in University Division.

We hit the streets at about midnight. Cunningham drove while I took the reports, handled the radio and kept the nightly Activity Log. After we left the station parking lot, it didn't take long before we received our first radio call.

"3Adam81, see the woman, victim of an assault, 30th and Vermont at the bus stop. 3Adam81, your call is Code 2."

"3Adam81, roger," I responded. And with that we started the long drive from the station to the scene.

At 30th and Vermont, Cunningham made a left hand turn that took us into the darkness of 30th Street. We travelled about half a block when on the right hand side, concealed in the shadows, we saw the bus stop. As we approached, I saw a large black woman standing next to the bus stop sign. She was wearing a white nurse's uniform that was soaked in blood. Over her shoulder was slung a large purse.

As Cunningham pulled up, I yelled from the open window, "Are you all right?"

"I'm all right," was the rather sarcastic response, "but that sucker that tried to rob me, he ain't all right. No sir. I got him good."

"That's not your blood?" I asked as I stepped from the car.

"No it ain't my blood. It belongs to the little sucker who tried to rob me!"

Realizing that an ambulance was not needed, I asked her to have a seat in the rear of the police car and I continued my interview.

"Why don't you tell me what happened?"

"Well," she said, "I work hard for my money. I'm a Licensed Vocational Nurse with six children and no sucker who ain't workin' is going to take my hard earned money."

"I understand, but what happened tonight?"

"Well, Officer, What's your name?"

"Whitaker."

"Well Officer Why-taker, I was standing at this here bus stop like I do every night. And out of the darkness steps this skinny little black dude. He comes up to me and demands my money. I ain't giving you my money," I said. "And then he made his big mistake. He grabbed my purse. Well, he didn't know that I carried this for protection."

The woman then pulled a ten inch screwdriver from her purse.

"When he pulled at my purse, he got tangled in the straps. So, while he was pullin', I stabbed that little sucker with my screwdriver. As we fought, I stabbed him and stabbed him. I stabbed him in the face a bunch of times and then in the chest. I stabbed him all over. With his hands caught in my purse straps, he couldn't get away. And anyway, I was bigger than him."

Now it all made sense; as did the large amount of blood that stained the sidewalk.

As Cunningham began the crime report, I started to follow the blood spots. Drop after drop hit the ground on a regular basis. At the scene of the assault, the distance between drops was longer due to the fact that the suspect was running. Then, apparently exhausted from the fight and weakened by the loss of blood, the distance between drops decreased, as did their size.

Slowly, I walked down the sidewalk, crossed the intersection of 30th and Vermont and continued east into the darkness. The light of my flashlight jumped back and forth across the uneven sidewalk illuminating the crimson trail where drops shone and sparkled brightly as they caught the flashlight beam.

Suddenly the drops stopped. I searched further and saw that the drops left the sidewalk and continued up a small concrete walkway that led to the backyard of an old home. Walking up the side path I came to a gate. Cautiously, I pushed it open and stepped into the darkness of the backyard. With my flashlight in my left hand and my revolver in my right, I walked until I came to an old weather-beaten screen door that led to a dilapidated enclosed patio. I turned off my flashlight, pushed open the door and stepped into the patio area. It was dark and all was quiet.

When I snapped on my flashlight, I found minute blood spots on the floor that led to a far corner of the room. In the corner I saw an old mattress and the all but lifeless body of the suspect curled in a fetal position. I approached and placed the barrel of my revolver in his ear, while circumspectly nudging him with my foot.

"Hey slick, it's the Poo-lice, get up."

He didn't move nor utter a sound. Blood covered him from the top of his head to the bottom of his feet. I placed the flashlight under my left arm, put my service revolver in my left hand and with my right hand checked his neck for a pulse. I found one, but it was weak. He was nearly dead.

Rolling him over, I checked him for weapons and after finding him clean, I handcuffed him, left the patio and started looking for Cunningham who pulled up as I stepped to the street.

"Did you find him, Whitaker?"

"Ya," I responded. "He's lying on a dirty mattress on the back patio, dying, so we've' got a couple of options."

"Options…what options?" asked Cunningham, irritation raking his voice.

"Well, we can leave, come back in thirty minutes and then call the Coroner. That would save court costs and our time. Or, you can call the guy an ambulance. My vote, let's leave."

"You're cold, Whitaker," Cunningham said, cutting distain on every word. "I'll call the guy an ambulance," he barked gruffly. And so he did. It was apparent he didn't like my style.

The ambulance arrived and the suspect was transported to County General Hospital. The fact that we never received subpoenas for the preliminary hearing led me to believe that he expired from his wounds.

Following the incident, Cunningham went directly into the Lieutenant, explained my comments and told him he refused to work with me again.

Shoot Out the Lights!

It was a cold winter night in South Central Los Angeles when a "Woman with a gun, shots fired" radio call hit the airwaves. Immediately, University Division started to respond.

I was working a black and white and when we rolled up to the scene I saw that a small "L" shaped apartment building was the center of activity. Moving in the shadows, I found a position near the front door. Beyond the door was a long hallway dimly lit by a single yellow stained light bulb that hung from the ceiling. Three apartment doors lined the right side, and as I stood at the front, I watched a number of policemen converge at the rear of the hall.

Since the hallway was straight, we were now in each other's line of fire. Suddenly, a shot rang out and everyone hit the ground. I do not know who fired that shot, but the smoke had not cleared when some cop started yelling, "Shoot out the lights, shoot out the lights!"

I could not believe what I was hearing! No one had a clear shot at a light without shooting in the direction of a fellow officer. Exasperated with the stupidity of the moment, I looked up from my crouched position and found that I was staring directly down the barrel of some recruit's service revolver. The kid had become so engrossed with the situation that he let his gun barrel drop to where it was about two inches from the top of my head. With this turn of events, I turned to my partner and told him it was time to leave. As we did, the banter of "Shoot out the lights, shoot out the lights," erupted again.

Moving away from the building, I watched a veteran cop slip the service revolver of a recruit from his holster and start shooting. He fired a number of rounds in the direction of the light and the other officers down the hall. When the gun was empty, he slipped it back into the holster of the shocked recruit.

I later learned that an old lady had become frightened when two cops mistakenly thought her apartment belonged to a bad guy, so they started banging on the door yelling for her to open it up. Instead of opening the door, and since she was unable to discern who was trying to break in, she did what any normal senior citizen would do, she fired two rounds through the door to scare them off.

A major investigation of the incident took place and a number of disciplinary days were meted out for the incorrect handling of the situation and especially for the unauthorized firing of a service revolver.

Fortunately, no one was hurt, but I was very thankful that I had left the scene before taking a round to the top of the head.

A 77th Division Stolen

The roll call room filled as uniformed cops working the Wilshire Night Watch filtered in, each found a seat on the hard wooden benches and placed their coffee cups on desk tops marred by years of cigar and cigarette burns. Steam spiraled skyward from the white Styrofoam cups and mixed easily with the gray clouds of cigarette smoke to form a haze reminiscent of Los Angeles smog.

I sat in the rear, and as the new guy, waited for roll call to begin.

The car assignments that night revealed that my partner was an older black officer who had six, five year hash marks decorating his sleeve and appeared to have little desire to hit the streets. Once in the car, he looked at me coldly and said, "You handle the radio; I'll take the reports and drive." Basically, he wanted to ensure that once on the street, we only did what he wanted, which turned out to be nothing.

It was mid-week and quiet when we received a radio call to take a burglary report in the southern end of the division known as Baldwin Hills. We pulled up to the small apartment and he told me that he would take the report and I should just sit and keep my mouth shut.

"Fine," I replied.

Inside the apartment, he sat down with the victims, a man and a woman who were also black. As they talked about the burglary, I casually walked around the apartment as if conducting more of the initial investigation. However, my focus was not on the so called "victims," but a very large, new, RCA color television that sat taking up an entire corner of the front room.

As my partner jovially conversed with the couple, I casually moved the television to the side, shone my flashlight on the serial number plate and jotted the numbers down in my small officer's notebook. I then walked out to our car and slid into the front seat.

"7Adam56, requesting a want on the following serial number."

"7Adam56, go ahead," responded the Radio Telephone Operator (RTO).

I proceeded to describe the make and model of the television and also gave the RTO the serial number. Then I waited. About five minutes passed and I received a response.

"7Adam56, the television is a Seventy-Seventh Division stolen; taken during the Watts Riots."

"7Adam56, roger and thank you."

That was all I needed. I requested another unit to meet us at the scene to transport the female for booking, and when I received confirmation that the unit was on its way, I walked back inside the apartment.

My partner sat comfortably on the sofa and causally looked up as I walked in. When the crime report was signed, he thanked the "victims" and started for the door.

"Oh, there is one more item of business," I said.

"And what would that be, Whitaker?" asked the surly old cop.

"The television in the corner is a Seventy-Seventh Street stolen."

Then, I turned to the couple and said, "You're both under arrest for Receiving Stolen Property, a Felony."

The old cop's jaw dropped and his eyes became as big as saucers.

"You can't do that, Whitaker," he stammered.

"Watch me."

With that, I handcuffed them both. You should have seen my partner. He went nuts. Not that it mattered to me, for he couldn't do a thing or I would have arrested him for interfering with a police officer, and he knew it.

As far as I was concerned, they had broken the law and were going to jail. His wearing a badge and carrying a gun meant nothing if he was not going to sustain the law.

The transporting unit showed up, the suspects and the television were loaded into the police cars, and off we went. You can imagine how quiet that ride was back to the station as I sat in the back seat with the male suspect, and my stewing partner drove.

When we arrived at the station, my partner refused to assist me with the booking or any of the reports. So, I did it all.

While I finished the reports, he walked into the Lieutenant's office and advised the Watch Commander that he "refused to work with Whitaker again."

Fortunately for me, his wish was granted and my reputation continued to grow.

Officer, My Head Hurts!

One night while working the Morning Watch in University Division, Roger Fiderio and I received a radio call, "3Adam9, shots fired, see the man, victim of a shooting. 3Adam9, handle the call Code 2."

As we approached the scene which was in the vicinity of 39th and Normandie, our headlights illuminated the front porch of one of the small single family residences that dotted the division.

I parked and Fiderio and I walked up the front sidewalk. As we approached the house, we saw a man sitting on the front porch with his head in his hands. He was alone and all I could hear was him moaning.

"I got a headache, oh my head. I got a headache!"

"Sir, did you call the poo...lice?" I asked.

"Yes, Officer, I called. Oh my head. Oh my head."

"O.K. pal, I give up, why did you call?"

"Officer, I've been shot. Shot my man, shot!"

"Where?" I asked.

OFFICER, MY HEAD HURTS!

"In my head, Officer, I been shot in my head. Right here, Mr. Policeman, right here. In my head. I do be shot, my man. I do be shot, right here in my head!"

Slowly, he lifted his head and moved his hands. To our astonishment, protruding from under the skin in the middle of his forehead were seven .22 caliber bullet slugs! Seven times he had been hit in the back of the head and not one of the seven rounds penetrated the skull! Each circled under the scalp and not being able to break the skin, protruded in the middle of his forehead leaving seven small mounds.

Caustically, Fiderio said, "I can't understand why you'd have a headache."

We called an ambulance and the victim was transported to Central Receiving Hospital where the seven bullets were removed. They bandaged his head and an hour later he walked out of the hospital!

When it came to filing a crime report against the perpetrator, he declined. It appears that it was his common-law wife. And to file a crime report and have her jailed might mean that he would not be so lucky the next time.

Officer's Need Help, Shots Fired

It was 1968.

I was partnered with Roger Fiderio and we were working 3Adam9, the black and white assigned to the north end of University Division, so named because it was the area that surrounded the University of Southern California.

Although nearly three years had passed since the Watt's Riots, the city had not completely bounced back from those days of devastation. To the contrary, the Black Panthers were in full swing, political riots were erupting across the country, the hippie culture was bent on destroying all that was moral and the common street criminal had become more bold and vicious.

The situation on the streets was not one of civil unrest, it was war. Each night, we who wore blue uniforms and a badge were targets as we patrolled the streets of South Central Los Angeles. Under these circumstances, one either became hardened and alert, or was quickly injured or killed.

On one night as we patrolled our area, we heard a broadcast from 77th Street Division that advised all units in South Central Los Angeles that a homicide had occurred, and the perpetrator was believed to be a Black Panther. A description of the suspect was given along with a possible vehicle. As I drove west bound down Adams from Hoover, Roger maintained the log.

Within minutes a radio call erupted over the air waves as the operator anxiously broadcast: "All units in the vicinity and 3Adam9, Officer Needs Help, shots fired, Figueroa just south of 28th Street. 3Adam9, handle the call Code 3."

Roger snatched the mike from its holder and with adrenaline flowing, responded, "3Adam9, roger."

With the snap of a finger, I flipped the toggle switch that activated the two red lights on top of the police car and with my left foot, punched the chrome button on the floorboard that worked the siren.

With my right foot, I slammed the accelerator to the floor and the throaty Plymouth jumped forward. In another motion, I snapped the steering wheel making a quick U-turn. With the pedal on the floor, red lights flashing and siren blaring, the black and white screamed eastbound on Adams Boulevard towards Figueroa. Again, the radio waves were broken as the operator broadcast, "All units and 3Adam9, the suspect's vehicle is southbound on Figueroa with 3Zebra56 in pursuit."

3Zebra56 was a plain clothes unit belonging to the University Special Operations Squad. These units had no sirens or special emergency equipment. If you wanted a red light on the car to make a stop, you went out and bought a hand held white spot light and then a red plastic cover. The light was plugged into the cigarette lighter, covered with the red plastic lens and clicked on when you wanted to use it. To make stops, you either put the light on the dashboard or held it out the window. Not sophisticated by today's standards, but it worked; most of the time.

The street lights blurred as the black and white raced down Adams Boulevard. As we approached the intersection of Adams and Figueroa, I hit the brakes sending the Plymouth into a sideways slide toward the intersection. When the car slid into the middle of Adams and Figueroa, I punched the accelerator to the floor and snapped the steering wheel. Once headed south bound on Figueroa, I again slammed the gas pedal to the floor. In the distance I saw our Zebra unit.

"All units, the suspects are now approaching Figueroa and Exposition."

Down Figueroa we flew. I watched as the suspect's vehicle made a sudden right turn on Exposition and bounce wildly across the railroad tracks going airborne. When it landed, it skidded wildly across the sidewalk and smashed into a small duplex with 3Zebra56 right behind.

In seconds, 3Zebra56 slid to a stop behind the suspect's car. I watched as both officers jumped from their vehicle and chased the two suspects who were now on foot. As our car rolled to a stop behind the Zebra unit, both Fiderio and I were out, weapons in hand, and running. Fiderio ran in the direction of the driver of the suspect's vehicle while I sprinted in the opposite direction toward the passenger suspect and the plain clothes officer who was running with a shotgun in his right hand.

When the passenger suspect reached the end of the pathway separating two duplexes, he spun and faced the officer. Something was in his hand. Exactly what I could not plainly tell, but it must have been obvious to the officer, for the night air suddenly was shattered by the blast of his shotgun.

BOOM!

The impact of the magnum round struck the suspect in the upper left side of his chest and slammed him against the corner of the building. He took the full load of the shotgun blast and slumped over. His eyes stared in cold hatred as he began to lift his right hand. The officer froze. I watched, waiting for a second blast, but none came. I was certain that the officer would fire again. I was wrong. He didn't.

In a daze, he let the shotgun barrel fall towards the ground as he stared back with a glazed look spreading across his face.

I stood at the officer's side with my weapon extended and my finger squeezing the trigger. As the suspect raised his right hand in my direction, rather than fire, I kicked forward catching him fully in the face with my right foot. That kick snapped his head back and sent him to the ground. As he slumped forward, knowing that he had just attempted to murder a police officer, I cracked him on the back of the head with the barrel of my gun. With that blow, the fight was over.

And although I knew that the suspect and plain clothes officer had exchanged gunfire, not seeing a weapon, I wasn't going to become this guy's executioner. Throwing him onto his stomach, I handcuffed him and turned toward the officer. He hadn't moved since the first shotgun blast. The shotgun barrel still faced the ground and as I looked into his eyes, I knew that the incident had taken its toll. He was in shock.

Had I fired and killed the suspect, it would have been considered in police language, "a good shooting" for earlier that evening, the suspect, a Black Panther, had murdered a rival in 77th Street Division. Then he and his companion headed north into University Division where they were spotted by 3Zebra56. As the suspects slowly drove their vehicle down Figueroa from Adams, the SOS unit pulled in behind. When the hand held red light was put on the dash, the suspects pulled to the curb.

When the passenger officer exited his car, the passenger suspect began to exit from the passenger side of their car. In his hands he held a sawed off .12 gauge shotgun. The same shotgun he used earlier in the evening to murder his victim.

When not quite out of the car, the suspect spun towards the police officer, but the shotgun prematurely fired sending the deadly pellets harmlessly into the air blowing out a street light that was directly overhead.

With the shotgun blast, both officers opened fire. The rear window of the suspect's vehicle was blown out as they began their flight from the scene, yet this only proved beneficial to the suspects for it allowed the shotgun toting murderer to continue blasting away at 3Zebra56 all the way down Figueroa and up until the time they lost control of the car and crashed into the small duplex.

And what happened to the nineteen year old suspect who took all nine double aught buck shotgun pellets? He lived and was convicted of the 77th Street homicide and attempted murder of two police officers. And that's how it was in the decade of the sixties.

A Drunk with a Gun

It was in the early morning hours and I was working 3Adam9 out of University Division. My partner was Tony Nardone. We were working a black and white; Nardone was driving. The call came out as "Two 390's (drunks) in a vehicle," and then the street location. We slowly made our way into Newton Division and just as slowly drove toward the location of the call. These calls were not responded to in great haste since we would much rather find the drunks gone when we arrived.

As we pulled around a corner, we spotted the suspect's car sitting next to the curb with two occupants in the front seat. Nardone shut off our headlights, and we quietly pulled in behind the car. It appeared that we had not been seen.

Quietly, we walked up to the suspect's car. Nardone stopped just short of the driver's door and was out of sight. I walked to the passenger window which was down and shouted, "Police officers, put your hands on the dash!"

As I stood to the rear of the window, I held my service revolver in my right hand and I placed the barrel on the lower part of the window ledge about two inches behind the right ear of the passenger suspect.

With my flashlight in my left hand, I shined the beam into the passenger's eyes as he turned to look in my direction.

Suddenly, I saw his left hand come across his chest in my direction. In his hand was a chrome .22 caliber revolver. Before I could move my head away from the window, the suspect shoved the gun into my face and slurred a profanity.

Instinctively, I began to squeeze the trigger, but as I glanced across the front seat at my background, I was shocked to see that Nardone was in my line of fire. And even using the weak 158 grain .38 caliber round, if the head shot was through and through, there was a chance I would not only kill the suspect but also my partner. That was a chance I did not want to take.

With a forceful smash, I struck the suspects gun hand with my service revolver and knocked the "Saturday Night Special" to the floorboard of the car. Although stunned, the suspect still was able to lunge forward for the gun. As he did so, I struck him on the side of the head with the barrel of my gun knocking him unconscious.

While this was happening, Nardone drew down on the driver who sat frozen behind the steering wheel. Both suspects then were removed from their vehicle. On the floorboard I recovered the fully loaded, six shot, .22 caliber revolver.

A Three Time Loser

It was a dark, quiet night and Nardone and I were in a black and white assigned to 3Adam9 in University Division. At about 3:00 a.m., Tony pulled into the darkness of a gas station on the corner of Adams Blvd. and Hoover Avenue.

As we sat in the darkness, I switched on the small light attached to our hot sheet holder. As I wrote, I heard a car approaching from the rear. I turned and saw a 1967 yellow Mercury Cougar. The driver didn't see us, and as he drove slowly past, I saw that the car was occupied by four males. I noted the license number and checked the hotsheet.

Unlike today, the stolen and wanted vehicles were not on a computer, but were hand typed onto a light brown sheet of paper and then mimeographed for distribution. We then placed the paper in a holder attached to the dash of the car and would often illuminate the sheet by turning on our flashlight and then placing our hand over the light thus allowing only slivers of light to shine through our fingers. We did this in an attempt to diminish the ability of the bad guys to recognize a police car sitting in the darkness, not that it wasn't hard to determine who we were, but we did everything we could to gain an advantage.

As I looked to the far column on the hotsheet, I found the Cougar's license number. It was a University Division stolen.

"The Cougar that just went by is on the hotsheet, Nardone. Let's go."

"You're kidding, Whitaker."

"Nardone, it's stolen. Go!"

Tony started the Plymouth and pulled out of the darkness onto Adams Blvd. Accelerating, we soon were directly behind the suspect's vehicle. As we looked through their rear back window, we confirmed that we had four suspects: two in the front and two in the back. Grabbing the hand mike, I ran the license number over the radio for confirmation.

"3Adam9, your vehicle is a University Stolen, armed and dangerous."

"3Adam9, roger. Be advised we are stopping the vehicle at Adams and Magnolia. We are Code 6 at that location." Code 6 meant that we were out of the car for an investigation.

Nardone activated the red lights, the Cougar, instead of pulling to the curb, slowed down, and the driver stopped in the middle of the street.

Normally, I didn't take the shotgun out of the rack, but because the Cougar was stolen and the occupants identified as armed and dangerous, I slid the Ithaca .12 gauge out of the rack and when I stepped from the car, I placed my left hand on the wooden slide mechanism and my right hand on the stock just below the receiver. My right index finger slid above the trigger guard.

Using my door for protection, I ordered the occupants of the car to place their hands out the windows, fingers spread. First, the passenger in the right front was ordered to open the car door from the outside, slowly step out and prone himself on the ground.

Slowly, the front passenger opened the door from the outside and stepped out. He stood about six two and weighed about two hundred pounds. His appearance was that of a black militant, and his demeanor was surly and confrontational.

With Nardone covering the car and its occupants, I stepped forward, and again ordered the suspect into a prone position on the ground. Insulting my family pedigree, he turned and faced me. With an air of antagonism, he made some more profane remarks and abruptly turned and began to walk away, not realizing that he just had made a terrible mistake.

I ordered him to freeze. He stopped and turned facing me. I held the shotgun waist high, the barrel pointed at his stomach. With a coldness brought about by time on the street, I stepped forward and commanded him to prone himself on the ground. As I spoke, he lunged and grabbed for the shotgun barrel. Instantly, I responded.

With the wooden slide receiver in my left hand and my right hand firmly gripping the smaller portion of the stock, I dropped the shotgun butt down, buckled my knees for leverage and then with all the power I had, snapped the shotgun butt in a vertical butt stroke directed at the bottom of his nose. The shotgun struck where it was directed, just under the nose and above the teeth. Bones shattered, teeth flew and the face disintegrated under the impact of the blow. The ferocity and force of the blow sent the man to the pavement like a sack of potatoes, while shattering the wooden shotgun butt, severing it from the receiver.

So there I stood, my right hand holding the stock of the shotgun and my left gripping the receiving portion of the weapon. The shotgun was now in two pieces.

The suspect didn't move. Whether he was dead or not, I didn't know. What I knew was that we still had three dangerous suspects to remove from the car.

I shot a glance at the figure on the ground and watched as a large pool of blood formed around his head.

No one in the car moved or said a word. They had watched as their partner was felled. It was obvious that he was the leader of the pack, and no one wanted to test the system a second time.

Still unaware of what the remaining suspects had in mind, Nardone directed them out of the car and onto the ground. Slowly, and moving as directed, each exited the vehicle and obediently placed himself in a prone position on the asphalt with arms outstretched and fingers extended. Once each had been searched and handcuffed, I walked over to the police car and called for back-up and an ambulance. The suspect on the ground had not moved or made a sound.

Whether or not the blow killed him, I didn't know. What I did know was that had he taken the shotgun from me, it would not have been the suspects on the ground, but Nardone and I.

Time passed and we waited for an ambulance and a supervisor. Still no movement or sound from the suspect on the ground. Blood continued to flow down the asphalt and soon formed a small stream as it headed toward the gutter.

Once the ambulance arrived, so did a sergeant who had never been a fan of mine. Getting out of his car, his first words after seeing the suspect and the river of blood were, "Is that your doing, Whitaker?"

"Ya *Sarge*, I answered. "That's my doing."

"I might have known it," he said. "Whitaker, if you're involved, I don't want anything to do with it. Oh, by the way, is he dead?"

"I don't know, I'm not a doctor."

With that, he walked back to his car, climbed in and drove away.

This action was not unlike him. On the night Fiderio and I were in a shooting not five blocks from this location and another suspect died, this same sergeant, not wanting to get involved, refused to respond quickly, and when he finally did, he immediately left the scene when he saw who was involved.

When the ambulance arrived, the still unconscious suspect was placed in the back and transported to Central Receiving Hospital.

I later was told that the suspect taken to the hospital barely lived. The blow had pulverized his face from the front of the mouth to the bottom of the eye sockets. All that was left had the texture of oatmeal. How long he lived after that incident is anyone's guess. He later was released from the hospital and failed to show up to his preliminary hearing. Word on the street was that was taken somewhere by his partners and left to die.

Additionally, he had just been released from prison for armed robbery and had been on the outside only for two days. He had a long rap sheet or arrest record for crimes of violence.

Did he want to go back to prison? No. Would he have gone back being in a stolen car? Yes. So in his mind, he had only one option and that was to kill two cops.

Get Out of the Car!

Many years ago, Roger Fiderio and I built a strong relationship of trust. The relationship began while we worked a patrol car together on the streets of South Central Los Angeles and continued through our University Division Special Operations Squad (SOS) assignment and throughout the time we were partners in University Detectives.

The patrol assignment was in uniform while the SOS assignment was in plain clothes. The SOS unit was considered elite and was made up of five, two man teams. It was one of the foremost crime suppression units in the city and we were considered to be some of the toughest street cops in the City of the Angels.

It was the summer of 1968, and we hit the streets at about 11:30 p.m. We headed for our area, which included the neighborhood surrounding the Los Angeles Memorial Coliseum. Our call letters or unit number was 3Zebra9. Many years before, this area had been the Beverly Hills of Los Angeles, but now it primarily was a black neighborhood, poor, run down and violent.

Roger and I had worked together long enough that we could go long periods of time without speaking. We usually knew what the other was thinking, and we had many ways of creating excitement if the night was slow. One was to park the car in one of the toughest areas we could find. If in uniform, we would remove our hat, Sam Browne belt and badge. Then we slipped our gun into our waistband and went off in different directions to see what we could find. If we were working in plain clothes, we would just separate and walk the alleys. We did this often and called the exercise, "The Most Dangerous Game." The "game" pitted us individually against whatever or whomever we encountered. Fortunately in all these "games," neither of us ever lost to an opponent.

One quiet night while we were working a plain clothes assignment, Roger drove us to our area and the hunt began. Prior to leaving the station I checked out a hand-held walkie talkie unit.

As we traveled down 23rd Street and idled through the darkness, I heard a still small voice whisper, *Richard, get out of the car.* I had heard that voice many times in the past, and although it was not an audible voice, it was very loud and clear.

"Roger, let me out of the car on the corner to see what I can find."

Roger never questioned my requests no matter how strange they might seem, so immediately the car slowed and I got out.

"I'll call when I want you to pick me up," I said.

With that, Fiderio drove into the darkness. Nearly fifteen minutes passed and with it went the problematic feeling as well. I contacted Roger via the walkie talkie and told him to pick me up. Within minutes we were back looking for some excitement. Not ten minutes passed when I again heard, *Richard, get out of the car!* In this admonition there was an urgency I could not ignore.

"Roger, let me out again. I'll be in touch."

Once again, Fiderio pulled to the curb and I got out, not knowing why, but only that I was admonished to do so. Slowly, I walked into the darkness leaving Roger and the police car behind.

Within seconds I heard the throaty acceleration of the Plymouth as the car roared into the night. Soon the noise was gone, and I stood alone in the darkness. With the walkie talkie in one hand, my flashlight in the other and my four inch, six shot .38 Smith and Wesson revolver shoved in the holster of my Alfonso custom made gun belt, I proceeded down the first dark alley I found. Darkness encompassed me as I soon found myself lost in the still silence of the night that can, in its own way, ring loud in the ears of one accustomed to the sounds of the ghetto at night.

I walked the alleys and dark streets of the area for about thirty minutes before I tried to raise Fiderio on the radio. I tried over and over, but there was no response. Walking slowly back onto Adams Boulevard, I stopped just east of Hoover. A patrol unit pulled around the corner and stopped.

"Whitaker," the passenger officer yelled, "where have you been? Fiderio was in a pursuit and there were some problems. Get in and we'll take you to him."

I jumped in the police car and we drove up the darkened side streets until we hit 23rd Street. The driver made a right on 23rd and punched the gutsy Plymouth. Within minutes we had traveled the route taken by Fiderio.

Twenty-Third Street was very narrow with cars parked on both sides of the street making passage difficult and cutting access down to a single driving lane each way. The street lights were old and dim. Old apartment buildings and small single family dwellings lined the street. The lack of adequate lighting provided easy pickings for the thieves who traveled to the area knowing that many naïve and rich students attending the University of Southern California lived in the neighborhood.

The street remained almost pitch black until it reached Figueroa which it intersected forming a "T." As the black and white pulled up to the intersection, I saw our car sitting in the middle of the street parked directly behind an old Buick that had crashed into a telephone pole. Before the patrol car came to a complete stop, I was out and walking rapidly toward some officers who were standing near our car.

"Where's Fiderio?" I asked.

"Over here," yelled Roger.

From across the street, Roger emerged dragging a handcuffed suspect. And while Roger looked as if he had been in a good fight, the other guy looked worse. His extra six inches in height and nearly one hundred pounds in weight did him no good when he faced off with this feisty Italian. In combat, Fiderio gave no ground. And he never lost. Pound for pound he was by far one of the toughest cops assigned to the streets of South Central Los Angeles.

One must picture Fiderio and the bad guy. Roger stood no more that 5' 8" and dripping wet, weighed no more than 150 pounds. The suspect he had in tow was about 6'2" and weighed a good 250 pounds. Again, both looked like they had been in a fight. But it was apparent that Roger had won. He always won.

After he deposited the suspect into the back seat of our car, I asked him what happened.

"I dropped you off and started down 23rd Street and when I looked in the rearview mirror, I saw this Buick coming up behind me. They were flying. They hit their high beams and honked at me a couple of times to let them pass. When I didn't, the guy flew past me at about ninety. They didn't make me as a cop because when they came along side, the dude driving tried to run me off the road. Once he got past, I pulled in behind them and grabbed the mike.

As he told the story, his face remained expressionless.

"Here I am, alone…..no partner…… driving with one hand while handling the radio and running the license plate. When I put the red light on the dash the pursuit began. We were both doing over a hundred down 23rd when the plate came back to a Wilshire stolen, suspects armed and dangerous. When we got to Figueroa, the dude driving couldn't make the turn and crashed into the pole. What happened next was kinda funny.

"OK, what happened next?" I asked.

"When they hit the pole, both dudes bailed out of the car. But the passenger instead of running, stopped and turned towards our car. He was still standing there when I went into foot pursuit of the driver. I cornered the driver in a doorway and the fight was on. He was big Rich, but I won. And that's it!"

We impounded the Buick, drove the suspect back to the station and placed him in an interrogation room in University Detectives. During our interrogation, we learned that he and his partner had robbed a home at gun point in Wilshire Division earlier that night and had stolen the victim's car. When I asked the driver why his partner had jumped out of the car and waited, he looked at me and said, "You is lucky…"

"Why?" I asked.

"Cause my partner and me talked about what we was gunna do if we got stopped by the poo…lice. And we decided that we ain't going back to jail. So my partner, who had the piece, was going to off the pig sittin' in the passenger seat when he got out of the police car. But that was the problem."

"Why?" I asked.

"Cause' there weren't no passenger ridin' in the poo…lice car, only the dude drivin'. My partner waited, but no pig got out. If he did, he woulda been dead."

Slowly, I stepped forward, leaned in close and stared into his hate filled eyes. The seconds passed. It seemed like minutes.

"You got no right lookin' at me like that!" he shouted.

Barely speaking above a whisper, I said in a mocking tone: "My man, let me tell you something. Had I been in the car, and had I stepped out, I would have had a shotgun in my hands. And Slick, I would have blown not only you…but also your partner…….both to hell before he got off a shot."

The small interrogation room was quiet. The suspect dropped his head and broke away from my gaze. There wasn't another word from him. He knew what I was saying was true. It was not idle talk, nor a threat. In that moment, I knew I had made my point.

Stealth in the Shadows

One night, Fiderio and I while assigned to the University Special Operations Squad found ourselves working an area that contained a large social hall called "The Old Dixie." The place was located on South Western Avenue and when not used for weekend dances, it was a watering hole, or a place frequented by cops who wanted to have couple of drinks when they got off duty.

When there was a dance, parked cars often became targets of auto theft and burglaries. On this particular night, I told Roger that it appeared to be a good night to get out and walk. We parked our car on a residential street some distance from the hall, and staying in the shadows, we walked toward the location.

Foot traffic was light since most who were attending the dance were inside the hall. The night was cool and clouds covered the moon. The conditions were perfect for our operation.

As we walked, we hugged the houses and stayed in the shadows. In the distance, I saw a figure in dark clothing walking in the street looking into the windows of the parked cars.

Staying in the shadows, we walked closer to the unsuspecting thief. When he crossed to the far side of the street, I motioned to Roger that we should slip onto a front porch, hide in the darkness, and sit and watch. We walked down two houses and then stepped onto a porch. When we slid into the darkness, the suspect crossed the street and began to look into the cars located directly in front of us.

Slowly, he made his way toward us, stopping to look in each car until he found what he wanted. He stopped directly in front of us, a distance of about twenty-five feet. We sat silent and watched as he slipped a tool between the door window of the locked car, then quietly opened the door and slid into the front seat.

In less than twenty seconds he was out of the car carrying a purse. Looking around, he glanced at the front porch where we were sitting. Not seeing us, he walked toward the house and the porch. As he approached, we moved deeper into the darkness. The bandit sat down directly in front of us on the front steps. Quietly, he emptied the purse onto the porch and began to rifle through the contents. Not wanting to lose this guy, I stepped up behind him. He still had no idea we were there. With my service revolver in my right hand, I placed the barrel of the gun behind his right ear and cocked the hammer back. Although not a loud noise, the sound can be deafening. With the gun behind his ear, I then very quietly began to give the bandit some specific directions explaining to him what I planned to do should he decide not to comply.

He began to shake violently. Compliance was immediate. Without any resistance, we handcuffed the suspect, scooped up the purse, completed the appropriate crime report and booked him into University Division jail.

A Unique Request

The year was 1968. Cheryle and I were living in our small two bedroom single car garage home at 5628 Bellingham Avenue in North Hollywood. I was working University Division Patrol and assigned to the Morning Watch.

One day, one of my partners asked if he could store a few items in our small garage. He said that it would only be for a short period of time.

"Sure," I said, not knowing exactly what he intended to store. Late one night, Daryl called and said he was on his way with the "items." A couple of hours passed and undercover of deep darkness, a pickup truck pulled into the driveway, honked twice and parked. When I approached the driver's door, Daryl got out and asked if I would help unload the "items."

"Let's do it," I answered.

He opened the back of the truck and reached in, grabbing the first item. To be honest, I had no idea what was in the bed of the pickup until my hand wrapped its self around the barrel of what felt like a long, very heavy weapon.

I was right.

We first removed a .50 caliber, air cooled aircraft machine gun! The second item was a World War II mortar.

"Where in heavens name did you find these?" I asked.

With a large grin covering his face, he said, "Oh, it wasn't hard. I have contacts. A bunch of cops are into this stuff. I even have a large waterproof box buried in the backyard with other items. All bought and paid for. It's all legal. I am a collector, have the licenses and have paid the taxes!"

Smiling, he then said, "Hey Whitaker, I got a real deal for you. How would you like a new, .45 caliber Thompson submachine gun, just like Elliott Ness used with a fifty round circular magazine, the works? It's legal. Just need to pay the taxes and fees on it."

"You're kidding," I answered.

"Nope. We have some in the original brown wrapping paper, brand new. Only three hundred bucks and we also have a freight car loaded with .45 caliber ammunition. Interested?"

"I think I'll pass."

The weapons only sat in our garage a few days. When Cheryle figured out what they were, coupled with the fact that we had two small children at home, she told me that the "items" would be removed…immediately. And they were.

I made a call and they were gone the next day. Where they went and what was done with them, I will never know.

Adams and Hoover

It was a beautiful afternoon. Fiderio and I were assigned to the University Division Special Operations Squad. We were working plain clothes in the area of the University of Southern California. It was about 1:00 p.m. and traffic on Adams Blvd. was heavy because of the lunch hour.

Standing on the sidewalk on Adams just east of Hoover Ave., we watched a male Negro exit one of the fraternity houses that surrounded the university. He was dressed in a karate uniform and there was no doubt by his appearance and demeanor that he didn't belong to a fraternity. As he walked in our direction, it was apparent that he made us for the police. Turning, he headed in the opposite direction. However, before he could start to run, Fiderio was behind him with me in front. Throwing open my windbreaker, I identified myself, showed the suspect my badge which was attached to my belt and ordered him to freeze.

Quickly, he took a step to run. With my weapon drawn, I again ordered him to freeze. We stood about two feet apart and I held my revolver in front of me with my right elbow braced snugly against my side. Like a cat, he sprang, grabbed the barrel of the revolver and pulled it into his stomach in an attempt to wrench the gun from my hands. Had I not had my right arm tightly against my body and a solid grip on the weapon, it would have been his. The fight was on.

When the suspect grabbed the barrel of my gun, Roger jumped behind him and threw a bar arm choke hold across his neck. The man reacted by standing straight up and lifting Fiderio off the ground, and then, with Fiderio hanging on for dear life, the suspect began to swing Roger from side to side while never releasing his hold on my gun. While Roger's feet flew back and forth, he never loosened the choke hold.

"He's got hold of my gun, Roger," I yelled. "Let go of him, he's dead!" As I shouted, I started to squeeze the trigger, but to my astonishment, Fiderio never released his grip.

"Let him go Fiderio," I screamed. "He's dead!"

"No," Fiderio yelled as the suspect tossed him around like a rag doll. "I got him, Rich! I got him!"

Releasing the pressure on the trigger, I increased my fight knowing that if he got my gun we were dead. The fight took us out into traffic, which caused four lanes to come to a standstill. Finally, I was able to rip my weapon free, but that didn't end the fight. Minutes passed and cars stopped to watch. Then as suddenly as it began, it ended. Exhausted, the suspect fell to the ground and we snapped the handcuffs on his wrists. He was later identified as an area burglar who preyed on the students at USC.

A Tragic Comedy of Errors

"I need to talk to someone!" she shouted from behind the heavy glass. "Please, talk to me. I have some information you cops want," pleaded the woman who was handcuffed to the bench inside the small holding cell.

When the rear station door swung open, Officer Jerry Brooks stepped into the hallway and heard the final pleading words of, "I have some information!"

No sweeter sound could be spoken to one of the best and toughest street cops to work South Central Los Angeles.

"Who does she belong to," asked Brooks as he walked past the Watch Commander's office.

Looking up from his paperwork, Lieutenant Rudy Brillon slowly removed his pipe, shot Brooks a look and said, "Vice brought her in on a prostitution charge, but I'm sure you could convince them into letting you talk to her."

That was all Brooks needed. After finding the Vice cops, he received permission to talk to their arrestee. The frantic street walker was escorted to an interrogation room located in the Detective squad room. It was there that Brooks began to work his magic.

The conversation between Brook's and the street walker began. Before long he determined her name was "Rosie," and the group she was associated with planned to burglarize the apartment of Ike and Tina Turner, two popular Rock and Roll singers of the day. Following the burglary, they planned on renting a truck and burglarize a restaurant in Culver City.

Further interrogation led to the details. Apparently Rosie had become angry with one of the players involved in the plot, and wanted revenge. However, her plan ultimately would backfire.

Working as a unit, the University Special Operations Squad arrived at work late one evening to begin what would become one long and funny weekend. We formed our teams, held roll call and then hit the streets. Then we waited.

The unit composition was unique. There was myself and Roger Fiderio. We had been partners in patrol and now were partners on the Special Operations Squad. All in all, Roger and I spent close to five years working together in various assignments. I believe that our longevity was partly due to the fact that no one really wanted to work with either of us because of our aggressiveness coupled with the fact that we both were considered to be a little crazy.

Then there was Jerry Brooks and his partner, Bob Gosnell.

We had Bob Stemples, Roger Niles, both of whom were excellent cops, Charles "Froggy" LeFrois and John Inglis. Inglis was another interesting story. John loved to party. He was not tall, but rotund and porky by most standards. One night, while off duty, John got mixed up with a young lady who became angry at him and proceeded to shoot him using his own off duty weapon. The bullet hit Inglis in the leg leaving him with a permanent limp and in remembrance of the night, John faithfully wore the slug on a gold chain around his neck. This was often a topic of discussion by others when we were off duty, and John played it to the hilt.

Before we hit the street, Brooks again talked to Rosie and told her to call him at the station when the bad guys were on the move. We waited nervously until the call came. It was a Saturday afternoon when our surveillance began. The tail meandered in and out of the city streets and with each sudden turn, we thought for sure that we had been made, but it was only in our minds. The suspects never knew we were there.

After a lengthy day of watching the bad guys stop at what appeared to be every liquor store in the division, we found ourselves at the apartment of Tina Turner. Now the long wait began.

I was placed in a tree directly across the street from the apartment building and to my consternation, my companions were small black ants that not only drove me nuts as they crawled over me, but also hurt when they stung exposed skin. I was in this tree six hours before the bandits finally made their move.

During the morning the suspects picked up a large flat-bed truck with plywood sides. After getting the truck, they drove to a dump and loaded it with trash filling it nearly to the top of the stakes. All of this was observed by our helicopter unit, Air 3 from an altitude of five thousand feet.

So there you have it, a truck crammed to the gills with trash, three drunken bad guys driving around the city awaiting the time to caper, eight cops anxious to make a bust, and one frightened prostitute who knew that if her complicity in the matter was revealed, she would be killed.

After six hours, the suspects carried the loot from the apartment and placed it under the trash in the truck. Once it was hidden, they began the drive to Culver City. As they drove, we followed and again enlisted the assistance of our helicopter unit which stayed with us until the tail ended the next morning.

It was after midnight when the suspects parked the truck in the restaurant parking lot. Now it became a waiting game. Although we were in plain clothes and driving unmarked cars, we were concerned that we would be seen by the suspects.

It seemed that we sat for hours, but eventually the restaurant closed, all the employees exited, and at about four in the morning our bandits made their move.

We watched from a distance as two suspects moved cautiously to the rear door, and without much trouble, kicked it in. The third suspect then backed the truck to within four feet of the door. With the rear door open and the truck in position, all three entered the restaurant. On the ground, we had the location surrounded, and in the air, Air 3 continued to circle at five thousand feet.

One hour passed then two. It was close to sun-up when we saw one very drunk suspect stagger from the rear of the restaurant. Then the others stepped from the doorway struggling with what appeared to be a heavy, floor safe.

We watched as they tripped, stumbled and fell on the slippery floor and wet concrete just outside the door. They struggled for at least an hour but were unable to get the safe through the door. Frustrated, they tried to rip the back off the safe. When that failed, they decided to wrap tied table cloths around the safe and then tie an end around the bumper of the truck. With tires burning, the truck lunged forward, the knots slipped and the safe careened back into the restaurant.

In the melee, two of the suspects sailed helter-skelter and slipped in grease and fat left on the restaurant floor. Infuriated at their inability to get the safe out, and being too drunk to realize that all they had to do was turn it 180 degrees, they decided on another option. And to them, it must have been considered to be a stroke of genius.

The driver erratically pulled the truck forward, put it in reverse and punched the accelerator. Again, the rear tires spun and rubber burned while the truck plunged backward at a severe angle. Before the drunk driver realized his predicament, the truck slammed into a telephone pole that stood adjacent to the door. With a loud crash, trash was rocketed skyward while the truck shimmied to an abrupt stop.

It was now daylight and the safe had outwitted these remarkable criminal masterminds. Yet, not wanting to feel that all was for naught, they reentered the restaurant and loaded the truck with bags of onions, potatoes and some slabs of frozen meat. With this loot, they fled along the deserted city streets of Culver City not realizing that paralleling them were four police cars and above them was the air unit.

Cautiously, we followed the bandits until they reentered the City of Los Angeles where we had jurisdiction. When we were sure that everyone was within the city, we surrounded the weaving truck and pounced mightily on the still drunk suspects. As we pinned the truck in, you can imagine their shock when the three bandits looked out the cab windows and saw M-1 Carbines, shotguns and all manner of artillery aimed in their direction!

The surveillance and arrests went like clockwork. We learned that once inside the restaurant, the reason they took so long was the lure of "free" alcohol. They drank themselves into oblivion tasting and sampling all the liquor in the place.

Brooks received filings on the suspects, but when we went to court, one thing dimmed the operation. It seemed that just prior to the Preliminary Hearing, Rosie disappeared.

Sometime later we learned from street sources that she had been killed by members of the group for snitching them off. This was all just hearsay from the other prostitutes and street people, but since she never was seen again, we believed that she was eliminated for helping us.

A Most Dangerous Game

It was a quiet night, so Fiderio and I decided to go on foot and walk the area of 39th Street between Normandie and Figueroa. We were in plain clothes and neither of us looked much like cops. I wore an old green fatigue Army jacket, and Fiderio looked like a drunken Italian as he walked down the street with his black hair messed up and his ill-fitting clothes hanging from his slender frame.

After separating, we took opposite sides of the street, with one walking in plain sight and the other in the shadows.

Often, I would walk slowly, stumbling and staggering which made it appear that I was either drunk or high on drugs. I would talk to myself and mumble, all in hopes that if a bad guy was prompted to commit a street robbery, he would choose me as his victim. While this was a dangerous ploy, it was also highly successful.

As I walked, I looked up the street in Roger's direction and saw two bandits walk past him and speed up when they saw me. Once they passed Roger, he turned and headed back to provide me some back-up.

As the suspects approached, I saw the larger of the two reach into his waistband and pull out a chrome plated semiautomatic pistol. Stepping directly in front of me, he shoved the gun into my stomach. With my gun still in my

155

waistband, I thrust my left arm up in a sweeping motion knocking his gun hand across his chest hoping that by doing so the bandit would be caught off-guard and not be able to react quickly enough to pull the trigger. I was right.

Now the fight for the gun was on.

"He has a gun!" I shouted to Fiderio.

Shocked at my quickness and shout that identified me as a police officer, the second suspect bolted into the night and was lost in the darkness.

As I struggled with the armed suspect, I could hear Fiderio running up behind us. Without hesitating, Roger jumped into the melee. His sudden attack from the rear and my vicious assault from the front found the man on the ground, and after an additional struggle, he was subdued, handcuffed and arrested. Needless to say, he also was provided the necessary medical treatment to care for his injuries sustained in the struggle.

The Bus Bench Bandit

University Division had been racked with a rash of bus robberies, so in an effort to stem that flow before someone was killed, the University Special Operations Squad was asked to keep a watchful eye on the bus benches during the early morning hours. The suspect was described as a male Negro, medium afro and medium build. His weapon of choice was a .45 caliber semiautomatic.

It was midweek and Fiderio and I were assigned 3Zebra9. We were in plain clothes and I was carrying a four inch Smith and Wesson .38 caliber revolver in a custom made Alfonso gun belt.

The weather was warm; it was about midnight and Roger was driving our unmarked police car.

After we left the station, we made a right onto Santa Barbara Avenue and drove toward Vermont Avenue. The streets were quiet and void of both vehicle and pedestrian traffic.

As we approach Vermont, I glanced to my left and saw a male Negro sitting alone on a bus bench waiting for the southbound Vermont bus. From a distance, he fit the description of the suspect wanted for the robberies.

"Let's check out the guy on the bus bench," I said.

Slowly, Roger pulled into a driveway just behind the suspect and hit the bright headlights.

The suspect turned his head, looked into the lights and then got up and walked to the end of the bench.

When the police car stopped, Roger and I got out and separated; Roger going to the left while I approached the suspect from the front.

As I stepped to within ten feet of the man, I heard a still small voice that whispered; *He has a gun.*

Since my revolver was already out of the holster, and hidden behind my right leg, it took only a second for me to bring it up even with the suspect's head.

"Keep your hands in your pockets and don't move."

The suspect froze, never taking his eyes off the dark barrel of my gun that was now only six feet from his forehead.

Drawing my elbow close into my body so as not to allow the suspect the opportunity to grab my gun, I stepped forward, reached into his waistband with my left hand, and pulled out a loaded .45 caliber semiautomatic.

"He has a gun," I yelled to Fiderio.

As I slipped his gun into my waistband, I ordered him to prone himself on the ground. Once proned with arms and legs outstretched, he was handcuffed and a more detailed search conducted. With that arrest, the Bus Bench Bandit was put out of business.

Protected by the Holy Garment

The garment worn by those Endowed in the House of the Lord is provided for a number of sacred reasons, one of which is that it acts as a protection. This was reinforced on a spring afternoon in 1972 as I worked in University Division in a detective assignment. Roger Fiderio was my partner.

Roger and I were assigned to the Burglary table and in our travels we had regular contact with a career burglar, heroin addict and receiver of stolen property named Bennie Washington. Bennie was well known on the street and lived in an apartment on Budlong Avenue with his common-law wife, Beulah and their children.

One beautiful afternoon, Roger and I decided to pay Bennie and Beulah a visit. They lived on the second floor in a building inhabited by nothing but thieves, addicts, bandits and prostitutes; our type of clientele.

It was mid-day when we pulled up in front of the building. On the bottom floor to the left, lived Ta-Ta Williams, a shotgun bandit who primarily robbed pharmacies in and around his own neighborhood. He was called Ta-Ta because of his stuttering; stuttering that eventually cost him his life when he went into the neighborhood pharmacy and while in the process of saying, "Thiiiis isssss aaaaa robeerrrryyyy," he was seen and heard by a clerk stocking shelves. The clerk, not seen by Ta-Ta, came up behind

Williams and shot him in the back of the head killing him instantly.

But on this particular day, Ta-Ta was alive and well. That is, he was as alive and well as a hard core heroin addict could be. After we parked our car, Roger decided he wanted to visit Williams before going upstairs.

"I'm going up to Bennie's apartment," I said, and so we separated. When I arrived on the stoop in front of the apartment, I knocked loudly and said, "Bennie, it's Whitaker, open the door."

Within a few seconds I could hear the first of eight deadbolt locks being slipped open. Then the vault like door opened and Beulah invited me in.

As I looked into the small front room, I saw that it was crowded. There were at least twenty-five bandits, prostitutes, thieves and addicts sitting around the room, some crammed onto the couches while others were sprawled across the floor. When I entered, all conversation ceased and it became deathly quiet. It appeared I had interrupted something.

Stepping in, I heard the door close and the deadbolts thrown into a locked position. However it was not the locked door that bothered me; it was the .32 automatic that I knew was under the cushion of the flea ridden couch. Seeing bandits and addicts seated directly above the weapon's position, I calmly stepped into the middle of the room and said, "If any one of you places your hand under the cushion of that couch or into your jacket pockets or waistbands, I'll blow you out the front window."

No one spoke. Not one of these fine citizens of South Central Los Angeles moved, because each knew from prior experience that this was not an idle threat.

Looking around the room, I found that I knew or recognized everyone except one large man. "Get up," I said. Slowly, he got up off the couch. "Come here."

With a swagger, he walked over and stood in front of me. He was much bigger than I and outweighed me by about seventy pounds. Cautiously, I began to search him for weapons. I asked his name. He gave me a name and told me that he had just been released from prison.

As I continued my weapons search, he suddenly pivoted and took a swing at me. As we struggled, I forcibly advised all others in the room that should they move I would kill them. They knew I was serious. No one made a move and as the man and I struggled, we made our way to the bolted door. "Unlock the door Beulah or I'll kick it down," I yelled.

As I struggled to handcuff the suspect, I found that as a joke, one of the Law Enforcement Explorer Scouts working at the station had double locked my handcuffs making them inoperable until the small pin on the handcuff key was inserted releasing the locking mechanism. Since I was in a brutal fight with the suspect, the unlocking of the mechanism was impossible. Therefore, my handcuffs were useless.

As we fought our way to the bolted door, a very frightened Beulah threw the deadbolts and opened the door. Still fighting, the suspect and I made our way to the small second floor landing. As he turned to swing, I caught him in the face with a hard right cross that sent him tumbling backwards down the flight of stairs. He landed at the foot of Fiderio who by now had heard the noise and had stepped out of Ta-Ta's apartment.

"Cuff him, Roger," I yelled. "Cuff him!"

Roger snapped his cuffs on the dazed suspect, and we shoved him in the direction of our car. As we did so, a loud and belligerent voice was heard from across the street yelling at us. Looking in the direction of the voice, I realized that it was a man doing his best to incite the neighborhood to forcibly remove the suspect from our custody.

Turning in the man's direction, I yelled, "Shut up or you're going to jail." That only brought out a louder string of profanities.

As Roger put our prisoner into the back seat of the car, I started across the street toward the second man who by now had been able to get nearly two hundred neighborhood residents either to peer out their windows or start into the street.

I approached the screaming man, grabbed his arm and shoved him toward our car. I knew that if I didn't get him off the street and do it immediately, the entire neighborhood soon would surround us, and the situation rapidly would go from bad to worse.

"I'm gunna get you," the man screamed. "I'm gunna get you."

I had heard that before, so I kept pushing the man toward the car. Louder and louder he screamed, "I'm gunna get you, honkey, I'm gunna get you!"

As we neared our vehicle, I pushed him up against the side of the car and placed him in a prone felony search position with his hands on the top of the car with his feet back, and legs spread. With his body in this position, it forced him to lean at an angle. With him thus proned, I wrapped my right leg around his right leg and with my left hand, grabbed the rear of his shirt collar. With both of his hands placed on the car, my right hand grabbed his right wrist and began the search. Throughout this preparation for the felony search, he continued to yell, "I'm gunna get you!"

As I slid my right hand from his hand to his wrist, the suspect suddenly, and with lightening speed, thrust his right arm back in the direction of my right front side. Unknown to me, he had up his sleeve a sharpened piece of metal identical to the type made by prisoners in correctional facilities which they use to stab other inmates. It was basically a homemade knife or shiv.

Before I knew it, the full force of the metal blade struck me in the right side ripping through my white shirt and cotton garments. After the initial driving force of the weapon, the suspect then ripped it down and across the center of my abdomen. With the impact, I snapped his right leg out from under him, slammed him face first into the asphalt and drilled my knee into the small of his back. As I did this, I yelled to Roger, "I've been stabbed!"

With the quickness of a cat, Roger was on the suspect. As I struck the man to ensure no further attack, Roger, thrust his .38 caliber service revolver into the assailant's ear, cocked the hammer and with some very descriptive expletives, told the man he was dead. Seeing the hammer cocked I screamed, "No Roger, don't, we've got too many witnesses!" For by now the entire neighborhood was running toward us from all directions.

Without another word, I grabbed the suspect on the ground, disarmed him, and as I threw him into the backseat of the car with our first suspect, Roger jumped in, started the car, and in seconds, we were gone.

During this incident I was wearing the older style one piece cotton garments which had bunched up around my waist exactly where the blade entered. When the blade struck, the suspect tore down, ripping a four inch gash through my shirt and into the garment. Then he tore it across, tearing another two inches of clothing. Amazingly, even with the ferocity of the blow, and the fact that it literally knocked me back and tore through two layers of clothing, the blade barely cut the skin. When my side and abdomen were examined, one could see the four inch downward stroke and also the two inch horizontal slash, but both only scratched the skin.

I will be eternally grateful for the protection those garments offered that day. I still have them put away, a constant reminder to me every time I look at them of the many different ways the Lord can and does protect His children.

Prayer in an Interrogation Room

I was working University Detectives when I had a very different experience in one of our interrogation rooms.

One night we arrested a suspect for burglary, and as I sat in the small stuffy interrogation room, the man broke down and began to sob. We spoke for some time, and then I was prompted to ask him if he would like to kneel down and have a word of prayer. Why I did this I do not know, except that I was prompted by the Spirit to ask.

He stated that he wanted to have a prayer, so in that small room in the jail, we knelt and I offered a prayer asking the Lord to bless this man and help him to put his life in order.

Tears streamed down his face.

I will never forget the Spirit that filled that room. To this day, I do not know what happened to that man or if that prayer ever had any lasting effect on his life, but what is important is that I was not ashamed of the priesthood I held and did not hesitate to speak when moved upon by the Holy Ghost. I have learned over the years always to respond to the Spirit when prompted, for often, there is no second chance.

A Blessing Given
In the Back of an Ambulance

"Shots fired, officer down. Any Southwest unit in the vicinity identify to Control and handle the call Code 3."

When the dispatcher finished I realized that I was only two blocks from the scene. Working a detective assignment, I responded. "3W42, show this unit at the scene."

In less than a minute, I was at the location. In front of me was a young uniformed officer sitting on the curb holding his bloody face in his hands. After a closer look, I realized that he had taken a head shot from a shotgun, and the blast had ripped off the entire right side of his face including his nose and part of the eye socket. Miraculously he was not only still alive, but his eye had not been hit by the pellets.

As I embraced him in my arms, the ambulance pulled up. After the paramedics loaded him into the ambulance, I climbed in. The paramedics started to work on the young officer, but he was losing blood and was in shock. It appeared that we might lose him.

Suddenly, cutting through the commotion and the shrill whine of the siren a still small voice said, *Richard, give him a priesthood blessing.*

Although I did not have consecrated oil with me, I slid forward on the stretcher and took the young man's head in my hands. The ambulance attendant said nothing, just watched as I closed my eyes and silently poured out my heart to my Father in Heaven requesting that this young warrior's life be spared and that he be granted the opportunity to heal, return to work and continue in his chosen profession.

The blessing ended as we arrived at the hospital. I watched as he was wheeled into the operating room. I had done all I could, so I returned to the scene to assist Jimmy Steele and Jerry Bova in the investigation. Some hours passed before we were notified that the officer miraculously had lived. For me it was not a miracle, just the priesthood of God in action.

As time passed, the young man began to heal and soon the physicians realized that he would be able to resume work as a police officer after sufficient plastic surgery was completed to rebuild the missing portions of his face. It took long grueling months of surgeries and rehabilitation, but he was able to return to work.

He was a large man and when he returned to work he had another dimension: the entire right side of his face was scarred and he looked like one of the meanest guys you have ever seen. The bad guys feared him and his reputation spread.

But the bottom line is that the experience gave me an additional testimony of the promptings of the Spirit and the power of the Priesthood. Our Father in Heaven loves all His children unconditionally, and we are richly blessed when we live righteously and exercise our priesthood in such a manner as to glorify our Father in Heaven.

We later recovered the missing firearm and arrested the suspect. It seemed that the shooter was wanted for another crime and was hiding in a garage when the officer walked by a glass window. As the policeman passed, the suspect put the shotgun to the glass from inside the garage and pulled the trigger.

The Thunderbird Bandits

In 1972, I transferred from Southwest Detectives to Devonshire Detectives and was assigned to the Auto Theft detail. My partner was Jim Murawski. Although Auto Theft was not considered the cream of the crop assignment for detectives, both Jim and I enjoyed the challenge. There was no glory associated with the assignment, as most detectives wanted to work Robbery, Homicide or Narcotics. While they opted for the bright lights and big city, I opted for anonymity. Additionally, working Auto Theft provided me the ability to continue serving at church since I was guaranteed my weekends off.

As time passed, Murawski and I identified a problem. A number of vintage Ford Thunderbirds were being stolen and stripped with the car shells dumped in and around the division. The vintage or Classic Thunderbirds were made between 1955 and 1957.

Using a large divisional map, straight pins and colored string, we plotted out the locations where the shells were recovered. It was not very academic by today's standards, but it worked. It is important to remember that during this time we had no computers. We compiled and analyzed all our crime related information by hand. In the process, we noted not only a pattern, but also that the dropping off points were located within a small area. We also realized that the cars were coming from all over Southern California.

Each day Murawski and I would sit and read the stolen and recovered vehicle reports. Then we would map things out and try to find the pattern. After nearly two months, we hit pay dirt. Looking at the large map with all the pins and connecting threads, we were able to determine what appeared to be an area in the center that remained void of any activity. We now had somewhere to start.

We sent a request to the three different patrol watches and advised them of our findings and the area where we wanted them to concentrate their efforts. They also were asked to look for specific things: one being any oil slicks into or out of driveways. After giving patrol the information, we didn't have long to wait.

Within a week, we got a call from one of the Day Watch units advising us that they had found a fresh oil slick coming out of a driveway in the exact center of our target area. It ran out a driveway, down the street and within four blocks they had located a stripped Thunderbird. It appeared that the thieves were getting lazy and over confident.

Murawski and I drove to the location and met the patrol unit. The officers pointed out the house and oil slick. The rest was now up to us. The driveway was part of an old home and it ran about fifty feet into the rear where it entered an old, single car garage. Both the driveway and the house were surrounded by large trees and overgrown shrubbery. Nothing was visible from the street.

We set up our surveillance on the house and waited. All black and white police cars were ordered out of the area.

We sat hidden for nearly six hours before we saw any movement. At about 4:00 p.m., an old car pulled slowly out of the long driveway. It contained one very scraggly, disheveled male occupant. As our subject departed from the scene, our tail began.

Driving an unmarked brown Plymouth, we followed the suspect through Devonshire Division and then onto the freeway which led south toward Van Nuys. I was driving and Jim handled the radio.

Over and over we tried to get a helicopter for surveillance. Not only were we unable to get a chopper, but we weren't even able to get any additional detective units for support. We were on our own.

It's an exciting experience to be involved in a tail, especially when you are the only car. You can't allow yourself to be "made," or spotted, nor can you lose the suspect. It takes all the driving skills you have to stay close enough to follow, but not so close to blow the operation.

Down the freeway we traveled into Van Nuys Division. The suspect's car wasn't stolen, and was registered to the address back in Devonshire. As we followed him, we tried to gather all the critical information we would need to identify the players in this drama, namely cars registered to any of the subjects, codefendants in previous arrests, etc.

Once we entered Van Nuys, the suspect drove from one location to another, and each stop provided us more license numbers, addresses, times, and descriptions of his partners. Soon the sun set, night fell, and we still had no back-up.

Late that night the suspect returned to the Devonshire home with us still right behind. Because of his movements, we had identified a number of different players. Back at the station we secured police records or rap sheets on each person identified. We also were able to identify accomplices who were listed on prior arrest reports. As we analyzed the information, a pattern began to appear. The players had been heavily involved in auto theft, not only in California, but also across the country. The case now was bigger than originally thought.

When we had all our information gathered and our ducks in a row, we raided the small garage where the oil tracks first had been noticed. In the garage we found numerous parts and pieces of classic Thunderbirds. We made the arrests, and during the course of the investigation, we determined that the thieves were placing many of the cars into large semi-trucks and transporting them across the country to South Carolina where a relative of the ring-leader changed the serial numbers, created phony paperwork and then resold the stolen classics.

Each member of the gang was a hardened criminal who had served jail time in one of a number of state prisons, and none relished the idea of returning. For me, this was a chess game; a game I enjoyed and one I wasn't going to lose.

After searching the Devonshire garage and adjacent house, we returned to Van Nuys. At one of the residences searched, we found paperwork that connected the group to a major car parts dealer in Southern California that dealt primarily in classic Ford Thunderbird car parts. We learned that most of the cars or specific parts were stolen on consignment. The owner of the classic car parts business would place an order, the thieves would identify the location of a car they wanted and after stealing the car, the order was filled.

Often, the cars were identified and notes made when an owner took the vehicle to a car agency to have the oil changed or minor work done. One of the suspects working at the location would note the home address and within a day, they would steal the car. This happened repeatedly, not only with the car agencies, but also with suspects working in car washes and even traveling the street. If they saw a car they wanted, they would note the license number, go to a Department of Motor Vehicles where another suspect was employed and get the home address from the registration information. One way or another, the car was theirs.

During the case, we used different methods of interrogative techniques. For example, with the original suspect that we tailed from the Devonshire location, once he was arrested and thought about returning to state prison, he broke and sang like a bird. He laid out the methods of operation, times and places, and even sat down and physically reviewed the hundreds of crime reports we had accumulated, being able to pick out those he had stolen.

Now what we needed was the master mind behind the operation. He was identified as a career criminal named Smith. He lived in a nice home in Van Nuys and had served hard time in the state penitentiary. Once we had sufficient evidence, we went to his home and made the arrest.

During the arrest, we swept up everyone, Smith, his estranged wife who was visiting, and even his six year old son. Smith and his estranged wife were both booked into the Van Nuys jail, and the little boy turned over to the juvenile authorities for placement.

When I went to the Van Nuys jail to interview Smith, he refused to talk. He not only was angry, but also threatening. We had cleaned out his home, his garages, the storage areas, his business, and sorely disrupted what was left of his family. But none of that seemed to matter to Smith, at least not at first. He was arrogant and adamant that he would get it all back and be out of jail the next day. The intensity of the game increased.

This was fun.

On the day prior to our being required to either release Smith or go to the District Attorney for the filing of criminal charges, I decided to change tactics. I walked into the jail facility and had the jailers bring him not into the normal interrogation room, but stand him on the other side of the jail bars. In doing this, it appeared to Smith that my mind was made up and I wasn't really interested in anything he had to say. I was there to make statements of fact, not request information. Arrogantly, he stepped closer to the bars. He was just close enough to hear my words, look into my eyes and see the coldness that was a part of my persona.

In his usual cocky manner, he sneered. Then the curtain raised and I was on stage. I stepped up so that only inches separated our faces. Then, in a whisper, I spoke.

"Smith, you're mine."

The sneer never left his face.

"I have you......."

"And I'll be out of here tomorrow, Whitaker. We both know that."

"That I doubt. But remember, I also have your wife."

He threw his head back and laughed.

"What makes you think I care about her? We've been separated for two years. You can have her!"

Expressionless, I continued. "And I've got your son. He's mine Smith. And he's gone!"

Suddenly, the laughter stopped. Anger filled his eyes and his face reddened as he squeezed the iron jail bars in a vice like grip. "You can't touch my kid," he yelled. "I'll kill you!"

"Are you threatening me?" I asked.

He began to shake as his hands gripped the bars causing his knuckles to go white.

"It appears to me that you're an unfit parent, and so is your wife, so that leaves me no choice. The boy is going to be placed in Foster Care. Trust me Smith, the kid is mine."

Suddenly, the hardened criminal began to change. I had found his Achilles Heel. The boy! Still clenching the gray iron bars, the color left his face.

"And I can guarantee you, pal, that I will see to it that he is bounced around from one foster home to another. Have you ever heard what happens to good looking little boys out there, Smith? It's not much different than the joint. Is it?"

The trembling increased as he looked into my eyes, his own became glassy as tears formed, but as his softened, mine remained hard, cold and unblinking.

"You wouldn't really take my son, would you? He's all I have. He's the only thing I care about."

Smith was mine.

"Unless we have a long talk, you've seen him for the last time, and I will do everything I can for as long as it takes to see that you don't see him again. The paperwork is already on my desk."

The transformation in the hardened ex-con had begun. With tears streaming down his cheeks, he no longer was the hard guy.

"Yes sir, I understand. What do you want?"

"We're going to talk. I want to know who is behind this operation. I want names, and if I at any time think that you're lying to me, the boy is gone. Do you understand me?"

Softly he said, "Yes, sir. Just let me have my son back."

Smith, just like the others, began to tell everything he knew, and that included the operation in South Carolina.

In that one incident, I learned that every man, no matter how hard he is, or how tough, has one weakness that when identified, will break him. And with that, they are yours.

The organization that had caused so much anguish to so many now toppled like a deck of cards. Preliminary hearings were conducted and all suspects were held to answer. Trial dates were set, and as the trials began, Thanksgiving quickly approached.

One day when I entered our small Detective squad room, Captain Jack McGilvray said he wanted to talk to me. When I stepped into his office, he asked me to close the door and have a seat.

"Whitaker, a patrol unit in Foothill Division stopped one of the guys involved in the Thunderbird ring that you and Murawski broke up. During his interrogation, the suspect commented that a Detective named Whitaker better watch out. He went on to say that it was common knowledge on the street that the gang was looking for someone to kill you and that they had found someone."

McGilvray then continued. "I want you to go with some of your team and move your family out of the house for a period of time. We'll have Metropolitan Division conduct surveillance on your place and see what happens."

Following my conversation with Captain McGilvray, I left the office with some of my colleagues and we drove to our Morella Avenue home. It was a Friday afternoon when I walked into the house with two other detectives.

"What are you doing home at this hour?" Cheryle asked.

"We have a slight problem and we need to talk."

I then explained the danger the family was in.

When I finished, Cheryle's only response was, "I have these children, I am pregnant with the fourth, and if anyone thinks that I am packing up and moving out of my house because of some threats, they are crazy. The answer is no."

So that was the answer I took back to the captain. I think that he had anticipated the response and told me to be careful and that units would be placed around the house beginning that night. With that, I finished work and went home.

That night was the North Hollywood I Ward Thanksgiving dinner, so not long after I arrived home, we packed up the family and drove to the dinner.

Prior to leaving the house, I contacted Devonshire Detectives and told them where I would be. I also gave them the telephone number at the building.

We had not been at the dinner thirty minutes when the hallway phone rang. The call was for me. When I got to the phone, the voice on the other end of the line identified himself as a police officer and went on to tell me that they had apprehended two suspects breaking into our house through the rear window. He asked if I would immediately return home.

Leaving Cheryle and the kids, at the ward, I drove home where I was met by a number of plain clothes Metro officers and uniformed patrol officers from the North Hollywood Division.

"We watched you leave," said one of the Metro officers. "We were parked back into one of your neighbor's driveways just across the street. After you left, we sat and watched as two guys walked up to the house, looked around and then started for the rear. We knew they were there to make the hit, so we let them get to the back and part way through a window. When we got to the back, we were going to let them get all the way inside the house, but not knowing where you kept your guns, and not wanting to confront two armed suspects in the house, we nailed them as one was just inside the house and the other was crawling through the window. You were lucky Whitaker; it appears the threat was real."

"It seems so," I answered.

Then the other Metro officer began to laugh. "And you should have seen your neighbor! When we came around the corner of the house with our shotguns, the guy panicked and went screaming into the house."

Cheryle and I later were told by our neighbor's wife that he, upon seeing the plain clothes Metro officers running down his driveway and thinking they were bandits, went running into the house screaming. Once inside, he threw himself on the front room floor and while rolling around in fear, yelled to his wife, "Call the police, call the police, they've got guns and they're going to kill us, they're going to kill us!"

Neither Cheryle nor I ever had much contact with this neighbor prior to this incident, but it was even less frequent after that day.

Although this was not the only death threat I received during my career on the Los Angeles Police Department, it was one of the most memorable.

Later, I talked to the patrol officer who conducted the street interrogation and he told me that when the suspect first made the comment that a cop was going to be "offed," the suspect immediately found himself on the ground with the barrel of a .357 Magnum in his mouth. It was in this way the interrogation continued. Needless to say, the cops on the street did not share this information with the LAPD brass, and while not considered to be the most legal interrogation technique, it certainly persuaded the bad guy to talk, and it possibly saved my life.

The Spider and the Fly

I was assigned to the Detective Bureau at Devonshire Division, and Mike Moen was my partner. One day I received a Burglary Report. The victim was a twenty-three year old white, single, female who lived alone in an apartment building on the west side of the division. The crime report stated that an unknown suspect forcibly entered the ground floor apartment through the bedroom window and ransacked the victim's underclothing drawer. After becoming sexually aroused, he fled through the same open window.

Because of the nature of the report, a physical examination of the crime scene was required. For some reason I felt uncomfortable going alone, so I asked Moen to accompany me.

"I can't Whitaker," he said. "I'm swamped. It's all yours."

I drove to the location, but before knocking on the door, I walked around back and examined the bedroom window. It didn't appear to be damaged or tampered with. The dust on the window sill was not even disturbed.

I walked around front and knocked on the door. It was opened by a very attractive young woman. I identified myself and she told me she was the victim.

"Please come in, Detective Whitaker."

With that invitation, I felt like the fly who had just been invited into the parlor of the spider.

As I entered, I pushed the front door wide open. The victim invited me to have a seat on the sofa.

I sat down and we began to discuss the elements of the crime. As we talked, I noticed a large blue hard bound book on the couch. Picking it up, I realized that it was a copy of the California Penal Code identical to the one the police academy issued me. On the inside was the serial number and name of a police officer who had the same last name as the young woman seated across from me and his serial number was the class after mine. Noting my interest, she said, "Oh, that book belongs to my ex-husband. He is also a police officer."

Interesting, I thought.

"Don't you want to see where the suspect broke in?" she asked.

"Yes, I do."

She led me into the back bedroom where underwear still lay on the bed.

"He came in through that window."

For the victim of what was a burglary with sexual overtones, she was far too calm. She explained that the suspect had used her clothing to become sexually aroused and then left the evidence on the bed.

I walked over to the window, and after a very careful examination found that not only were there no signs of forced entry, but also the inside dust had not been disturbed. Neither did I find any trace of bodily fluids on the underwear.

And then it felt as if the walls were closing in and the spirit in the room became cold. There was no doubt about what I needed to do. I needed to flee. But as I started for the living room, she stepped in front of me and quickly shut the front door.

"Wouldn't you like to talk some more?" she asked.

"Miss, thank you for your time, but I need to leave." With that, I opened the front door and left.

Was it a phony burglary report? Who knows? What I do know is that as I stood in that apartment, I knew I was in danger and had I accepted the offer to sit and "talk," disaster surely would have struck.

Chaos at Thirty-five Thousand Feet

It was 1981 and I had started the security consulting firm of RBW and Associates.

One of my associates was a Burbank Police Department detective named Randy Pastor. Randy was a member of the church, and we had a great relationship and traveled frequently conducting seminars and providing security training for individuals and corporations.

One day, Randy and I were required to fly to San Jose, California to provide a seminar for the California Restaurant Association. We checked in at the Southwest Airlines desk at the Burbank Airport and told the desk personnel that we were police officers, showed the proper identification and advised the airline personnel that we were armed. We then asked if they wanted us to turn our weapons over to the captain as I had done in the past. On one occasion I had been told by the captain to keep the gun, but give him the ammunition. He never asked if we carried spare ammo! That was interesting.

The airline personnel went to the captain and he asked to speak to us. As we boarded, he stepped out of the cabin and approached.

"Gentlemen," he said, "I understand that you are both armed?"

"Yes sir, we are," I replied.

"Well, considering the times, that's fine. If anything happens, just do me a favor and shoot up or to the side. Whatever you do, don't shoot down. Down is where all the hydraulics are located. Cut those and we are in real trouble."

With that, the captain smiled and reentered the front cabin.

Following that brief discussion, Randy and I headed to the rear of the plane. We found two seats on the right hand side in the last row, sat down and relaxed. Randy sat next to the window, I was on the aisle. Directly behind our seats were seated the two female flight attendants.

The plane filled quickly. We began to liftoff and the flight attendants stood in preparation of making their safety presentations. One attendant stood next to me in the aisle. In front of her and to her left was a single male passenger about twenty-five years of age. Soon we were airborne and the presentations began.

The attendant to my left took the oxygen mask and when she dropped it representing what would happen should we lose pressure, the young man in the seat in front of her jumped up and began screaming profanities. The attendant attempted to calm him, but the violent explosion continued. He then stepped forward and pinned the attendant against the bathroom door still yelling. Both Randy and I sat very still and watched as a male attendant came from the front. The disturbance continued drawing all eyes to the rear of the plane. On and on he went making threats toward the flight attendants and the pilots.

Turning to Randy, I softly said, "We have a problem, and if that clown heads for the cabin and the controls, I will put one in the back of his head."

"I'm right behind you," Randy said. "Just don't miss or shoot down."

After some time the flight attendants were able to get the man back into his seat. Once they accomplished this, my eyes never left him. There was no doubt that he was high on drugs. And there was no doubt in my mind or Randy's that were he to bolt to the door of the cabin, he would never get to the controls. That flight was the longest forty-five minute flight of my life.

As the plane touched down, it was obvious that we had two very frightened flight attendants seated directly behind us. When we came to a stop and before the overly aggressive passenger could unbuckle his seat belt, I was out of my seat standing in front of the flight attendant who had originally dropped the oxygen mask and who was the focus of the verbal assault.

"I'm a police officer, you can relax."

"I know," she responded still shaken.

"I am going to stand directly in front of you until the plane is empty. My partner will keep his eye on your violent friend."

Her eyes filled with tears. "Oh thank you," she said.

The plane emptied from both the front and tail section. As I stood guard over the flight attendant, Randy stood next to our seats like a mountain guarding the valleys below. Fortunately nothing further occurred.

I never will forget the feeling of concern I had as I watched and listened to that young man make threats and do his best to disrupt the brief flight. And I never will forget the fact that it didn't take very long to decide that we were not going to allow a drug crazed passenger storm the cabin while we were at thirty-five thousand feet.

A LONG, DARK TUNNEL

Preserved by Angelic Hands

As I reflect on the past, I more fully understand the brevity of life. At any time, we can find ourselves instantly on the other side of the veil.

It was August 30, 1966. I was twenty-two years old and assigned to Wilshire patrol. We spent the day in cleanup activities following what were referred to as "mini-riots." I was driving a 1967 red Volkswagen Bug and left the division parking lot at a little before five in the afternoon. The weather was warm and I drove with both the driver and passenger windows down. I also wasn't wearing a seat belt since the car was not equipped with them.

As I drove home, I noticed that traffic was heavy, so I decided to change my route and drive down Fulton Avenue which ran past Los Angeles Valley College. After exiting the Ventura Freeway, I drove north toward the intersection of Fulton and Oxnard streets. At the corner, a tri-light traffic signal controlled the traffic.

As I drove down the slight hill, I saw that the signal was green, so I entered the intersection. Suddenly, out of the corner of my eye to my left, I saw a white Cadillac racing toward me at a high rate of speed. Instantly, I knew that he was going to run the red light and hit me broadside. I also knew that I was going to die. That registered immediately.

Then the following occurred.

Seeing the Cadillac, I grasped the steering wheel...then, the impact. When the Cadillac slammed unabated into the driver's side of my car, I felt an impact and force beyond description. I also felt something else. There was a tremendous pressure on either side of my neck. It was a pressure that felt as though large, powerful hands were gripping my shoulders. Suddenly, I was ripped from the seat in the direction of the open passenger window. Then, with the hands under my back, I realized that I was in a prone position traveling rapidly away from the accident.

Then the warmth. It encompassed my entire being. It was accompanied by a peacefulness I had never known. I recall thinking that it was much like the warmth experienced just as the anesthesia for an operation takes effect, but multiplied a thousand times.

Instantly, I realized that my spirit body was standing directly over my physical body. I lifted my arms, examined my hands, then turned them over and saw that my spirit form was identical to my physical body. I looked down at the physical form below me. My eyes were closed and I appeared at peace. Then I looked just beyond it and saw that an angel, the same who had pulled me from the car, had his hands under my back and was transporting my body down a long black tunnel toward a brilliant light.

I felt more an observer than a participant; then I had the sensation of travelling at a rapid speed down the tunnel. Again I looked to my right toward the light that seemed to be drawing me toward it.

The warmth increased, and I realized I could comprehend and see all that surrounded me. I was totally aware of everything without moving my head in any direction. It was as if I was standing in a transparent bowl and everything was open to my view with no front or back, no up or down. All of this occurred while my spirit stood above and next to my body.

The light drew nearer. The peacefulness increased.

Then the voices.

"He's dead; cover him up," they said, "cover him up." My mind raced. *Don't do anything we'll all regret.*

With the voices, I heard the wailing of a siren. As suddenly as the experience began, I was back. No pain, no discomfort, just awake, laying on the sidewalk, covered with a blanket and surrounded by voices.

I sat up.

The crowd gasped.

The blanket that covered my head and chest slid to the ground.

"I'm a police officer. I need to get my guns out of my car."

I stood up and walked to my car that was wrapped around a tree just west of where my body had been placed. The car was lying on its side, so I climbed up onto the passenger side, slipped in, found my service revolver and back-up gun, then climbed out and sat on the curb to wait for the ambulance.

The crowd had grown, and I sensed a feeling of amazement as they watched me walk over to the ambulance and climb in.

When the distance I had traveled through the air was measured, it was determined to be one hundred and twenty-five feet from the point of impact to where the angel had placed me on the sidewalk. The Volkswagen had been thrown approximately sixty feet and was wrapped around a tree on the corner of Oxnard and Fulton.

I had traveled across four lanes of rush hour traffic before I was placed on the sidewalk. It was estimated that I had lain on the sidewalk, dead, for nearly ten minutes before my spirit reentered my body and I was able to sit up.

The experience had a tremendous impact on me and I later would spend a great deal of time on my knees seeking a greater understanding of exactly what had happened and why I was spared.

One night as I knelt in the dark, the Lord permitted me to see the accident, the impact, and observe the angel with his blessed large and powerful hands as he pulled me out of my seat, across the gearshift column and through the open passenger window; all before the car began to roll and careen across the street.

I want to impress on you the reality of my experience. Under normal circumstance in an accident of this magnitude, one would be dead and their body mangled in the wreckage. But I live, breathe, and testify to you that angels attend. As I was permitted to view the accident unfold, I watched my body literally be pulled out of the car through a small window. I saw angelic hands placed under my back, and then carry me gently to where I was placed on the sidewalk.

The windbreaker I wore was not damaged, but my white cotton T-shirt was shredded. Physically, I suffered no injuries except for a few minor abrasions on my back, but following the accident I felt as though I had been in a violent street fight, and lost. At the hospital the doctor examined and released me, but the soreness lasted about two weeks before slowly subsiding.

With the passage of time came the realization of the miracle that occurred. I also received a testimony of the fact that someone from the other side had again been sent to protect me; protection that has been my gift through-out my life, a gift which I never will take for granted.

THE POWER OF
DISCERNMENT

Cheryle Captures a Crook!

As I reflect on some of my experiences, I realize that some might think I was the only one in the family who had the instinctive capabilities required to be a police officer. Such is not the case. Cheryle also had this ability which surfaced many years ago.

It was 1968 and we were living in our second apartment which was located in Van Nuys, California. I was assigned to the University Division Morning Watch. Our first two little girls were quite young, Shannyn being about three and Cindy only two.

I worked from midnight to eight, so I was sleeping soundly when Cheryle ran into the bedroom, shook me and yelled, "There's a burglar out front. Get your gun and get him before he gets away!"

Not fully awake, I got out of bed and tried to get more of the story as I put on my Levi's, slipped a .357 Magnum in my waistband, grabbed my handcuffs and threw on a nylon windbreaker.

Excitedly, Cheryle continued: "I was in the back carport with the girls when a young man jumped the fence. He was holding a brown paper bag in his hands and looked suspicious, so I walked over to him and asked him what he had in the bag, which surprisingly he handed me. It was full of money, jewelry and watches. He then grabbed the bag back and shouted, 'I don't need to show you anything!'"

When I walked out the front door and looked toward the street, I saw a male Caucasian, nineteen, dressed just as Cheryle described holding a brown paper bag. I pulled the Magnum from my waistband, walked up next to the suspect, put the barrel of my gun to the side of his head and told him he was under arrest for burglary. Immediately, he began to tremble.

Then I explained to him what I would do if he decided to resist or run. I ordered him to his knees and he complied. As I stood over him, a car drove by and backfired.

"He's going to kill me," he screamed. "Don't let him shoot me."

"If I shot at you, slick, you'd be dead. Now get up and walk over to the bridge."

Trembling, he got up and walked over to the wrought iron bridge that provided entrance into our apartment complex.

"Sit down and put your arms through the grating."

Once this was done, I handcuffed him to the bridge.

Behind me I heard yelling. I turned and watched as six bikers boldly approached yelling profanities and advising me that the suspect was their friend and they wanted him released.

When they were about fifteen feet away, I pulled my gun, cocked the hammer and aimed the weapon at the head of the nearest man. With that, they stopped. I then "politely" advised them I was a police officer, the suspect was under arrest for burglary and I would kill the first one of them that made any attempt to take the suspect from my custody. The sight of the cocked Magnum and my pleasant, meek personality made the necessary impression, for the bikers immediately turned and walked in the opposite direction. Within moments, the police arrived.

When they got there, I had to laugh. The first patrol officer jumped out of the car and frantically asked, "Did you shoot at the guy?"

"If I shot him, he'd be dead," I answered.

I later learned that when Cheryle was on the phone and the car backfired, she yelled, "My husband just shot him!"

The police arrested the suspect and were able to identify the victim of the burglary. While testifying at the trial, the defense attorney, noting Cheryle's youth, pressed her as to how she even would have thought that the suspect could possibly have committed a crime. With great poise, she explained her list of reasons, each giving her great probable cause, including the burglaries in the area, the brown paper bag, and then finally she said, "My husband is a Los Angeles Police Officer."

"I have no further questions," responded the defense attorney.

Because of his prior record, the judge sentenced the suspect to prison.

An Unlikely Participant

It was a Fast Sunday in the Morning Sun Ward. Larry Burns was the Bishop and the Melchizedek Priesthood had been asked to pass the Sacrament. I agreed to help and sat in the front row on the aisle seat in front of the Sacrament table. But before the Sacrament, came the blessing of babies.

Bishop Burns stood at the pulpit and asked all who had been invited to participate in the ordinance to please come forward. The first baby to be blessed belonged to the Manuele's.

As invited, ward members walked forward. From behind me, I could hear movement and then someone walked past me who reeked of alcohol. Without seeing who it was, my left arm shot out and grabbed the man by the coat, stopping him dead in his tracks. When he turned to look at me, not only was it apparent that he had been drinking heavily before the meeting, but it was someone I had never seen before. I stood up and said, "Don't go any farther pal. Just turn around and leave."

Seeing me stand and stop the "uninvited participant," Bishop Burns left the stand and since it was his ward and his problem, I sat back down and let him handle it.

It appears that the individual was a homeless man that Brother Greg Manuele had met on the street near his store.

Befriending the guy, Greg invited him to the blessing of the baby. The man, thinking it a pretty good idea, decided to tank up before the meeting and when Bishop Burns asked for those invited to assist in the blessing to come forward, up popped our neighborhood drunk.

After a conversation with the Bishop, the man weaved his way to the back door and left. As the guy walked out, Bishop Burns looked at me and said, "Thanks President!"

TITHING

Twenty-Seven Cents

I remember the faith that was required by our family as we were severely tried following my stroke. The stroke hit one night in May 1981. I was a few weeks shy of my thirty-seventh birthday. It was followed by eleven years of migraines and seizures, but before that, it was necessary for me to leave law enforcement; a career that I had sought since the age of fourteen and one which I greatly enjoyed.

The process required to secure a pension from the City of Los Angeles is complicated. They did everything in their power to discourage and place despair into one's life. And that was the case where I was concerned.

The city sent me to doctor after doctor. I believe that the final total was approximately twenty-four. Some you would consider reputable, others not so. And during the process, we exhausted our savings, for even when one is ill, children still need to eat and bills must be paid.

And then it finally happened. We were out of money. We had done everything we could and I was at a loss, so I called a family council meeting.

It was June 1982. We were living in our home on Robin Avenue, in Saugus, California. Shannyn, our oldest child was just seventeen. Scott, the youngest, was four.

In the Robin Avenue home we had a very large dinner table that I had made especially to seat all nine of us. It was eight feet long and four feet wide.

On the night of the council, we all took our seats, and after dinner I told the children that we needed to talk.

I explained to them that the money was gone and that all we had left was what I would put on the table. Slowly, I placed on the table two shinny dimes and seven old pennies.

"That's it kids," I said. "All we have is twenty-seven cents." The room was silent.

"Now, what should we do?" I asked.

The silence was soon broken as each of the children said, "We pay our tithing, Dad."

So that is what we did. Slowly, and deliberately, I removed three pennies and placed them in a tithing envelope. When that was done the silence was broken by Becky, our family comic, who was nine.

"I hope that doesn't mean we're going on welfare, Dad."

That comment sent the entire family into a state of uncontrolled laughter. Becky was one who always could see the funny side of a situation, and she never hesitated to share her opinion with all others.

The tithing was paid; three old pennies. And although the times did not get better immediately, as a family we were able to face another day knowing that in the Lord's own time the windows of heaven would open. And they did. Within two weeks, I was offered and accepted a security position at Lockheed Aerospace in Burbank, California.

A SACRED
RESPONSIBILITY

Sherwood LaCount

Sherwood LaCount was a character actor and a convert to The Church of Jesus Christ of Latter-day Saints. When we met, I realized that I had seen him in a number of television shows and also church films written, produced and directed by my uncles, Scott and Judge Whitaker. Sherwood had a wonderful family which consisted of his wife, Louise, and a young nine year old son, Mark.

Brother LaCount joined the church later in life and always regretted not hearing the Gospel of Jesus Christ as a young man. He also regretted that he had smoked for many years before his conversion. This habit eventually would cost him his life.

During 1971 and 1972, I served as the President of the Third Quorum of Elders in the old Burbank, California Stake. During this time I had another significant assignment in that I was the Home Teacher to the LaCount family. In a short period of time, Sherwood and I became great friends.

As the time passed, my relationship with the family continued to be strengthened. One day in late 1971, I received a telephone call from Sherwood.

"President, this is Brother LaCount."

"Well, how are you Brother LaCount?"

Sherwood's voice seemed strained and very somber.

"I need to talk to you about something, President. I have been diagnosed with lung cancer and have only about three months to live. I would like to take this time to plan my memorial service. I will organize the service and would like you to conduct it."

Brother LaCount was in his early fifties and me in my mid-twenties. Yet, when one has the mantle, the Spirit takes over, so on that afternoon, I took copious notes as Sherwood described exactly what he wanted and who he desired to participate in the service. I wrote every word as he gave detailed instructions.

Days turned into weeks, and although I saw him becoming thinner, he continued to attend church and function as best he could as a husband and father. Then one night, I received another telephone call, but this time, it was from Sister LaCount.

"Brother Whitaker, Sherwood has taken seriously ill and appears to be dying. The doctors believe that he won't make it through the night, and he has asked that you come to our home and give him a blessing."

"I'll get my counselor, Sister LaCount, and we will be there in twenty minutes."

Getting on the phone, I contacted Brother Bill Oleson who was my first counselor.

"Brother Oleson, I need you to meet me at the LaCount home. Brother LaCount is dying and it appears that he won't make it through the night. He's asked for a priesthood blessing."

Within twenty minutes, Brother Oleson and I met in front of the LaCount home which was located on a secluded tree enveloped lot in North Hollywood. Getting out of our cars, Bill and I walked a distance into a grove of trees and when alone, knelt and I poured my heart out to the Lord asking for the divine guidance needed to provide the blessing that the Lord would pronounce if He were standing in my place.

Following the prayer, Bill and I walked to the front door where we were met by Sister LaCount who welcomed us and ushered us into the bedroom.

On entering the room, I saw Brother LaCount lying in bed. I hadn't seen him in a few weeks and during that time he had lost more weight, and it now appeared that death was near. He could not have weighed more than ninety pounds.

Unable to raise his head, he slowly opened his eyes when Sister LaCount told him we were there.

"Thank you for coming, President," he whispered. Then he softly directed that Brother Oleson should anoint, and I should seal the anointing and give the blessing. So that is what we did. However, the blessing was different from what was expected by everyone in the room, including me. For although it was my voice, it was the Spirit that pronounced the blessing and made some very specific and remarkable promises. I was directed to tell Sherwood that his work on the earth was not yet completed and that that Lord would give him sufficient strength to rise from what the doctors perceived to be his death bed, and as his strength improved, he would be allowed to complete his work upon the earth.

Upon the completion of the blessing, I looked across the bed at Brother Oleson and saw that his eyes were open wide in astonishment. Then I looked at Sister LaCount. She too wore an expression of astonishment which was magnified as she looked at her eternal companion who appeared to lie dying.

After Bill and I walked out the front door, he turned and said, "President, do you know what you promised Brother LaCount?"

"I didn't promise him anything, Brother Oleson. The Lord did, and what He promised will come to pass."

Brother LaCount slept well that night, and after a week, he began to regain strength and gain weight. As the weeks passed, he got stronger and his weight increased. He even attended church, and with the aid of crutches was able not only to attend Sacrament meeting, but also was able to walk to the Sacrament table and administer the Sacrament.

Then one Sunday while I was standing in the back of the North Hollywood Ward Chapel, I saw Brother LaCount enter through the rear door with a smile on his face.

"President, I did it, I did it!" he exclaimed.

"Did what, Brother LaCount?"

"The paper work came through this week, and I was sealed to my parents in the Los Angeles Temple. Sister LaCount's ninety-three year old grandfather, who is a Patriarch, came down from San Francisco and was with us. I didn't think I would be able to do it, but it is done. We are now an eternal family!"

And so it was. About a week passed when I received another telephone call from Sister LaCount telling me that Sherwood was in Saint Joseph's Hospital in Burbank and he wanted to see me. It appeared that the final curtain call had come and he soon would exit this stage called mortality.

I drove to the hospital, found his room and quietly walked in. It was apparent that the veil was thin between this side and the other. Gently, and in great love, I took his hand. He slowly opened his eyes and began to whisper. As I moved closer, I listened carefully.

"President, I didn't understand the meaning of your blessing at the house, but now I do. We are now an eternal family and I am ready to leave. Thank you."

Sherwood then closed his eyes and fell into a deep sleep; a sleep that is preparatory to leaving mortality. With tears in my eyes, I reverently placed his hand under the covers, kissed him on the forehead and bid a dear friend good-bye. Later that night I received the final telephone call from Sister La Count.

"President, Sherwood is gone. I was holding his hand when he said good-bye and slipped away."

The memorial service for Sherwood La Count was exactly as he had planned. As I spoke and addressed the family and many friends in attendance, there was no doubt in my mind that not only was Sherwood pleased with the service, but that he had been allowed to attend.

Releasing a Parent

On Monday, December 6, 1995 my youngest daughter Jamie and I drove to Los Angeles. The purpose of the trip was to allow me to give my mother a blessing as she lay dying in the hospital.

After checking into a hotel in Santa Clarita, we drove immediately to St. Joseph's Hospital in Burbank where Momo had been for the past two weeks. Upon our entering her room, it was apparent that she was close to death, but for some reason was waiting.

As we talked, both Jamie and I noted that although her speech was strained, she was extremely alert and coherent. It was apparent that her body had gone through a tremendous amount in the last two weeks and she was weakening. As I stood next to the bed, we had the opportunity to reminisce about years past and holidays that had meant so much to the family when I was growing up.

During the conversation, she stopped and looked at me, and with tears in her eyes softly said, "I have seen the Savior's face. It is radiant and so very beautiful. There have also been others in the room who are from the other side. I told them I was not ready and they smiled and left."

As I stood next to the bed, I knew that what she said was true, for the Sprit bore witness to my soul that it had occurred.

During our visit, Jamie sat on the bed with tears in her eyes and carefully listened to the conversation, interjecting words of love for her grandmother. Mother and I continued to speak, and then she stopped and asked who the other people were in the room. In the eyes of the world, only Jamie and I stood in that room, but I knew that the angels, who had been there before, were again in attendance.

We continued to talk and as I leaned over the bed, she stopped and asked if I had just turned the light on because it was now very bright. The room was radiant with the Spirit, and I asked if she would like me to give her a blessing. She said yes. She took Jamie's hand and held it tight, but Jamie later told me that as soon as I laid my hands on her head, the grip relaxed and her entire body went limp.

I then had the privilege of releasing my mother from this earthly probationary period, seal her unto death and tell her that those in the room would soon escort her to the other side. In the blessing the Lord noted her faithfulness, commended her for her return to activity in the church and blessed her for withstanding the great physical trials she faced. She was also told that many on the other side of the veil awaited her return. As usual, I cannot remember all of the blessing, but Jamie was in the room and knows what Momo was told. On Tuesday, following our return to Las Vegas, Cheryle spoke to Momo on the telephone and although she sounded very tired, it was apparent that she was at peace and putting things in order and saying her good-byes.

On December 18, twelve days after the blessing, Mother passed away.

A Change of Assignment

I was serving in the Nevada Las Vegas Mission presidency when I received a request to give a blessing to a three year old girl who drowned in a hot tub. I knew the family because they were members of our ward and both parents had recently been reactivated.

Cheryle and I arrived at the hospital and were met at the Intensive Care Unit by about twenty ward members which included a number of priesthood holders.

I said my hello's and then talked to the parents. The small girl was a foster care child who had slipped from the house and after climbing some steps, had fallen into an above ground hot tub. Although she had not been in the water long, when I saw her I noted that she was connected to a Life Support System.

"How long has she been like this?" I asked.

"Twelve days," the parents replied.

Walking to the bed, I stopped and looked into the small face. There was no sign of distress, just a daughter of God who lingered between mortality and eternity.

As I stood next to the bed and pled for guidance, the Spirit counseled me that the child should be released from her mortal journey to continue on into the eternities. The prompting was such that it could not be ignored.

I also knew and felt the presence of unseen others in the room who had been sent to accompany this sweet spirit to the other side.

With that, I asked one of the brethren to anoint and I would then seal the anointing and give the blessing.

As I looked into the eyes of all present, I saw that they were all confident that after the blessing was given, this beautiful child would be well on her way to recovery.

I knew differently.

My priesthood companion anointed the little one, and then I, with the other Melchizedek Priesthood holder, laid our hands on her head and I sealed the anointing and gave her a blessing.

While I cannot recall exactly what was said, I remember telling her that she was not alone and that others, unseen by many, were in the room to assist her in her departure. When I ended the blessing and looked around the room, I saw faces filled with disappointment and eyes that emanated distress.

I stood at the bedside, and was able to speak to the child, not as one would speak as an adult to a child, but as two adults conversing. She understood the blessing, was grateful for my presence that evening and told me she was ready to leave.

I bid her goodbye, and then Cheryle and I quietly left the room.

Approximately six hours later I received a telephone call from the foster parents advising me that the child had quietly passed away.

IN THE PRESENCE
OF PROPHETS

President David O. McKay

It was 1972, and I was a young Elder's Quorum president in the Burbank Stake in California. One night I went to bed concerned that possibly I was not doing all I could as a young president. I had barely fallen asleep when the following vision was opened to my eyes.

I found myself sitting at the rear of an old chapel. The interior was constructed of dark wood, and the rear seats were elevated so that from the rear you had a perfect view of the stand and the pulpit.

I sat alone on the hard bench in the back row and looked down on the stand and pulpit where I saw three men seated in hard, straight-back chairs. In the middle was President David O. McKay, who was deceased. On his right was Elder Howard W. Hunter, a member of the Quorum of the Twelve Apostles, and to his left was James D. Pratt, the Burbank Stake president.

The meeting ended and I felt no better at the end than I had at the beginning, so I walked outside and was standing alone on the sidewalk when President Pratt and the other Brethren approached. As President Pratt walked up and extended his hand, I shook it, and then President Pratt turned to President McKay and said, "President McKay, let me introduce President Whitaker of the Third Quorum of Elders."

I extended my hand to President McKay. He stepped forward, took my hand in both of his and smiled. Then he stepped even closer, looked deep into my eyes and in a soft voice that penetrated every fiber of my being said: "Richard, the Lord is well pleased with your efforts. Keep up the fine work."

With that assurance, the dream ended, and I found myself awake. I immediately got out of bed, dropped to my knees, and prayed for confirmation that what I had seen and heard had occurred. In that prayer the Spirit confirmed the reality of the dream. The Spirit also confirmed the fact that although I had been introduced to President McKay as "President Whitaker," he knew me personally and used my first name rather than referring to me as, "President."

I have had other experiences with modern-day prophets and stand firm in my testimony that each was called by God, in his time and season, to preside over the Lord's affairs upon the earth.

Stick by Your Guns

While serving as an Elders Quorum president, I was asked to speak at one of the leadership meetings in which Elder Howard W. Hunter of the Quorum of the Twelve Apostles was in attendance.

After I spoke, Elder Hunter stood and as he addressed the priesthood, he turned to me and began to ask questions pertaining to statistics and figures applicable to the level of activity in my quorum. Without hesitating, I recited the figures from memory and had an answer to each and every question. President Hunter was somewhat taken back and asked me if I was sure of the figures. I was, but before I could answer, President Jim Pratt leaned over to me and said, "Stick by your guns, president."

I had planned on it and answered Elder Hunter with the same figures as given previously.

Elder Hunter was happy with the response and the meeting continued.

President Spencer W. Kimball

In 1976, the First Presidency scheduled an Area Conference at the Rose Bowl in Pasadena, California. When the brethren coordinating security asked for volunteers, I declined. This is not a church where you volunteer for this and that. This is a church where assignments are made and follow-up conducted. Time passed and finally the man who was coordinating the security called me and asked if I would accept an assignment and serve. "Of course I will," I responded.

On the day of the conference, my assignment was to stand in a long tunnel that allowed ingress and egress to the floor of the Rose Bowl.

When I arrived at the location, I found that other than a large motor home across from me, the tunnel was empty. Those in charge instructed me to watch the motor home for in it was a VIP.

As a good soldier, I positioned myself just outside the door and waited. Time passed and then suddenly, the door opened and out stepped President Spencer W. Kimball. With a large grin on his face he bounded down the steps and headed directly for me. As I put out my hand to shake his, I said, "Good afternoon, President." He ignored my outstretched hand and as he stepped up to me, he grabbed me in a large bear hug, and squeezing me soundly, said, "It's a great day for a conference, isn't it Elder!"

"It sure is President!"

President Kimball then stepped back, looked me in the eyes, hesitated and smiled.

With me at his side, we walked into the conference. I never would forget that hug and a Prophet of God stepping back and looking deep into my eyes as he searched my soul.

A Solemn Assembly

It was 1977 and I was serving on the North Hollywood Stake High Council. As a council, we were invited by the First Presidency to attend a Solemn Assembly at the Los Angeles Temple with twenty-five hundred other priesthood leaders from Southern California. Additionally, the Brethren requested our stake to form a singing group of twelve men selected from the High Council. Although not one to jump up and volunteer to sing, I gladly accepted an invitation to be part of that group.

The day of the meeting we formed a line outside the east entrance of the temple where we waited until ushered into the main assembly hall on the second floor.

The assembly hall encompassed the entire floor with room for the General Authorities as they sat by quorums. Our choir sat patiently in the front awaiting the arrival of the Prophet. The room was crowded. Sacrament tables had been set up in the front. Selected stake presidents were asked to bless the Sacrament while Bishops were invited to pass it to all in attendance.

As we sat, suddenly all conversation ceased and a silence washed over the room and like a wave on the ocean, everyone stood as President Spencer W. Kimball walked from the rear to the front podium. It was a marvelous feeling as the Spirit of the Lord fell heavily on all in attendance.

The meeting began and we then had the privilege of singing. That meeting was one of the highlights of my life. Not often does a man have the opportunity to attend a Solemn Assembly in the House of the Lord, and it is even rarer to be able to sing within these holy walls for those on this side and those sent from the other.

President Gordon B. Hinckley

To be in the presence of an Apostle of the Lord Jesus Christ and future Prophet of God is a unique experience; one which I had in January 1995 when Bishop Larry Burns coordinated the security for a Nevada Las Vegas Area Conference held at the Thomas and Mack Center.

It was very early on a Sunday morning, and Bishop Burns and I were scheduled to meet Elder Dennis Simmons and President Gordon B. Hinckley at the Thomas and Mack Conference Center. President Hinckley was then First Counselor in the First Presidency, and President Hunter was the Prophet, but seriously ill.

Bishop Burns and I arrived at the Thomas and Mack at about 6:00 a.m. There was not a soul around except us. Suddenly, the van carrying President Hinckley pulled up. Larry went to the van to assist the President, while I opened the glass door to the side entrance.

As I held the door open, President Hinckley walked up, stopped and stood directly in front of me. We shook hands and then he looked directly into my eyes. It was a look that penetrated deep into my soul. He did this without saying a word. Five seconds passed and then ten. After nearly twenty seconds of silence, President Hinckley broke into a large grin and said, "Thank you Brother Whitaker."

"You're welcome President."

That was the most intense Personal Priesthood Interview I have ever had. Later, I had the opportunity to spend time in the Green Room with President Hinckley and Elder Russell M. Nelson, a member of the Quorum of the Twelve Apostles.

It was during this time that I was able personally to view the great and unselfish dedication of Elder Nelson.

As I stood near President Hinckley, a telephone call was made to Salt Lake and I heard him ask about President Hunter. After he received an update, he turned to Elder Nelson and asked him how his daughter was. Elder Nelson shared that she was not doing well, and that they did not expect her to live long.

I learned during that conversation that his daughter was a young mother with children and she was in the final stages of terminal cancer.

President Hinckley walked over to Elder Nelson and then said, "Russell, why don't you leave and go be with your daughter?"

Without hesitation, Elder Nelson said, "President, I am on assignment from the Lord and I will stay and finish that assignment."

President Hinckley smiled and both went on to participate in the conference. Not long after the conference, Elder Nelson's daughter passed away.

Something More to Do

Our second mission to Quito, Ecuador was winding down and I was finishing my responsibilities as the Director, Fondo Perpetuo para la Educación, Ecuador or in English, The Director of the Perpetual Education Fund, Ecuador. One night I had the following dream.

I found myself in the Primary Room of a ward building. The dress was casual and as I sat on the floor, I saw the late President Gordon B. Hinckley also in the room. He dressed casually and sat enjoying the laughter of the children.

While children's voices permeated the room, President Hinckley arose from his chair and asked me to join him. We walked from the building to a grassy spot located directly outside the building. A large smile crossed his lips as he asked me to have a seat. Once we both were seated, his tone became serious.

"Brother Whitaker, the Lord has something more for you to do."

Before President Hinckley could tell me the nature of the assignment, the dream ended.

Not long afterward Elder Richard E. Cook contacted me and asked if Cheryle and I would return to South America and fill a special assignment in Lima, Peru. We accepted and it was this assignment that saw me develop a church-wide program to rescue many who were struggling in the Perpetual Education Fund.

SERVING IN THE KINGDOM

A Thief in the Ranks

While serving in the North Hollywood Ward bishopric, President Keith Barton approached me and asked if I would serve on the High Council and accept the assignment for all the North Hollywood Stake Physical Facilities. Within two weeks, I was on the council and had begun to organize the work.

The year was 1976. The excitement then began.

My assignment encompassed total responsibility for the five stake facilities as well as the responsibility of hiring and terminating custodians, purchasing all supplies and coordinating all work schedules and building projects. I conducted the salary negotiations with Salt Lake and brought custodians from as far away as Idaho. When Salt Lake informed me that I could pay my custodians only a certain amount which, according to the standard of living, was very low, I negotiated for higher pay, documented needs and got what I requested. It paid to ask.

Once I asked one of the custodians to do some work in his assigned building. He refused. I then turned up the heat. Eventually, he quit. But before doing so he made it a point to quote me the 121st Section of the Doctrine and Covenants and tell me I exercised unrighteous dominion. First of all, he failed to understand the scripture. Secondly, the church paid him from the sacred funds of the Lord. His was not a calling, it was employment.

The assignment was difficult and I was not the most liked person in the stake. On one occasion, I was told that I was the topic of discussion in a stake meeting. As the stake presidency sat with the Bishop's, President Barton was asked, if, "Brother Whitaker is following Whitaker's program or that of the stake?"

President Barton responded by stating, "Brother Whitaker is following neither. He is following the Lord's program with the total support of the stake presidency." There was no further discussion.

Time passed and soon I became aware that I had another custodian who refused to work. I asked him to keep the stake center restrooms cleaner and told him not only what I wanted, but also how to do it. He refused.

One day I drove to the stake center armed with a toothbrush. Before this day, I had made a point of requesting that the tiles and grout in the restrooms be cleaned because they were absolutely filthy. Normally, the task could have been accomplished using standard means, but with his refusal, the recommended process changed.

When I asked him a second time, he again refused.

I waited a few days to give him the benefit of the doubt, and then walked into the stake center and found him sitting and listening to the radio. I asked him to come with me to the restroom. Reluctantly, he did so. Once inside the bathroom, I handed him the toothbrush and a bottle of solvent.

"Brother, I have asked you to clean the restrooms. It appears that you didn't understand my request. Now I am telling you that I want the grout between the tiles cleaned; and I would recommend that you use this solvent and this toothbrush. I will be back tomorrow to see how everything looks."

"I don't have to do this," was his reply.

"No, you don't. And you don't need to work for the church either."

"You wouldn't dare fire me. I can sue."

With that, the discussion ended.

When I returned, the bathroom was still filthy. Remembering that this "good brother" also had a custodial business on the side and did this type of work during his off hours, I decided to check our custodial supplies in the two buildings this man maintained. As I examined the records and then evaluated the daily usage of supplies, I noted a discrepancy. I went to the stake accountant and found that when compared to the previous year when this man was not employed, we now were consuming far more supplies. I then checked the type and brand of supplies purchased for the stake and found that many were sent from Salt Lake, and because of the church contracts, the supplies carried a specific brand name not available in Southern California. With this information, I turned my collar around and went into the investigative mode.

Checking the schedule, I determined when this man would next be working at the stake center on a late shift. With this information, I decided to monitor his activities, or in police jargon, conduct a stake-out.

One evening after my meetings ended, I pulled my car into the darkness of the stake center parking lot and watched. Time passed. Soon it was time for the custodian to leave. It was about 11:30 p.m. But before he did, something interesting took place.

I sat in the darkness and watched as he exited the building time after time with arms loaded with supplies. I watched as he filled his trunk and back seat and then stepped to the driver's door and entered the car. Once he was in his vehicle, I started my car and with my bright headlights on, I pulled in front of his car blocking his exit. Getting out, I walked over to the driver's door. As I stood next to his window, I shined my flashlight beam into his face and then onto the supplies loaded in the backseat. Suddenly, he went white. The ensuing discussion was very short and brief with me doing the talking and he doing the listening.

"Brother, those supplies do not appear to belong to you, but to the church. So, you have two choices. The first is to replace all the supplies taken this evening and then tomorrow morning resign from church employment, or, refuse and I will arrest you for grand theft and book you into the North Hollywood Division jail facility. Oh, and Grand Theft is a Felony."

As I said this, I pulled out my badge, and I am confident that as he looked at it, he also saw the gun on my hip.

"But I'm a member of the church...."

"You're a liar and a thief and one who delights in robbing God. Make your decision and do it now."

Slowly he unloaded the supplies and returned them to the stake center. The next morning, he quit.

The next day, I briefed President Barton on the activities of the following evening and left any further decisions about discipline in his hands.

Always Temper Your Comments

In 1980 while we lived in Saugus, California, I was called to serve as an alternate High Councilor to the Santa Clarita Stake High Council.

The calling was difficult and my relationship with the stake president, strained. After a year of tense situations, a counselor in the stake presidency stopped me in the hallway one Sunday and said, "Brother Whitaker, in the nine year history of this stake, no one has ever made the stake president as uncomfortable as you have. Therefore, you will be released next week."

And what was the cause of the discomfort? I did nothing more than ask questions. However upon reflection I found that it was not the questions asked, but the manner in which they were presented.

It was my understanding that if one was in a position to make observations and recommendations and was asked for counsel, then it was his responsibility to voice his opinion. After that was done, then it was also a responsibility to raise one's hand to the square and sustain the presiding authority in the final decision. That is precisely what I did, but in retrospect, I see that I was too direct and at times, too abrupt.

We all must learn to temper our opinions and keep them to ourselves unless the Spirit prompts us to speak. We must learn to speak in loving tones remembering to preface the comment with, "If I might make an observation and recommendation," or, "It seems that we might want to look at the alternative," or, "If you're open to a suggestion, the thought occurs to me that….," etc.

Because of some difficult experiences, I have learned never to give ultimatums to those who preside or make them feel that I do not respect them or their calling. I have learned the importance of always respecting the position one holds. In doing so, I will respect the individual in the position and not do or say anything hurtful, argumentative or contentious.

ANGELS OF DARKNESS

Do Not Turn Around

In 1960 at the age of sixteen, I had my first encounter with the forces of evil.

I was living with my parents in our home in North Hollywood, California. At about 4:00 p.m., feeling tired, I decided to go into my bedroom and take a quick nap before dinner. I shared the bedroom with my brother Greg. I entered the room, shut the door and lay down on my bed with my back to the door.

Greg was down the street playing with his friends, and my parents were in the kitchen. Not long after closing my eyes, I heard what sounded like the bedroom door open and close. A few seconds passed and I felt an unnatural coldness surround me. Then there was a tap on my shoulder and suddenly I found myself paralyzed, unable to move or open my eyes. It was then that I heard a still small voice caution me and say, *Richard, do not turn around.*

I don't believe that I could have turned around had I wanted, but since I was unable and counseled not to, I just lay on the bed facing the wall. A feeling of great foreboding engulfed me and as the moments passed, the feeling increased and the darkness became thicker. I tried to speak but was unable to open my mouth, nor could I move my arms.

Another tapping on my left shoulder, and a second time I heard the same still small voice caution me and say, *Richard, do not turn around.*

I was terrified and could think of only one thing to do. In my mind I said, *In the name of Jesus Christ, and by the authority of the Aaronic Priesthood that I hold, I command you to leave!*

I had no more finished that command than I felt the presence diminish, my body released from the paralysis and a deep sense of peace surround me.

When I felt all was safe, I rolled off the bed and went into the kitchen where my parents were standing and talking.

"Did either of you just come into my room?" I asked.

"No," they answered.

"Did Greg come home, or is he still outside?"

"He is still down the street, Richard. Why? What is the problem?" asked my mother.

"Nothing, I was just wondering."

I had no doubt what had happened, nor did I forget the feeling of total paralysis and darkness that engulfed me at that time. Nor have I ever forgotten the power in using the name of Jesus Christ to vanquish evil.

An Evil Presence

Before Cheryle and I attended the temple to receive our own endowments and be sealed as a family for time and all eternity, the forces of evil did all they could to thwart the effort.

During the two week period before we attended the temple, I felt a dark presence in our home. On a number of occasions I saw a vapor in the corner of the room, and on two separate nights, I awoke to see a dark figure standing at the end of the bed. Each time, I commanded these entities to leave and did so in the name of Jesus Christ. When this Holy name was uttered, they vanished.

Thursday night before our Saturday temple session the attacks became more personal. As I lay in bed, I felt uneasy and knew Cheryle and I were not alone. Although the room was dark, when I looked toward the end of the bed, I again saw a dark figure. It stood silent and did not move, but only directed its gaze in my direction. It was a figure that had not entered the room through the door and emanated evil in and through its presence. I commanded the presence to leave in the name of Jesus Christ and watched as it formed into a mist like vapor and exited the room through the left hand corner of the ceiling.

On two other occasions, I found myself in bed, totally paralyzed, barely able to breath and unable to move. I felt as if

I would die if the tremendous pressure upon my chest was not removed. Unable to speak, I formed in my mind the command that had worked before and which I knew was the only name under heaven that the powers of darkness would obey; the name of Jesus Christ. As soon as the thought had been formed and the command made, the entities left.

During all of these experiences, Cheryle was next to me, saw my breathing become labored and realized that I was sweating profusely, but during each experience, she neither saw nor heard anything.

It didn't take me long to realize that I was at war with an unseen enemy determined to destroy me. And although I knew the threat was real, I never realized that I posed such a threat to the powers of darkness that it would cause them to take such an interest in me.

It was Friday, the day before we were to receive our endowments. In the early morning hours, I suddenly was awakened as I felt a tremendous pressure being exerted upon my chest. So great was this pressure that I thought I soon would stop breathing and die. And although I had felt this same type of pressure on previous occasions, this experience was far more severe.

As I attempted to move, I found myself paralyzed. And when I tried to open my eyes or speak, I found that also impossible. Then suddenly, I saw the most vicious, ugly female personage I had ever beheld kneeling on my chest with her hands wrapped around my throat. She flayed from side to side, her face distorted and her long dark hair flying from side to side. She screamed over and over, *I am going to kill you! I am going to kill you!*

The grip around my throat tightened. I felt as though it was choking the very life out of me. At first, the shock of the experience caused me to panic, but then, calmly and in my mind, I reflected upon times past and actions taken. So forming the words in my mind, I commanded, *In the name of Jesus Christ I command you to depart.* Nothing happened.

Again I gave the command, but the intensity of the attack increased. I felt as though the end was near. The viciousness of the attack was beyond anything I had ever experienced. I plainly could distinguish the distorted features of my female assailant. The entire personage of this attacker was devoid of any light. It was blackness accompanied by a screeching and wailing that was not of this world. Over and over my assailant screamed, *I am going to kill you! I am going to kill you!*

Her eyes were black pools void of any expression but hatred. The entire personage was the most evil and dark thing imaginable and filled with hatred for me and all I stood for. This was evil in its basest form, her only desire and mission was my destruction.

Struggling, I commanded a third time. This time was successful, for as suddenly as the attack began, it ended.

Finding my body released from the horrible grip which the demon had upon it, I discovered myself drenched with perspiration and exhausted. But I was alive and never would forget the power of evil and the fact that there is only one name under heaven that the powers of darkness must obey: the name of Jesus Christ.

The following day Cheryle and I, accompanied by Shannyn, Cindy and others from the North Hollywood I Ward traveled to the Los Angeles Temple where sacred covenants were made and a family was sealed for time and all eternity.

One Name Under Heaven

It was 1990 and I was working as the Technical Advisor for the motion picture, *The Hidden*. The cast included Michael Nouri, Kyle McLaughlin, Ed O' Ross and others who later went on to have very successful careers in the Motion Picture and Television Industry.

One day we were scheduled to film a scene using an abandoned jail facility. It had four stories above ground with the upper floor surrounded by barbed wire. It also had two floors below ground, the basement area housing the cells.

The floor with the cells had a main concourse running down the center and then aisles that extended off the main corridor. Each aisle contained three cells on each side for a total of six per unit. To enter the below ground facility required that you walk down two flights of concrete stairs, approach a desk, then pass through a large, barred jail door that was located to the left of the stairwell.

On the day of filming, we set up in the jail parking lot. Since we were shooting inside the cell area, I wanted to do some exploring just to see what it looked like. As I walked down into the lower levels of the facility, I felt a change in temperature as it became colder. When I entered the reception area, I turned to my left, opened the large barred jail door and entered the long concourse.

Walking down the long hallway, I immediately knew that I was not alone. Then suddenly they appeared. More evil spirits than I could count! I was surrounded. Their wailing and ranting filled my ears. Blood curdling screams caused the hair on my arms and neck to stand on end. I observed that their countenances were void of light and darker than night; a darkness that I had viewed before, but never this intensely since there were hundreds in this group that contained both men and women. Stepping through the gate, I had intruded into their world.

Suddenly, the circle of evil began to move closer. Calmly, I raised my right arm to the square. Then, with all the power and force within me I said, "In the name of Jesus Christ, and by virtue of the Holy Melchizedek Priesthood which I hold, I command you to depart!"

When I invoked the sacred name of Jesus Christ, hundreds of evil spirits bowed and started slowly to move away from where I stood. However, as they retreated backwards, the intensity of the wailing and screams increased as did the flaying of heads which sent long dark hair flying in all directions. Unadulterated hatred could be seen on their dark and evil faces as they bowed in obedience to the name of the Savior.

Slowly and with bodies bowed, they moved back, all the time screaming and throwing their heads from side to side.

As they moved, I walked slowly back to the open jail door and toward the stairs that provided an exit to the floors above.

Stepping back into the daylight, I soon was approached by one of the still photographers who told me he needed a photograph to be used on the identification card I was going to wear in my scene. Together, we entered the back of a truck that had been set up for taking pictures, and after the photographer shut the door, I stepped in front of a black cloth and he took my picture. I stepped from the van and about ten minutes later he again approached me.

"Whitaker, the picture we took can't be used. We need another."

"What was wrong with it?"

"Take a look," he said.

I looked at the photograph and it was apparent that another would need to be taken, for surrounding me was a very large aura of light. It was brilliant enough to be photographed and visible to not only me, but also the photographer, an aura that remained with me when I exited the cells and was visible in the photograph just moments after my leaving the confrontation with those whose realm I had entered.

The photographer took the second photograph, and being void of the brilliant light, it was used for the identification card. I watched as the photographer destroyed the first photograph and tossed it into the trash.

I have never forgotten that experience, nor have I forgotten the immediate response by the angels of darkness when the name of Jesus Christ was used by a representative of Jesus Christ holding the Melchizedek Priesthood.

THE MINISTERING
OF ANGELS

Spared At a Young Age

My life has been spared on a number of occasions in many remarkable ways.

The first experience occurred when I was two years old and riding in the car of my mother's uncle, Frank Struhs. I was packed in the back seat with a number of my cousins who were pushing and laughing as little children will do. My mother and dad were following in their car.

We were travelling at about thirty-five miles an hour when suddenly the back door opened and I was thrown onto the pavement. Thankfully, the car that was directly behind us was driven by a Catholic Nun who was able to slam on her brakes to keep from running over me.

My parents stopped and picked me up off the asphalt where I had bounced and rolled. As you can imagine, I was a mass of blood, and imbedded in my head were rocks and gravel from the street.

My parents drove me to the hospital where doctors removed the rocks and cleaned the dirt off my bruised and bloody body. When they were done, the hospital staff was amazed that I had not suffered one broken bone nor had I suffered any damage other than bruises, scrapes and abrasion's. They washed me up and sent me home.

And so the journey began, as did the protection provided by unseen hands that has continued throughout my life.

They Were Going to Shoot!

Because of its inherent danger, President McKee forbid the missionaries in the Nevada Las Vegas Mission from using small hand held laser lights. They could cause serious injury when directed toward the eyes of another and in some cases, the laser beam could be mistaken for the beam of light emitted from a weapon.

However, this did not stop one of our Zone Leaders from testing the system, an act that almost cost him his life.

With the knowledge that a young man in the Midwest had been shot by police when he pointed a laser light at them, President McKee told his leaders that under no circumstances would he tolerate any missionary possessing or using a laser pointer. I can remember him stressing this to all his District and Zone Leaders. He was clear; there were no exceptions.

One evening, President McKee and I had a meeting with a stake president. At its conclusion, he told me that he had another meeting to attend, so I was through for the night. I drove home and was about to change my clothes when the phone rang. It was Sister McKee. She told me that she was unable to contact President McKee and that she had just received a telephone call from the North Las Vegas Police Department advising her that they had one of our missionaries handcuffed and sitting in the back of a police car. She asked if I would go to the scene while she continued to try and get the President on his cell phone. She gave me the location, and I was out the door.

While I drove to the location, Sister McKee contacted President McKee and gave him the cell phone number of the sergeant at the scene.

When I arrived at the location, it was obvious that this was not one of the safer areas of the city. To the contrary, the street was dark and located behind one of the casinos in North Las Vegas. As I drove up, I saw two police cars parked directly behind the mission car.

I walked up to the scene and saw one of our Zone Leaders sitting handcuffed in the back seat of a black and white police car. At the scene were also a uniformed sergeant and two plain clothes officers. Near the plain clothes officers I saw two bicycles which indicated to me that the officers had been assigned bicycle duty and were working a special detail.

After introducing myself to the sergeant, he told me he was a member of the church and a ward mission leader. I asked him, "What happened?"

He explained that our Zone Leader and a twelve year old church member were sitting in the mission car, in the shadows, when two North Las Vegas police officers on bike patrol rode around the corner and headed in their direction.

"It appears that the Zone Leader, thinking that the two on the bikes were a couple of his missionaries, decided to shine a laser light on the helmet of one of the officers. Immediately, both officers, thinking that the laser light (which is identical to those placed on 9 mm handguns) was coming from a weapon, shifted into a combat mentally and began their approach to the car. With weapons drawn, the officers approached while they issued verbal commands to the occupants of the car. The Zone Leader and his young companion froze. That might have saved their lives."

The sergeant continued his narrative by stating that, "The officers went through their commands for the pair to place their hands in plain sight and then individually exit the car. Once out of the vehicle, the officers searched both of them, and after taking the laser light from the Zone Leader, they handcuffed him and put him into the backseat of a responding police car."

As I stood and talked to the sergeant, it was apparent that both the Zone Leader and his young companion had been only moments away from dying. Whether they knew it or not, I was convinced that both officers had decided in their own minds that should the suspect with the laser light aim it again at them, the officers, believing it to be the sighting mechanism of a weapon, would have commenced firing.

Following President McKee's conversation with the sergeant and after my discussion with him as well as with the concerned officers, the police decided that our Zone Leader would be released into my custody and I would ensure his return to the apartment.

Once the missionary was out of the police car and unhandcuffed, I walked up to him and we stood toe-to-toe. Then, as commanding as a Marine Corps Drill Sergeant, I told him to get his car, get his underage companion and drive directly to his apartment. Once at the apartment, I would have something to say about the incident.

Without a word, he got into the mission car and with his companion in the front seat, drove to his apartment building where he parked the car, told the young man to go home and waited for my arrival.

Silently, and with his head bowed, the Zone Leader stood on the driveway. He knew that I was not happy and he also knew that his mission president was very disappointed with his actions, especially since he was in a key leadership position and openly had been disobedient.

When I walked up to him, I positioned myself so we were nose-to-nose and toe-to-toe. Again I went into my Marine Corps Drill Sergeant impression. Something you might call "controlled anger." The entire dialogue only took about thirty seconds but in that short period of time the ground shook and this Elder trembled. I never will forget the last thing that I told him.

"Elder, I would recommend that you go directly into your apartment and the first thing you do is get down on your knees and thank God that you are still alive."

With that, I abruptly turned, walked to my car and drove off leaving him standing alone in the middle of the driveway.

I returned home and forgot about the incident until I received a telephone call the next day from President McKee.

"Do you know what happened to our Zone Leader last night after you left him?" he asked.

"I have no idea. What happened?"

President McKee went on to explain that the first thing in the morning he received a telephone call from this Elder. During their conversation, he told President McKee that after he drove back to the apartment, "President Whitaker stood in front of me in the driveway and really chewed me out."

He continued to tell President McKee that, "The last thing President Whitaker told me to do was go into my apartment, immediately get down on my knees and thank God I was alive. So that's exactly what I did. If President Whitaker said to do it, I was going to do it."

While on his knees in prayer, this usually very obedient young man experienced something that he would never forget.

"I was praying, when suddenly I found myself out of my body, out of my room and back at the scene where I shined the light on the two policemen. But President, I was not on the ground. I was above everything looking down. It was like a movie. I could see everything. I saw my car, me in the front seat with my split and the two policemen with guns drawn approaching the car. I knew what the policemen were thinking, I heard their thoughts. They were going to shoot us.

"Then as I looked at the policemen, I saw surrounding them a number of spirits, or angels doing everything they could to try and persuade them not to shoot. They were doing everything they could to try and talk the policemen out of killing us. As I watched, I knew the policemen had made up their minds to shoot. Then I looked at my car and it was surrounded by even more angels protecting us. They, too, were pleading to the policemen not to shoot. I now know that if it hadn't been for the angels sent to surround the policemen and my car, we would have been killed."

I am convinced that this was a very frightening way for a young man to learn a very valuable lesson, a lesson that I am sure will be indelibly fixed in his mind and always reinforce the importance of obedience with exactness.

Following this incident, President McKee released the Zone Leader of his leadership responsibilities and made him a junior companion. After his mission, he married a wonderful young lady, has been sealed in the temple, is raising a fine family and has told me on a number of occasions the impact that experience had on his life.

Angels Protect the Lord's Anointed

I had many wonderful experiences while I served as a full-time first counselor in the Nevada Las Vegas Mission. One in particular testified to the thinness of the veil and the fact that angels attend the Lord's anointed.

At mission conferences, my role was primarily that of the Sergeant of Arms. I kept the peace and maintained reverence until the arrival of President and Sister McKee.

I kept things as reverent as possible by saying very little and casting looks that many have said could crack stone. It was a talent I developed on the streets of South Central Los Angeles.

President McKee and I had been together for quite a long time and could read each other like a book. At one particular transfer conference, I did what I was assigned and then retired to the back row of the chapel. Why the back row? That was because the Assistants to the President were to sit with him on the stand, not a counselor.

The meeting started and it was no different from many other transfer conferences President McKee had conducted. We prayed, recited My Commission, by Bruce R. McConkie, Doctrine and Covenants Section 4, sang, and then President McKee stood up to teach his missionaries.

As he spoke, the Spirit increased. Suddenly, there appeared a brilliant band of light that surrounded him as he stood at the pulpit. He continued, and as I looked to his left, I saw six brethren suddenly appear and take seats on the stand. At first I saw only their silhouettes, then, in prayer, I asked that the veil be parted. It was. I saw that they were dressed in white clothing and their demeanor was businesslike.

While they sat quietly on the stand, I had the impression that their being in attendance was not just to hear President McKee speak. Tears filled my eyes as I had confirmed to me in power, how pleased the Lord was with this mission president and a man I had grown to love, a man I called an eternal friend. But it wasn't until the next day that I understood the reason why six brethren from the other side of the veil were sent to a Nevada Las Vegas Mission transfer conference.

Elder Morris Carrillo, a senior missionary and being the "car czar" for the mission, had as one of his jobs the responsibility of driving missionaries north when they were transferred. Therefore, the minute the conference ended, Elder Carrillo loaded up the mission van and hooked up the enclosed trailer used to transport the bicycles and suitcases. Once packed, they started north. He was accompanied by five Elders who were being transferred to various locations in the northern part of the state.

Their journey went well until just south of Elko when the transfer van hit black ice and began to fishtail. Struggling, Elder Carrillo tried to keep the van and trailer from sliding off the highway and into the deep ravines that lined both sides of the road. Then he saw it. A large gasoline tanker was bearing down on the out of control mission van and trailer. With all his strength, Elder Carrillo muscled the steering wheel back and forth as he lightly applied the brakes and tried to accelerate out of the fatal direction which in seconds would see them collide head on with the tanker which we later learned was full to capacity with high octane fuel.

With brakes locked and smoke bellowing into the afternoon air from the tanker's burning tires, the two vehicles were destined to collide. The impact was horrific as the tanker struck the van on the passenger side just behind the front door tearing off the entire side and ripping out the back seat of the now spinning van. Then the tanker struck the fishtailing trailer destroying it, sending shredded baggage, clothing and bent bicycle frames flying across the rough terrain.

Upon impact, one missionary was thrown from the van into the desert. He later said that it was as if he had been lifted by unseen hands and set down on a large desert bush, one of only a very few in the vicinity of the accident.

Miraculously, he was the only one who suffered severe injuries. His leg was broken. The other missionaries suffered bruises, abrasions and scratches, but no one was killed. And when we saw the pictures of the van, no one should have lived through that terrible accident.

One of the great miracles was that neither the truck nor the van erupted in flames. For had there been a fire, the gasoline tanker undoubtedly would have exploded killing everyone.

The driver of the tanker suffered no injuries. Later it was learned that he was a member of the church who had dropped his son off at the Mission Training Center the day before the accident.

When interviewed by the stake mission president who was one of the rescue workers at the scene, the truck driver explained that with the collision, his door was jammed closed. Unable to get it open, he looked out the driver's side window and to his amazement saw his deceased father standing next to the damaged truck. Effortlessly, the father opened the door for his son, and then disappeared.

The next day when I was told of the accident and the results, the Spirit confirmed to me the reason the six brethren had been sent to the conference. And their assignment was not completed until they each ensured that five missionaries and Elder Carrillo were divinely protected during the accident. So, as it was unfolded to me, I knew why the truck driver's father and six angels were on the scene.

The accident pictures if viewed alone would leave one to believe that all perished. The fact that the Lord spared all involved impacted the Missionary Department to such a degree that not long after the accident, the Department sent pictures of the wreckage to missions across the world for training purposes.

Yes, angels minister to those involved in this sacred work.

Restrained by Unseen Hands

In the Spring of 2001, Cheryle and I were serving our first mission assignment to Quito, Ecuador. It was just before lunch when I finished my paperwork in the Employment Resource Center and found that I needed to walk to the Regional Offices to conduct some business.

Usually when I walked, and especially when alone, I spent the time praying. I did this during the five years I was in the mission presidency, and the practice continued.

I also did something else. Quite often I asked for the protection of the angels of heaven. I often requested that one be sent to protect me on the right hand, one on the left, one to the foreguard and one to the rear; and I testify that they are there, they are real, and they are known. So on this day as I walked down Amazonas Boulevard to the Church Office Building, I made this request and immediately knew I was not alone.

I arrived at the building, said my hellos, put my reports into the baskets and left. Since I wanted to miss the impending rain, I quickened my pace and again asked for the protection of angels. It was the height of the tourist season in Quito and the Avenida Amazonas was packed with people, cars and taxi cabs, all crammed onto the two lane one way street.

Suddenly, I heard a loud pop...pop, then another three in rapid succession. Pop...Pop...Pop.

Gunshots!

That is a sound you never forget. Then there were more in rapid succession. Automatic weapon fire! The first five shots sent people running in all directions, some diving and rolling on the ground in an effort to escape the bullets that were tearing up chunks of sidewalk concrete and shattering store windows. Others, ducking, went fleeing down side streets. In seconds, everyone deserted Avenida Amazonas except for the bandit driving the wrong way, the police who rolled, ducked and shot as they moved in my direction, and Elder Whitaker.

The scene moved in slow motion as it rolled up the street toward me like a wave coming ashore on a deserted beach. Closer and closer they came. I looked for some protection, but there was none; there was nowhere for me to run or hide. So I stepped back and placed my back against a brick pillar. Then I watched as the gun battle moved closer.

A few people near me lay on the ground covering their heads. The bandit's car slowly approached.
Thud...thud...thud. Police bullets slammed into it tearing and slicing through the metal like a hot knife through butter.

The police fired from all directions and paid little attention to the background or who might be in the line of fire. Chunks of concrete turned to dust as bullets ripped into the sidewalk in front of where I stood.

The bandit's car slowly drove by and the driver looked in my direction while police bullets continued to slam into the truck which now appeared to be driven by one who not only had been hit by the gunfire, but also appeared to be waiting for the police to close in and make the final kill. Throughout the chase, the driver never accelerated, nor did he move any faster than just above an idle.

Memories of days long past flashed through my mind. Times far distant when I was the shooter and the streets were located in South Central Los Angeles.

As the gun battle blazed in front of me, I reached under my left arm where I had for many years carried my gun in a shoulder holster. It wasn't there! I swore softly under my breath, something for which I later repented, but it seemed appropriate at the time.

Even though I thought I was out of the line of fire, I wasn't! Bullets chipped the bricks where I stood. Then it happened. Suddenly, with great force, two large unseen hands pinned me against the wall; hands that pushed with such force I was unable to resist or to move. Sharp posts of the window ledge painfully stuck into the back of my legs, but the choice was not mine. It was a position that offered safety, but one I probably would not have taken because of the posts.

The gun battle raged past, bullets flew, bodies rolled and the truck moved slowly up Amazonas tempting the police to score a final, decisive hit. As it passed, a policeman in front of me who had been firing at the truck waved down a car, commandeered it, and began a vehicular pursuit.

Once the gun battle moved past me, the unseen hands released me from the wall.

I took a long, deep breath, thanked the Lord for the protection of His holy angels, and as many of the population in Quito ran frantically after the continuing gunfire, I turned and walked in the opposite direction. I was one of only a few who walked away from the excitement.

I knew that with all the walking I did, the day would come when I might be a first hand witness to a real life Butch Cassidy and the Sundance Kid South American gunfight. But I really hadn't thought that I would be caught in the middle of the crossfire with 9 mm rounds hitting the concrete and building all around me. I honestly thought that it would occur in one of the banks which were robbed regularly.

Elder, He Has a Gun!

Tuesday, April 15, 2008. Quito, Ecuador.

It began much the same as every work day...hectic with heavy cloud cover and threatening rain.

It rained hard over the weekend and in between the rolling thunder that rocked our apartment, I counted at least fifteen lighting strikes on the surrounding mountains. It was quite a show, but far less impressive than the one I would experience in the afternoon.

We worked hard in the morning and as lunch approached, Cheryle and I decided that we would walk down Avenida Amazonas where she could go to the Banco International and turn in a bill for a man who had formerly lived in our apartment.

Because of the cold weather, I put on my black, three-quarter length leather jacket, pulled on my black leather gloves, slipped on my traditional Aviator sunglasses and out the door we went. Since I do not have a missionary tag that clips on, I never wear a tag on the outside of my leather jacket, however, I did have one attached to my suit coat.

When we reached the corner of Amazonas and Patria, we stopped to view the changes to the street in front of the Hilton Colon. Suddenly above the noise of the heavy mid-day traffic, I heard Cheryle scream, "He has a gun!" I snapped my head to the left and saw two males running past me with a third man in foot pursuit. The third man I identified as a plain clothes cop. In his right hand was a handgun. Without hesitation, I broke into a sprint. In three strides I dodged the traffic coming from my left and bounded across the middle divider and then in my best matador representation, I side-stepped an oncoming bus and two additional cars.

The cop and two suspects were now directly to my right. In full stride, I shouted, "Policia! Alto!" (Police! Stop!) To my amazement, the two bandits threw their hands in the air and stopped! However, the cop kept running. So, without slowing down, I sprinted past the two who had their hands high in the air and who were surrounded by a crowd, and I fell back into the foot pursuit directly behind the cop.

Side-by-side, we sprinted through the park dodging people and winding in and out of the trees. I glanced to my left and saw a third suspect about fifty yards away running down a concrete path with two uniform police in hot pursuit. One cop carried a hand gun while the other had an automatic rifle.

As we closed in on the fleeing bandit, he turned in our direction, extended his right arm and fired! Pop! The bullet sailed past me, striking a tree.

Realizing he was cornered, the suspect stopped running. The plain clothes cop was now only about ten feet ahead of me. In the blink of an eye, the two uniform cops grabbed the man and threw him to the ground. One reached down and recovered the suspect's weapon. Stepping to the side, the cop dropped the clip and then snapped back the slide ejecting a live round from the chamber.

Once the suspect was on the ground, I turned, and with the plain clothes cop, walked back to where additional police and an angry crowd had surrounded the first two suspects, forcing them to the ground.

I walked through the crowd and watched as a cop threw the third suspect onto the ground with his two companions. When all three were together, they were forced stomach down onto the concrete and a police officer commanded them to spread their arms and legs. Five police officers and a very hostile crowd now surrounded the prone bandits. When one of the suspects turned his head, I saw that his eyes had begun to shut from blows he had received.

Curious to see how they searched a suspect in South America, I stepped back and watched as a uniformed cop approached the first suspect from the rear, stepped between his legs that were wide spread, and gave him a brutal kick to the groin. When the suspect began to writhe in pain, the cop slammed his knee into the middle of the man's back forcing him into the concrete and preventing him from curling into a ball. As the suspect moaned and writhed in pain, the police jerked him into a sitting position and yanked his jacket down around his arms, pinning them to his body. After doing this, they again roughly threw him stomach first onto the pavement.

While this was happening, the other two suspects, which included the one who had taken a shot at us, remained obediently quiet and never moved from their spread eagle position. When the suspect being searched failed immediately to comply with each direction given by the searching officer, the police viciously punched him. This brought about immediate compliance.

As I stood silent, the policía never asked who I was, but I could sense that my presence commanded respect. All they knew was that in the middle of the foot pursuit and gunfight was a silver haired guy with dark sunglasses, a long black leather jacket and black gloves who, although they never saw me with a weapon, knew that I was there to back them up.

When everything was under control, I slipped from the group, walked back across Patria to Amazonas, and looked for Cheryle. A few minutes passed and she walked out of the bank.

"You should have seen yourself," she said laughing. "When you took off running, your leather coat was flapping behind you just like a cape. With the sunglasses and coat flapping, you looked like the Ecuadorian answer to Zorro!"

"Did you hear the shot?" I asked.

"Yes, but I knew you weren't doing the shooting since you didn't have a gun, and since I never have worried about you, I went into the bank!"

Of interest is the fact that I ran the foot pursuit with a left broken ankle. An ankle that remained broken for the final seven months of the mission and was not corrected until we returned to the United States and Dr. Rob Tait rebroke the bone and reset the fracture.

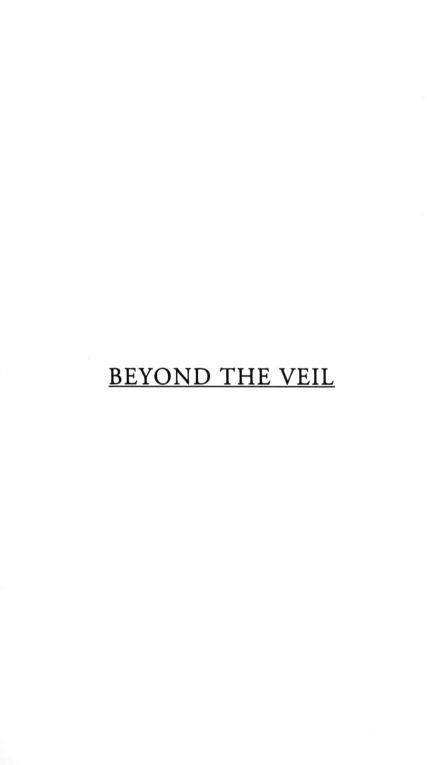

BEYOND THE VEIL

The Restoration of Sacred Blessings

In 1973, after thirty-two years of marriage, my mother and father divorced. At the time Cheryle and I lived with our family in North Hollywood, California where I served on the North Hollywood Stake High Council. We were members of the North Hollywood I Ward, and Ted Everett was the bishop.

One Sunday it came to my attention that a problem existed that would have a dramatic impact on my father's membership in the church. After prayerful consideration, the Spirit counseled me to advise Bishop Everett about what I had observed. Since he was also my father's Bishop, any recommendations for a disciplinary council would come from him. Walking into his office, I sat down and explained my concerns and what I had observed. I also recommended that the matter be presented to the stake president. Bishop Everett did this immediately.

During my life, my relationship with my father had not been good. There were a number of reasons, but as I reached adulthood and activity in the church, he felt that I was a little too rigid in my approach to the Gospel of Jesus Christ. Consequently, we didn't have much contact even though we lived in the same ward.

Although his relationship with me was strained, his relationship with my children was marvelous. He was a far better grandfather than he had been a father. The years had mellowed him.

It wasn't long before he was called into a High Council Court and excommunicated from the church. The year was 1981. With that action, he lost all the blessings associated with the priesthood which included all of his temple blessings. However, with the permission of the bishop, he was allowed to sing in the ward choir.

Then in 1984, the family held an Orson Adelbert Whitaker family reunion in Provo, Utah. Cheryle and I loaded the family into the big station wagon that Becky referred to as "the grocery getter," and off we went. Arriving in Provo, we settled in, met family members who had not been seen in years, and went to a park for the reunion.

It was fun to see the Whitaker Brothers; Dad, Bob, Berlin, Ferrin, Judge, and Jack, all with their silver hair, standing in the front of the entire family singing, joking and carrying on as though they were teenagers, reminiscent of days long past when as young boys they did the same with Grandpa O.A.

As the songs bellowed forth and the antics became more hilarious, I heard a very still small voice that said, *Richard, your father has cancer. He only has a year to live.* He had no idea what was in store, for the cancer had not as yet been diagnosed.

Upon returning home, I immediately talked to Bishop Everett and asked if he would speak to President Barton and determine if a second High Council Court could be reconvened to evaluate my father's progress and worthiness for rebaptism. By now the cancer had been detected and he was struggling.

One night, I received a telephone call. It was dad. "Richard, I have been given permission to be rebaptized. I would like you to do it. Will you?"

"Of course I will," I answered.

Dad by now was very weak and barely able to walk. The cancer was in the stomach and esophagus, and was spreading rapidly. He had about three months to live.

As a family we drove to the old Burbank Stake Center which was the same stake center where thirty-six years earlier he had baptized me. With help, he was assisted into the font where I performed the ordinance. Then after we dressed, I confirmed him a member of the Church of Jesus Christ of Latter-day Saints and he again received the Gift of the Holy Ghost.

Later, he told me that during the confirmation, a warmth covered him which he never before had felt, and during that time, the pain of the cancer disappeared.

Immediately after his baptism and confirmation, his illness permanently confined him to bed. The cancer spread quickly. On the final onslaught of the disease, he was readmitted to St. Joseph's Hospital in Burbank, California. I remember during one visit he said: "Richard, last night I had a dream. In the dream I was standing next to a person whose stature was that of a tree when compared to mine. So great in fact, that at first, because of his greatness in the church, I thought it was President Keith Barton, but as I looked up, I saw your face…it was you."

There was no doubt that not only did the dream surprise him, but the fact that it would be me standing in that position shocked him even more.

Knowing that he was going to die caused him to reflect upon who would restore his temple blessings, for he softly whispered, "I have asked Uncle Scott to have my temple blessings restored, so that is taken care of."

However, Scott could not fulfill the request because he died eleven years earlier. Standing next to the bed, I knew that the responsibility for having those sacred blessings restored would be mine.

During the years before his death, not only had he stayed close to Shannyn and Cindy, but he also grew very close to his other grandchildren and had a very special place in his heart for Becky.

After a brief stay in the hospital, my mother took him into her home where she tried to care for him, even though they had been divorced for twelve years. Soon the process of full-time care became too great, and we took him to a hospice where he died on January 1, 1985.

We held the funeral and I moved on. Before we knew it, Becky was graduating from Rosedell Elementary school. It was June, 1985.

As a family, we attended the graduation. The chairs were set up outside in an open area. Becky was going to receive a special award so we filed into a row and since I had the camera, I made it a point to sit on the end next to the aisle.

Slowly, the area filled and people sat patiently waiting for the ceremonies to begin. In the front was Mr. Clark, the principal and others sitting patiently while the last of the stragglers came in and found seats. When everyone was seated and the foot traffic had ceased, there was a lull. Suddenly, I felt someone standing in the aisle next to my right side. Looking up, I saw that it was my father. Without a hello or greeting of any kind, he stood, looked me in the eyes and in my mind I heard: *Richard, I need my temple blessings restored. I cannot go with Scott and the others and do missionary work until these blessings are restored. Please see that it is done.*

Then as quickly as he appeared, he was gone. Tears filled my eyes as I reflected upon the experience. Although it was brief, only a few words spoken and none by me, it was real.

And it testified that the blessings of the temple are eternal and critical for the work on the other side to be conducted. They are so important that dad was given permission to visit his eldest son and make a request that only could be accomplished by those in mortality, and only with the approval of a Prophet of God.

Yet, even as important and sacred as the experience was, I failed to act upon his request. Time passed; then a second time, the same appearance, the exact same words. No greeting, no small talk, only one simple request and after he delivered his message, he left.

Again, and I don't know why, I didn't act. The third time I was sitting on the floor in my office in our home on Robin Avenue in Saugus, California. I was conducting Father's Interviews with Richard and Becky. I had just completed their interviews and as we sat, talked and laughed, the room filled with a familiar spirit.

For a third time, my father appeared. Again, he spoke the exact same words and made the same request. Never did he say anything about my prior lack of response. Never was there any tone of unpleasantness in his voice, only the delivery of a message that to him was of critical importance. After he left, I looked at Richard and Becky, both still young children, and quietly said, "Angels have been in attendance this night." Both knew something was different and years later Richard told me that he remembered the experience.

It took three very sacred experiences before I finally sat down and wrote a personal letter to President Spencer W. Kimball detailing the events I have previously outlined requesting that the temple blessings for Lowell Dawn (Don) Whitaker be restored.

Time passed, and then one day a brief, but poignant letter arrived. It was from the Office of the First Presidency advising me that a member of the Quorum of the Twelve Apostles had restored all of dad's temple blessings in the Salt Lake Temple. That was in 1986 and since I completed the assignment, he has moved on, and I have not had any further communication with him.

James Clement Moran

It was a warm summer evening and I had just opened the garage door in order to go into the front yard. The Saugus, California sky was clear and the few visible stars were bright.

When I turned and walked back into the garage, I saw an elderly man, of normal stature standing at the rear of the garage just in front of the washer and dryer.

As I stopped, he spoke.

"Brother Whitaker, my name is James Clement Moran and I would like my temple work done."

Then, as quickly as he appeared, he was gone.

Since his name was unfamiliar to me, I went into the house and found Cheryle in the kitchen.

"Cheryle, who is James Clement Moran?"

She stopped what she was doing, turned and asked, "What makes you ask that?"

"Because he just appeared to me in the garage and asked for his temple work to be done."

Tears formed in her eyes. "He is my Great-Grandfather Moran."

Within a short period of time the necessary paperwork was submitted to the Las Vegas Temple and after Richard Jr. completed the baptism for his Great-Great Grandfather Moran, the other ordinances were performed.

Guardian's of the Temple Gate

I was just shy of my thirty-seventh birthday when early one morning in May, 1981 I suffered a stroke. As I lay sleeping, I suddenly was awakened by an explosion in my head that sounded as if a shotgun had been fired between my ears. I bolted upright, and when Cheryle turned on the light and looked at me, she saw my face contorted, speech slurred and my right arm wrenched into a position leaving my fist on my chest and the entire right side of my body seizing. I couldn't speak and drooled when I tried. My mind could form thoughts, but the speech would not come.

Thus began one of the most difficult periods of my life, and one of the most challenging we would face as a family. That one incident literally not only ended my law enforcement career, but also changed my life.

Following the primary stroke, smaller, mini-strokes or Cerebral Vascular Accidents (CVA's) would hit. On many occasions just before a CVA, I would feel the aura, then the right side of my body would begin to tremble and then seize. My right foot would turn in and the right arm would be pulled tightly against my chest. My speech would slur and if standing unsupported, I would fall. The CVA's were always accompanied by seizures.

Some seizures were more severe than others. I recall one where I was in the office of Marshall Handleman, the treating neurologist assigned by the city. While Cheryle and I sat in the waiting room, a CVA hit. I fell to the floor and began to seize. It required an injection of 50 milligrams of valium to stop the seizure. I don't know who was more nervous, Cheryle or Dr. Handleman.

The doctors identified migraine headaches as the root cause of the stroke. The headaches were excruciating with almost unbearable pain, and they struck almost daily, but I pushed on. I didn't take time off work, I didn't stop serving in the kingdom, and I didn't stop raising my family or working the two or three extra jobs sometimes required to make ends meet. Nor did I stop my pursuit of my education which saw me earn my Bachelor of Independent Studies from Brigham Young University and a Master of Public Administration from the University of Southern California.

On a number of occasions, I remember being assisted from Sacrament meeting in the Saugus I Ward by loving members of the High Priest group who would help me into the foyer allowing a seizure to run its course.

I suffered the migraines for seventeen years prior to the stroke and many times in agony I would go to Kaiser Permanente Hospital only to be told by my doctor that the migraines were all in my head and he could do nothing. Therefore, the pain continued.

Financially, we struggled. For a solid year we battled the City of Los Angeles for my pension. Eventually, it was Dr.

Handleman who emphatically stated that the migraines and the stroke were job related.

Eventually, I was able to secure my pension, but with a family of nine, things continued to be financially tight. Over the years, we fell deeper and deeper into debt. And although Cheryle did find work, and it helped, I think it was more to help her keep her sanity rather than for the money. In all reality, scooping ice cream at Thrifty's and working in a clothing and yardage store didn't pay much. So the debt mounted. Yet, on we battled. Then, one day, I knew that I needed to do something or we would sink below the waves.

After a long talk, Cheryle called her parents, and asked if we could borrow ten-thousand dollars. They agreed. It was now 1987. The loan helped to put things on an even keel, but I was determined to pay the money back as soon as possible.

The only thing that Cheryle and I had that afforded us any equity was our home. We knew that the house on Robin Avenue in Saugus had appreciated, but how much we didn't realize. Nor did we understand where we were to go once the house was sold and the debt paid. But, I knew that we were going to pay that debt even if it meant selling the house and moving to an apartment.

I continued to be very sick, yet I worked at Lockheed in the "Black World" of top secret security and afterward in the Motion Picture and Television Industry as a technical advisor and actor.

During this time, the headaches did not subside, and the drugs prescribed for the pain greatly hampered my mental acuity. Revelation was not as frequent as it would become in future years mainly because of the medications and constant pain.

On occasion, Cheryle and I talked about the future, both knowing that some dramatic changes were in store, but what, how and where remained a mystery. That is until one morning when she awoke, looked at me and said: "I had a dream last night and we are to move to Las Vegas."

The minute she said this, I felt it was what we should do. Under the circumstances and considering my health, I knew that what had been revealed to her was at least an option. But how were we to finance our fact finding trip to Las Vegas?

A few days passed when I received a telephone call. It was my cousin Orma Wallengren, or as she was known professionally, Claire. She wanted to know if she could buy dad's string bass which my father had left me when he died. This was his second bass. My brother Greg had the bass that was played in all the recording sessions.

"I will give you five hundred dollars for it, Richard."

That was the exact amount of money we needed for the trip to Vegas. Without hesitation, the bass was sold.

Cheryle and I made reservations in a downtown Las Vegas hotel, and after putting things in order, began the journey that would change our lives. It was a journey that eventually would see us lose a daughter to a tragic traffic accident and see four of our children find their eternal companions; a journey that would see my health miraculously restored following a priesthood blessing, and then find me serving full-time for five years in a mission presidency and developing eternal relationships with great and noble men. It was a journey that would see Cheryle and I called to serve four foreign Spanish speaking missions and one English speaking mission.

When we arrived in Vegas, we began to look around. Leaving the hotel one summer morning in July of 1987, and not having a clue where we were going, we drove out the parking lot and onto what we later learned was Bonanza Blvd. Once on Bonanza, we headed east. As we drove, we saw in the far distance a shinning roof that appeared to be copper in color; we drove closer and the Spirit grew stronger.

Crossing Nellis Blvd., we noticed that most housing and other developments literally disappeared. As we approached what we later learned was the intersection of Hollywood and Bonanza, the paved road ended. I pulled up to the intersection and stopped. The Spirit had increased greatly.

As I stopped the car, the building under construction was to my left. It was surrounded by a chain link fence with workers busily scurrying about moving dirt and climbing up and down the girders.

Suddenly, I looked in front of me and saw three large men wearing ancient armor and holding long swords in their hands. On my right stood two sentinels dressed in armament that appeared to be very old and worn. Their size was massive and countenance fearsome. They wore helmets on their heads, breastplates over their chests made of what appeared to be thick leather and protective pads on other areas of their bodies. In front of each man, being held with two hands was a long treacherous looking sword. The two sentinels stood stoically looking forward, never even acknowledging my presence.

On the left side of the roadway, standing just above the corner of the intersection in the dirt was another battle clad warrior. He was also large in stature and was dressed the same as his two companions. Unlike the other two, he turned his head and looked directly into my eyes and I felt as though he were reading my soul. At this time the Spirit so overwhelmed me that tears began to pour down my cheeks. There was no doubt in my mind that these three men were angels placed at this location to guard some sacred structure.

Cheryle, who was seated next to me watched, but later told me that she saw nothing except my reaction to something unseen. As this giant of a man and I looked at each other, time stood still. Suddenly, I realized where I was and what building was being constructed. The guardian of the gate, after searching the depths of my soul, slowly nodded approval for us to pass and then turned back facing forward. His face was deeply tanned and his eyes were dark and piercing. The face was handsome and the features appeared as though they were finely chiseled. The helmet hid his hair and it was apparent that under the leather armor, he was very muscular. There was no smile, no frown, just an expression that would have sent fear into the hearts of the wicked and would have caused them to flee and seek somewhere to hide.

He did not look in my direction again.

Barely able to see because of the tears, I drove up to the building and in front was a large granite block of stone identifying the structure as the Nevada Las Vegas Temple, The Church of Jesus Christ of Latter-Day Saints.

There was no doubt in my mind what had occurred. I was blessed to have witnessed three of the angels assigned to guard and protect that holy edifice during the building process.

After returning to Saugus, the Robin Ave home was put on the market and sold within a few days. And although many considered us crazy for our desire to move to Las Vegas, the Spirit confirmed our decision, and that was all I needed.

A Visit from Bruce Handwerker

Bruce Handwerker and I worked Operations Valley Bureau together on the Los Angeles Police Department. Bruce contracted cancer and died at the age of forty-two. I was honored to speak at his memorial service. It was interesting in that he was very Jewish and I very Mormon, however it was me who was asked to speak along with his Rabbi.

Since his passing and that of our daughter Becky, she has told me on a number of occasions that Bruce has accepted the gospel and requested that his temple work be done. However, for this to be accomplished requires the permission of his wife, Harriet.

After Becky told me of Bruce's desires, I prayed many times that the heart of Harriet Handwerker would be touched in order that permission for the work could be secured.

On one particular day, Bruce came to me and personally requested the work to be done. In the past, it was Becky who passed along the request.

Bruce thanked me for sending Becky and Doni to visit. He told me to go see Harriet when in Los Angeles, bear my testimony to her and request her permission. It was a wonderful conversation, and it is interesting that on many of these occasions when the veil is parted, I know I have been removed from this sphere and spiritually transported into a realm far more pure that allows me to understand to the fullest extent the glorious experience.

Bruce and I spoke for some time. He told me because of the nature of his life on earth and his righteous desires, he was granted permission on this occasion to visit and personally make the request for his temple work to be completed.

To date, permission has not been granted by his family, but I am confident that in the future the work will be completed.

A Family is Sealed

Allow me to share with you an experience that occurred as I filled a sealing assignment in the temple.

Once in the sealing room, the officiator asked me to offer a prayer. I did so and upon its completion, the Spirit in the room intensified.

With the abundance of the Spirit, it was difficult not to weep as the room filled with those from the other side.

The officiator asked me to be proxy for a father being sealed to his wife and son. The name of the family was Crooks. As the officiator began the ordinance, three individuals from the other side of the veil appeared just to the right and the rear of the altar. It was the father, mother and son for whom the work was being accomplished.

When they appeared, each held the hand of the other tightly. Suddenly, the officiator became emotional and stopped the ordinance. Again and again he tried to begin, but it was difficult. Finally after three attempts, he began, but not without great difficulty.

When the ordinance was completed, the young man grabbed his mother, hugged her and said, "We are a family mother, we are a family!"

Great joy shone on the faces of each family member. Then as quickly as they appeared, they departed.

At the end of the session, when the officiator and I were alone in the room, I asked him if he remembered the Crook's sealing. He said that he did. I then said, "They were here." He looked at me with tears in his eyes and said, "I know they were, for when I began the ordinance, the flood of Spirit was so overwhelming that it was difficult for me to continue, as you saw."

We shared with each other how beautiful this and other experiences are, bore our testimonies and told each other that we looked forward to meeting often in this sacred edifice.

Special Guests

A very special event happened one Saturday morning when Cheryle and I went to the temple and attended the sealing of a young couple. Before the ceremony began, the room filled and all seats immediately were taken except three located on the bride's side on the front row. Interestingly, no one ever attempted to occupy those seats even though the room was filled with many standing in all the corners.

As the ceremony began, the officiator mentioned how wonderful it was to see so many, and then referred to those allowed to attend from the other side. He said that they will be seen by some, but not by all, and after additional comments on the subject, he moved onto the next item.

As he spoke, an interesting thing occurred, for into the room entered three personages, one male and two females. They were dressed in white and walked directly over to the three unoccupied seats. I have learned that those from the other side will not occupy seats or places that are occupied by those from this side, nor will they allow themselves to be sat on or in any way interfered with. They, too, are entities and occupy space, and I beheld others from the other side standing in all areas of the room, all dressed in white. The session was beautiful and the officiator did a wonderful job.

Tuesday morning when I was walking, the bride's father pulled his car up alongside to visit. As we talked, the Spirit confirmed that I should share with him the experience in the temple. As I did, tears ran down his cheeks. He told me that all week he had prayed for permission to be granted for others to be allowed to attend from the other side of the veil. I told him that it was apparent that the Lord granted his petitions for many attended. His tears continued to flow when I described the three who occupied the empty seats. He told me who they were.

What a wonderful experience and how blessed we are as a people to have our prayers answered and to experience sacred manifestations of the Spirit.

A Special Day in the Temple

Today, May 27, not only did Cheryle and I celebrate our birthday, but we also went to the temple for the endowment of Dennis Archer and then the Archer's sealing session. It was a beautiful afternoon in that a number of things occurred. I had requested earlier that Becky, our nineteen year old daughter who had passed away before this day and was a close friend to the Archer family, be able to attend the Sealing. This she was able to do and she remained throughout the ordinance.

In the Sealing room, she first stood behind Cheryle and me, then moved to a chair in the front, and when another woman was about to sit in the chair Becky occupied, she slid over to another that was empty and stayed there until the ordinance was completed. Then, she said good-bye and left.

When the Sealing was over, I returned to the Celestial Room and sat alone in the rear. I was pleased to find that not only was Becky there to wish me a Happy Birthday, but also Grandpa Orson, (O.A.), Grandma Clara, Grandpa Don, Momo, and Doni, all who had passed to the other side of the veil. They each spoke to me and although they did not stay long, I was thrilled and overwhelmed with their expressions of love.

I imagine that some who observed me with tears rolling down my cheeks thought that I possibly had been overcome with the Endowment session, and although it was beautiful, that was not the cause for my emotion.

It was a wonderful afternoon and even though emotionally drained, I found myself very vibrant and refreshed upon leaving The House of the Lord.

My Name is Debbie

President Don Nesbitt, the Sunrise Stake Mission President, forwarded to me the following experience:

It had been our practice and policy as the Sunrise Stake Mission Presidency to have at least one of us attend every baptismal service. The Ward Mission Leader would conduct the service while the ranking member of the presidency would preside. The Bishop of the ward was invited and would be there with the other leaders of the appropriate organizations to welcome the new convert into the ward. The Bishop would speak as part of the service.

In order to maintain the intensity of the Spirit of the Holy Ghost at the services, we found that it worked out best to have the bearing of testimonies during the intermission while those directly involved in the baptism were changing their clothes. Then we would have the confirmation. This was prior to the policy where all convert confirmations take place in Sacrament Meeting.

This Saturday, three baptismal services were held. During the intermission, the Ward Mission Leader was invited to bear his testimony and then a member of the Stake Mission Presidency would bear his if no one got up right away. Our testimonies seemed always to ignite testimony bearing. In the first service, President Whitaker bore his testimony. In the second service, I bore my mine.

In the third service, a mother and her son who had been baptized in the first service were present and seated on the same

*row of seats as President Whitaker. The baptisms had occurred
and the testimony part of the service just started when I noticed
something happening with President Whitaker.*

*He stood up, walked to the front of the room by the font and
said, 'It is not my practice to bear my testimony twice on the same
day. But, a young lady, whose voice I didn't recognize, just spoke
to me and said, 'My name is Debbie and I have been given
permission to come to ask my family to do my temple work for me
as soon as possible. I was killed on Sunrise Mountain a few
months ago, and I have accepted the Gospel of Jesus Christ. I
need my temple work done as soon as possible so that I can
progress.'*

*President Whitaker finished bearing testimony of Jesus
Christ, of Joseph Smith and the Book of Mormon, and then he
sat down. The intensity of the Spirit was tremendous.*

*As he sat down, the mother with her son scooted over close to
him and said, 'I am Debbie's mother and this is her brother.
Debbie and a boyfriend were camping on Sunrise Mountain east
of Las Vegas. They were in their sleeping bags when someone
found them and they were shot and killed.*

*We noted the date. As soon as Debbie had been deceased a
year, we made sure to follow up and saw that her temple work
was done. We always have a fabulous outpouring of the Spirit at
our baptismal services, but this was the first time something like
this had happened.*

*President Don Nesbitt
Sunrise Stake Mission*

MISSIONARY
EXPERIENCES

What Do I Do If Gaylene Dies?

The 1960s were drawing to a close. The United States continued to be racked with riots and civil unrest, much of which stemmed from the war in Vietnam. These difficulties stretched major police departments around the country as never before. The Watts Riots in 1965 had set the stage.

Black militants surfaced in every city. In Los Angeles, we had the Black Panther's under Eldridge Cleaver and Huey Newton. We also had the US organization which Ron Karenga formed and ran.

In the regular street battles, sometimes we won, sometimes we lost. Unfortunately, it was usually the bad guys who had better weapons that often influenced the outcome of the battle. It was under these conditions that the Los Angeles Police Department decided to increase the number of personnel working the Metropolitan Division. This division proved to be the forerunner of the first Special Weapons And Tactics (SWAT) unit in the world.

When the requests for applications to work Metropolitan Division came out, those of us working the University Special Operations Squad (SOS) submitted our papers. Because of our reputations and work standard, we were confident that they would accept us. Many were; all except me.

Although I was looking forward to and enjoyed the combat of the street, the Lord had something else in mind.

One day as I was praying, the Spirit counseled me: *Richard, cancel your application for Metropolitan Division and submit an application to University Detectives.* I couldn't believe it. I didn't want to be a detective.

But Father, I argued, *all detectives do is sit around with their feet on the desk, drink coffee and smoke cigars. I don't want to be a detective!*

Richard, cancel your application for Metropolitan Division and submit an application to University Detectives. On three different occasions the Spirit gave me the same instruction, so that is what I did.

Two weeks after pulling my papers for Metro and submitting my papers to University Detectives, I received a telephone call telling me that I had been accepted into the detective unit.

Yet, I wasn't able to report immediately to my new assignment. The night before reporting, I broke my right thumb which placed me on the Injured on Duty roster. It would be six weeks before I was able officially to report, and upon doing so, Bob Van Drew, a very large and friendly man, met me. Bob would be my first partner as a detective. We were assigned to the Burglary Table.

Bob had a kind, gentle, heart-felt smile that warmed a room and a nature that emanated his love for most everyone with whom he came in contact, whether they were the good guys or the bad. He stood about six foot two, and weighed a healthy two hundred and thirty pounds. He reminded me more of a big hearted teddy bear, than a cop.

We immediately hit it off. Each day we would go into the field, and for lunch we would buy a sandwich and find a shady spot in Exposition Park. There, we would eat and talk.

One day as we sat in the police car having lunch, Bob became very quiet. This was out of character, for he normally loved to visit, and our conversations often would be interrupted by his contagious laugh.

"Rich," he began, "what do I do if Gaylene dies?"

I had no idea what he was talking about, even though I knew that his wife was named Gaylene.

"What do you mean?"

Bob went on to explain that his wife was in the hospital just about to give birth to their third child. With that introduction, the First Missionary Discussion began.

As we sat in the police car, the Spirit was strong. He asked questions and I answered them. However, I didn't give

Bob too much, but shared with him one principle each day. Day after day we did this.

I also had the opportunity to visit the hospital where I was introduced to Gaylene. Not too many days after our first conversation in the car, a baby girl was born to the Van Drew's, the date, April 6, 1970. They named her April.

As the daily discussions continued, the Spirit prompted me to submit a Missionary Referral Card for the Van Drew family. On the bottom of the card, I requested to be notified when contact was made and an update from the missionaries if they were teaching the family. Days turned into weeks and I heard nothing. Every day I asked Bob what was new. And every day he looked at me, smiled and said, "Nothing new. Why?"

Then a phone call.

"Brother Whitaker, this is Elder Brown. We have been teaching Bob and Gaylene Van Drew, and they have asked that you baptize them."

That was payday!

You could have knocked me over with a feather. Not once did Bob ever mention the missionaries. Not once had he even hinted that they were taking the discussions. But they were, and the Spirit touched their hearts. The Van Drew's made a baptismal commitment and set a date. Cheryle and I were thrilled.

So on that very special Saturday, as a family we traveled to Buena Park, and I was privileged to baptize Bob and Gaylene. One year later we were honored to be invited to the sealing of the Van Drew family in the Los Angeles Temple.

Time passed and Bob and I went on to different assignments and other partners. Where Bob found a home working University Homicide, I became a Detective III and an adjutant to Commander David D. Dotson, a staff officer in Operations Valley Bureau.

About six years after that day in the Los Angeles Temple, I received a telephone call advising me that Bob had been killed the night before in a traffic accident. It appeared that he fell asleep at the wheel while making the long drive home to Acton. Gaylene asked me to speak at the memorial service.

Five days after Bob's untimely death, I stood as the primary speaker at his Memorial Service. They held the service in the Granada Hills Stake Center and it was filled to capacity. Police uniforms filled both the Chapel and Cultural Hall. Most in attendance were nonmembers.

And so, as the relationship with Bob Van Drew began, so it ended, with the First Discussion.

But this time instead of a one on one taking place in the front of a police car, I preached the Plan of Salvation to over two thousand people as each paid their final respects and remembered the life of a man they came to love, one who was a special son of God.

Elders, Get in the Car, You're Teaching a First Discussion!

My first missionary experience on the Los Angeles Police Department was with Bob Van Drew. The second occurred while on assignment to Devonshire Detectives where I supervised a special unit comprised of detective's and patrol officers.

One of the patrol officers on my team was a young man named Steve Donaty. Steve was single and I could tell that he was not only searching for a wife, but also looking to answer some of life's basic questions.

Each day as Steve and I sat at the squad table prior to hitting the streets, the discussion would inevitably go to the Gospel of Jesus Christ. After a couple of weeks the Spirit prompted me to fill out a Missionary Referral Card and submit it. I did this and then I waited. Every day I asked Steve if he had any visitors or met anyone new.

"Nope," he said. "Nothing new, why?"

"Nothing, just wondering."

Day after day I asked, and day after day he gave the same response.

"Nope. Nothing new, why?"

After six weeks of this nonsense, I decided that something needed to be done.

One day Steve and I drove in an unmarked detective car down Reseda Boulevard. Although we were working undercover and were dressed in Levis and casual shirts, the car was easily identifiable as an unmarked police car and we were the first to realize that we fooled no one.

It was about two in the afternoon. I was driving and Steve was riding shotgun.

As we drove, I suddenly spotted two young men dressed in white dress shirts riding their bikes on the sidewalk. On the back of the bikes were tied their scriptures.

"Hang on Donaty," I yelled.

With that, I snapped the steering wheel to the right and quickly pulled into a driveway directly in front of the Elders. Simultaneously, each locked up the brakes on his bike and came sliding to a stop about five feet from the right side of the police car.

Throwing open the driver's door, I jumped out and ran around the front of the car.

As authoritatively as I could, I yelled, "Police Officers Elders……..Get in the car, you're teaching a First Discussion!"

Their mouths dropped open and their eyes became as large as silver dollars. In a state of shock and utter amazement, they dropped their bikes, grabbed their scriptures and jumped into the back seat of the police car. With Steve Donaty sitting in the front seat, a First Discussion began.

As we sat in the car with traffic speeding by, the Spirit began to work and Steve felt something that he had never felt before. Although the missionaries taught him the Second through the Sixth Discussion in quieter surroundings, the Spirit was never stronger than it was that day when I ordered two frightened Elders to get into the back of a police car and preach the Gospel of Jesus Christ.

Four weeks later I was privileged to baptize Steve.

Two Faithful Missionaries

While I served as the Ward Mission Leader in the Morning Sun Ward, Sunrise Stake, I had a number of wonderful opportunities to serve with and provide service to the full-time missionaries.

One morning I was at the computer writing when the telephone rang. It was Sister Kendra Hall, one of our full-time sister missionaries. She asked if I would give her and Sister Brown, a priesthood blessing. She said that the Zone Leader and District Leader were unavailable, so I said, "Sure, when?"

"Right now Brother Whitaker, if that's all right?"

I agreed and within ten minutes I shaved, dressed in a white shirt, a suit and tie and was prepared to act for the Lord as His mouth-piece when the Sisters arrived.

Before I gave the blessings, we talked and they shared some concerns. The Spirit prompted me to request that they each act as scribe for the other's blessing and take notes that could be used for future reference.

Under the direction of the Spirit, I gave the blessings and afterward I took the time to talk to them about the decisions of the past evening when an unmarried couple who were living together complained about the requirement to keep the Law of Chastity. They told me that they had been frightened of the man and had not stood firm in declaring what the Lord would have the couple hear. They said that they were up into the early hours of the morning praying and discussing the matter. It was then that they decided to ask for a priesthood blessing.

After the blessings, I told them how important it was for them to review with each other the content of each blessing, the words used, promises made, and then write their thoughts and feelings in their respective journals.

We shed tears as these two wonderful representatives of the Savior sat in our living room. The Spirit was strong, and prompted me to give some additional words of loving reassurance to them, and when I finished, Sister Hall stood, and told me that she had been on the verge of calling her father at home to ask his advice on the matter. He had been a bishop and former stake president and she respected his advice. However, she was prompted to call me instead.

She told me that when I was speaking to them, she heard inaudible words, spirit to spirit, and she saw her father in front of her, speaking. As I spoke, she heard his voice and his words. As tears ran down her cheeks, she could barely speak.

I explained the workings of the Spirit and stressed that the counsel of the Lord through worthy priesthood holders will always be the same. I explained that we often do not take advantage of the opportunities to receive priesthood blessings when they are needed. Pride, ego, many things get in the way of our humbling ourselves in order to receive the blessings of this great gift.

The Sisters went back to the couple and although they found only the woman at home, they counseled her regarding the Law of Chastity. The woman danced with the issues and said that they would live together without violating any laws of God, but after baptism if they were in the same house, then it was their problem not the Sisters.

Wrong answer.

The Sisters thanked the woman and left. They did not receive a call back for another discussion.

A Man Can't Think
When He's Smiling!

Bob McKee was a new mission president, and I mean new. Maybe two weeks on the job. Neither of us knew each other, and I know that he wondered who this counselor was that he got stuck with and how long would it take to replace President Whitaker.

Normally, a counselor did not speak at mission conferences. It was President McKee's philosophy that he who has the keys to speak, should speak. And not only was he right, but the Spirit bore witness to me on many occasions that this was the way the Savior wanted the work organized. However, on this occasion, President McKee wanted to hear from his new first counselor who was an unknown as far as he was concerned.

When invited, I got up and began to speak. Now you must remember that this was in front of the entire mission. As I spoke, I never looked behind at President McKee, but he was, as was his trademark, smiling ear to ear at his missionaries. I was the opposite, rarely smiling especially with the missionaries. So, with this in mind, I went on to say that:

"I believe in the philosophy of Tom Laundry, former head coach of the Dallas Cowboys. A newspaper reporter once asked Landry why he walked the sidelines with such a serious look on his face and never smiled. Turning to the reporter, Landry calmly said, 'A man can't think when he's smiling.' "

With that, there was a great burst of laughter from all the missionaries. I then realized that I was in trouble.

Slowly, I turned around and looked at President McKee. He met my gaze and still sat with a huge grin on his face. Instantly, I realized that I had opened mouth and inserted foot. Quickly, I tried to dance my way out of that one, but the horse was out of the barn. Cheryle, who was also seated on the stand, could only smile at me and shake her head.

Regarding my comment, President McKee never said a word. He didn't need to. His silently sitting behind me continuing to smile painted a picture worth a thousand words. I repented and tried my best to smile. Not easy for a street cop trained in South Central Los Angeles.

A Daughter's Influence

A child can greatly influence a parent, and when this is done for righteous purposes, it testifies to the power of this wonderful work and the fact that Father knows all of His children.

I was conducting a number of Mission President's Interviews in the mission office. As I walked out to meet the investigator, the Elders introduced me to a black woman in her early forties and her daughter who was seventeen. As was customary, I conducted the interview with the mother, and at the conclusion asked her how she heard about the church.

She told me that her seventeen year old daughter joined the church eighteen months ago while living in Kentucky. At that time her daughter tried to have her mother meet with the missionaries in Las Vegas, but the mother had no interest. Over and over the daughter tried to get her to contact the missionaries, but she refused. Slowly, her life slid downhill.

On a regular basis she communicated her problems to her daughter until finally the daughter told her she was flying to Las Vegas and wasn't going to leave until her mother joined the church. And that is exactly what she did.

The daughter got on a plane, flew to Las Vegas, located the missionaries and told her mother that she wasn't leaving until she listened to the missionaries.

The mother then realized that if it was that important to her daughter, there must be something to it. Somewhat reluctantly, she met with the missionaries and began to read the Book of Mormon.

"As I read, the Spirit touched my heart," she said. "And I knew it was true."

I can recall the powerful testimony she bore in that interview. It was a testimony firm in the knowledge that the Book of Mormon was the word of God and was true. It was a testimony born out of the ashes of a very dysfunctional life. And it all occurred because a loving daughter would not take no for an answer. Therefore, a mother was provided the opportunity to repent, change her life and enter the waters of baptism. Nothing can match the power of love and example.

Go into the Closet and Pray

During a President's Exception Interview, I asked a young Hispanic man how he heard of the church. He shared with me that he had married a member, but he had never been interested in religion. Over and over his wife asked him to go to church, but he refused. Her family even invited him on a number of occasions, but to no avail.

He said, "Years passed and then for some reason I decided to read the Book of Mormon. I did so and got to the section where it said to pray in secret. I didn't know what it meant, so I asked my wife."

"Go into the closet and pray," she told him. "It's that simple."

"So that's what I did. I went into our closet and asked the Lord if Joseph Smith was a Prophet of God. I will never forget the wonderful feeling that came over me and the feeling of happiness I felt. I knew I had my answer so here I am."

Liahona Left in a Casino Break Room

Let me share with you a story that one of my Ward Mission Leaders told me during a Personal Priesthood Interview. As I was discussing the activities of each stake missionary under his direction, he said "President, I need to tell you a story about Brother Espinoza." He then related the following:

Brother Espinoza, a faithful member of the church, worked in a casino as a dealer. In the past, dealers could not hold temple recommends, but that has changed, and he is a recommend holder and very faithful, so faithful in fact that he takes the Liahona magazine with him to work and reads it as he sits in the break room.

One day after reading an article, he placed the magazine down and returned to the floor. However, when he returned to the room for his next break, the magazine was gone. Rather angry, he accused the other dealers of taking his magazine. They knew how important it was to him, and he told them that he wanted it returned.

Everyone he confronted denied any knowledge of the missing magazine. One day passed, then two and then it stretched into weeks. Finally, a slight Hispanic woman who worked in the housekeeping section entered and sheepishly handed the magazine back to Brother Espinoza. She apologized for taking the magazine, but told him that she had seen him read it every time she was in the room and was curious about the contents. She said that she read the magazine from cover to cover and was very impressed by the writings from a Prophet, President Hunter. At this time she told Brother Espinoza that she would like to learn more about the church. Brother Espinoza offered to have the missionaries visit her. She accepted the invitation and was soon baptized. But the story does not end here.

After her baptism, she requested that other family members listen to the missionaries. To date, nine other family members have been baptized, all because one stake missionary was not ashamed to read a Church magazine in a place that some would have thought not to be conducive to the Spirit.

The Lord works in marvelous ways His wonders to perform. Our actions and example speak louder than our words, which is exemplified by this wonderful story of conversion.

Mission Extended

I cannot remember the birth of the Savior without remembering the last, great sacrifice He made. The Atonement: An ultimate sacrifice that could only be made by the Son of God: a sacrifice that is eternal.

Not many of us who serve in the kingdom of God will ever be called upon to provide the ultimate sacrifice of life, but then, some have.

I was serving with President McKee when I received the assignment to travel to Ely, Nevada and attend their stake conference. The experience of speaking at conferences was not new to me. I had the opportunity, under the direction of Ross McEachran, to travel quite often and speak, and this type of assignment continued under President McKee.

My assignments on this weekend required that I travel to Ely on Saturday, speak Saturday night in a special missionary meeting and then provide stake missionary training Sunday morning. Following the training, I was to speak in the general session of Stake Conference.

The drive to Ely took about four hours, depending on how often one was stopped for road construction, or by the police. Both of which occurred a number of times during the five years I made the trip.

The day was clear and beautiful and I made good time traveling toward Lund, Nevada, which was about thirty minutes outside of Ely.

As I drove over the last incline before entering Lund, I glanced to the right and observed a sign which read "Cemetery" and had an arrow pointing to the left. After looking at the sign, the Spirit prompted me to turn in and visit the location. I glanced at my watch and saw that I had plenty of time before I was to be in Ely, so upon coming to the turnoff, I made a left turn and traveled toward the cemetery. As I drove down the gravel road, I looked to the right where I could see the small, very old cemetery surrounded by a white fence.

Slowly, I pulled into the gravel parking area and parked. I entered the cemetery through a small, white turnstile. I could see that the sacred area had been in use for many, many years. Walking to my left, I stopped to read one marker, then another and soon found that I had made a complete circle and again was nearing the white turnstile. A spirit of calm overshadowed the sacred ground and I knew that I was not alone.

I started for the turnstile but suddenly stopped. For some unknown reason I felt prompted to turn around and walk to a specific row of markers that I had passed without reading their inscriptions.

Acknowledging the prompting, I turned back into the cemetery and stepped in front of one marker. As I stood looking down at the inscription, the flood of Spirit that surrounded me was overwhelming. Looking down, I noticed that engraved on the left side of this marker was the Los Angeles Temple.

Odd, I thought, *that the Los Angeles Temple would be on a grave marker in Lund, Nevada.*

I then looked at the name. It was a male. The Date of Birth: 1948 and the Date of Death, 1968. Then I saw the engraving just below the death date. It contained only two words; words that brought forth a flood of emotion.

"Mission Extended."

As I stood with tears running down my cheeks, the Spirit bore testimony to me that I was standing on sacred ground; ground consecrated as the final resting place for the mortal remains of one who had been and continued to be noble and valiant. And one who had been called home while on his earthly mission to continue the efforts on the other side.

The next day as I stood before the stake missionaries and shared this wonderful experience, I noticed one of the older brethren on the front row with tears in his eyes. As I finished, he softly said, "President, you are exactly right. He died on his mission to Los Angeles. That young man was my cousin."

Paul Rhuebottom

It was President McKee's first meeting with the stake priesthood leaders. The chapel was full and during his comments he stressed that as priesthood leaders they had the responsibility to open their mouths and talk to everyone. Then he opened the scriptures and quoted Doctrine and Covenants 29: 6-7, emphasizing, "...for mine elect hear my voice and harden not their hearts."

In the congregation that morning was President Trey Rogers, the Stake Mission President in the Nevada Las Vegas East Stake.

The meeting concluded and President Rogers and his two counselors started home. As they passed a bus bench on that early Sunday morning, they saw standing at the bench a very well dressed black gentleman with scriptures in hand. Trey drove past when one of his counselors said, "President, the Spirit is prompting me to tell you that we should go back and talk to that man."

Without hesitation, President Rogers turned the car around and stopped in front of the man.

"Can we help you?" he asked.

"I'm looking for a church," was Paul Rhuebottom's response. "I'm new to Las Vegas and a friend of mine told me about a church somewhere downtown."

"Get in," responded Trey, "and we'll take you there."

With those few words a wonderful relationship between Paul Rhuebottom and these brethren began. While in the car driving to the non LDS church located in downtown Las Vegas, the brethren invited Paul to attend church with them the next week.

"I'd love to," he responded.

And he did. At the invitation of President Rogers, Paul began the missionary discussions. Within a short period of time, I received a telephone call asking me to conduct a President's Exception Interview. We set a date and time.

At the time designated for the interview, I stepped into the hallway of the Sunrise Stake Center, and standing before me was Paul Rhuebottom. I observed that he was a black gentleman about sixty years of age. He was dressed very well and as he approached with hand extended, the Spirit confirmed to me the elect status of this wonderful gentleman.

The interview was not long, and in that interview the problems and baggage of the past were handled. As I sat with this wonderful man, the Spirit confirmed that he had been approved for baptism as far as my interview was concerned. His next interview would be with the District Leader. That interview also went well. They held the baptism, and after that, I lost track of Paul.

Occasionally, I saw President Rogers at the Las Vegas Temple. Whenever possible he updated me on Brother Rhuebottom's progress. Not only had Paul accepted a calling in his ward, but he had attended the temple and received his own endowments.

The last thing I heard prior to our first mission was that Brother Paul Rhuebottom, not only was strong in the church, but also was serving as an Assistant in the High Priests group. All of this came about because one very new mission president challenged the stake mission leaders to open their mouths and seek out the elect.

The Living Christmas Card

In the summer of 1998, I was asked by President McKee to develop a program that became the "Living Christmas Card." He outlined the basics and it was my responsibility to organize and see it implemented.

Preparation for the Living Christmas Card began in early November with the final touches put on it just in time for the Thanksgiving Holidays. We asked wards to become involved, and members to submit the names of nonmember neighbors and less active members to whom the missionaries could go. Many members caught the vision and participated; others, including some priesthood and auxiliary leaders, balked, offering one excuse or another.

As time passed and ward support waned, some of the missionaries had to use their own initiative and resources to guarantee success.

Just before Christmas, President McKee held a Christmas Conference. He taught that weekends and holidays were the ideal times for proselytizing because families were usually home and receptive to the Spirit, especially on Christmas.

"For during Christmas the Spirit of the Lord floods the earth," he said, "and hearts are softened and lives changed through the message of the Savior."

The Christmas Conference held just a few days before Christmas found Elder Skinner ill with the flu, and although miserable, he toughed it out, attended the conference, did his best to stay away from all others, and when the conference concluded, he asked for a priesthood blessing. Following the blessing, he and his companion went to work.

Repeatedly, people slammed doors in their faces and made rude comments. Over and over they knocked, they sang and they experienced rejection. To them it seemed that they never would realize the success promised them by their mission president.

Finally, they had a break in the onslaught of the adversary. Still not feeling well, the companionship pushed on and found another door. Knocking, they began to sing. Very slowly the door cracked open; first an inch, then two. They continued to sing and it opened further. When the door fully opened, a man stood before them. His face carried the heartache of loss and his eyes were stained with tears. Stifling the sobs he said, "You are my angels, come in."

Representing the Lord Jesus Christ, two ambassadors of the Savior, one fighting off illness and the other fear, stepped into the man's home.

"Oh, you don't know what this means to me," he said. "My wife died yesterday and I didn't know what to do. I was lost until you knocked on my door. You are angels sent from God."

So, under the continued direction of the Spirit, they presented the *Luke II: The Account of Jesus' Birth* video, shared scriptures and sang additional songs of Christmas. They learned that the grief-stricken man was taking his deceased wife's body back to Guatemala for burial, and then he planned to return to the United States.

Two valiant Elders shared their testimonies and then set an appointment to return and begin the Six Missionary Discussions.

During the entire experience of knocking on this special door, singing, sharing the story of the Savior's birth and then their testimonies, Elder Skinner felt no effects from the illness that had so severely hampered his health just hours before. But, upon leaving the man's home, the illness immediately returned and Elder Skinner was bedridden.

A Witness of the
Living Christmas Card

Bishop Don Nesbitt shared the following story with me:

Saturday evening, just prior to Fast Sunday in December 1998, the Spirit woke me in the night with the information that my Ward Mission Leader was ill and would not be able to coordinate the Living Christmas Card program. He instructed me as to the importance and urgency of the program and that I should call Richard Jameson as an assistant to the Ward Mission Leader to coordinate it. I don't recall exactly how the message came through the Spirit, but it was very clear at the time and still clear on Sunday morning.

At meeting time, Brother McKendry, the Ward Mission Leader was not there. He had been working six, ten-hour days a week for a couple months. As testimony meeting proceeded, the Spirit reminded me of my instructions. I have learned never to postpone a prompting of the Spirit. When the meeting ended, I invited Brother Jameson to my office. His radiance was very strong.

I explained to him that the Lord needed his help. I shared with him that since the Ward Mission Leader was ill, the Spirit instructed me to call him to assist in coordinating the Living Christmas Card program where we could help the missionaries sing and share the Christmas message with our friends. This assignment could be done on Sundays, since he had such a heavy work schedule during the week.

I explained how important the calling was and asked if he would accept this assignment for the month of December. It was explained that he would need to coordinate with the Ward Mission Leader and also report back to me. The Spirit bore witness. He accepted.

To begin with, we needed to make a list of ward member's names who we could enlist in the program. We were hurrying because it was almost time for Priesthood and Relief Society meetings to start. We couldn't find any paper with lines, so we went back into my office and began drawing lines on the blank paper that we had. As he was drawing lines, I was distracted and turned to look toward the picture of the Las Vegas Temple. It was then that I noticed the two individuals dressed in shining white robes seated on the two chairs just below the temple picture. The intensity of the Spirit increased.

While I watched my visitors, one of the brethren addressed me by name and began to explain that they had been sent to prepare four families from my ward to hear the Gospel of Jesus Christ and the Living Christmas Card was critical in that preparation.

I explained to Brother Jameson that we no longer were alone, that two individuals from the Spirit world had joined us. I related the urgency of work and that families were waiting to have their temple work done. I relayed other impressions that I just had received. Tears streamed down our faces.

By the time the tears dried, we were alone again. Brother Jameson went forward in this new calling, getting names and addresses and helping the missionaries. His testimony had grown. He was excited and shared our experience with the organizations as he asked for additional names of families to be visited. Many participated.

Further information was revealed as I pondered on this experience the following day. At noon, I shared with my LDS co-worker, James Cheney of Logandale, what had happened. He responded that they were there to coordinate the effort. The Spirit again confirmed to me that the two individuals who had come to my office were in charge of coordinating the preparation of the families that the missionaries would visit. The Spirit then impressed upon my mind how important it was that we held missionary correlation meetings, Bishopric meetings and presidency meetings. We are not alone in this work of saving and recovering souls. This is the kingdom of God and Jesus Christ is in charge. Those on the other side of the veil are anxiously engaged as well, and wanting temple work done. They will assist us, but we need to exercise the faith to be obedient. They will be in our meetings with us. The program was successful. Four families expressed interest in learning about the gospel.

My testimony of the ministry of angels continues to grow. As my love for the Savior grows in leaps and bounds.

Don O. Nesbitt, Bishop, Viewpoint Ward,
Las Vegas Nevada Sunrise Stake

The Scott Wiltrout Story

I never will forget the experience I had in interviewing Scott Wiltrout and the support he received from Bishop Huntsman of the Nevada Las Vegas North Stake.

When Scott entered his interview, I noted that he was in his mid-thirties, poorly dressed and looked homeless. As the interview progressed, Scott revealed that he lived in an old run down trailer with another man about his same age.

Work for both was sporadic and the basics of life hard to secure. As the interview concluded and the problems for which he sat in front of me resolved, I realized that although Scott could have been approved for baptism, it was not what the Lord desired at that time.

Under the direction of the Spirit, I advised him that he should go back and not just casually meet the Bishop of his ward, but sit down with him, secure counsel about the direction his life should take, and then come back in three weeks for a follow-up interview. I also advised him that he was to attend Sacrament meeting and with the approval of his Bishop, also attend Priesthood meeting. The interview ended and I moved on to the next one.

About three weeks passed and I received a telephone call from the Elders who told me that Scott had done as requested and now wanted his follow-up interview. We scheduled the date and time, and when he walked in, I immediately saw that he looked very different. His eyes were clear and his countenance bright. It was a look that definitely was missing during the first interview. The follow-up interview went well and I sent him to the District Leader for his final interview. Scott left the room beaming.

Another three weeks passed, and while I was at a stake meeting, I was prompted to ask Danny Smith, the North Stake Mission President, about the baptism of Scott Wiltrout. With tears in his eyes, President Smith looked at me and said, "Oh President, you wouldn't believe it."

With that, he went on to relate the following story.

Scott went into the Bishop as you instructed. I don't know what they talked about, but the meeting went well. Not only was he baptized, but the Elders also taught and baptized his roommate the same day.

Although both attended their meetings, their clothes were not appropriate for Sunday, so one day Bishop Huntsman drove Scott and his roommate to Deseret Industries and bought each a complete set of Sunday clothes. This was done in preparation for the next week when they would receive the Aaronic Priesthood and be ordained to the office of a Priest.

The next Sunday both men arrived at church looking like priesthood holders. Bishop Huntsman had interviewed both of them, and Scott was ordained first. Then the Bishop asked Scott to stand in the circle for his friend's ordination. With apprehension on his face, he stepped up and joined the circle. Following the ordination, the Bishop called his young twelve year old Deacons Quorum president over.

'President,' he said, 'I want you to take and teach these two men what they need to know to pass the Sacrament today.'

'Yes, sir,' said the young Deacons Quorum president. And off the three went into a corner of the Cultural Hall.

When the time came for the passing of the Sacrament, on the front row sat Scott and his roommate. I never will forget the smile on Scott's face as he nervously approached me and extended the plate. Although he was shaking like a leaf, his obvious fear was overshadowed by the big smile that was on his face.

What a difference a caring Bishop made in the life of two men. He was a Bishop who didn't kick against the pricks and argue that he was just getting two problems in his ward because missionaries were baptizing the poor and needy. Quite the contrary, this Bishop saw an opportunity not only to magnify his calling, but he also saw that through these two men, others in his ward would be blessed, and they were, one of them being a twelve year old deacons quorum president.

Later, prior to my release from the mission presidency, Bishop Huntsman was released and called to replace Danny Smith as the North Stake Mission President. Eventually, he was called into the Nevada Las Vegas Mission presidency.

The Worth of a Soul

One day as I sat in the office in Quito, Ecuador, the topic of discussion turned to missionary work and specifically to the missionaries in Quito.

Danny Miño, a returned missionary, mentioned that every time he saw a missionary on the streets of Quito they were looking down, not smiling and never, absolutely never, did they speak to anyone. "It's as if they don't want to baptize," he said. The other brethren in the office agreed with Danny.

Danny and Carlos then mentioned that when they served in the Guayaquil South Mission, missionaries were taught to smile and talk to everyone. However, they were told that they were not to baptize children, only families or adults. I couldn't sit there and remain silent. "The worth of souls is great in the sight of God, and a nine year old," I said, "is as valuable to our Father in Heaven as a fifty year old."

"But they go inactive," was the reply, "and they become ladrones, or robbers and thieves," commented Danny.

As the conversation continued, my mind drifted not only to the nine year olds we had baptized in the Nevada Las Vegas Mission, but also the "ladrones" and even murderers who, when given the time and opportunity, repented sufficiently to permit their entrance into the waters of baptism and the kingdom of God.

On the topic of baptizing nine year olds, I specifically remember three stories that emphasize the fact that "the worth of souls," all souls, "is great."

One of our finest missionaries in the Nevada Las Vegas Mission was a young man named Elder Christopherson. Although, in his words, he was only a mediocre student in high school, when President McKee provided him the opportunities to grow and develop his teaching and leadership skills, this Elder stepped to the plate and hit home runs.

He served in some fairly tough areas, and when other missionaries complained about the difficulty of the area, and that the area was all tracted out with no one left to teach, Elder Christopherson rolled up his sleeves, went to work and out baptized everyone else in the mission.

Because of his wonderful personality and dedication, he also touched the hearts of many, including one small girl who, on December 8, 1998, wrote the following letter which was presented by President Robert H. McKee in a mission conference.

Dear Elder Christopherson,

I'm so grateful for all that you have done for me! You've changed my life so much you'll never know. Thanks to you, I have been walking in the light of Christ. You are sort of my savior in a way! You mean so much to me and I'm so grateful for being able to know such a wonderful person like you. You've helped me get baptized, helped me find the straight and narrow path and find a good family and most of all helped me find out who I really am and find true happiness!

When you go back up to heaven, Heavenly Father is going to be so proud of you! I tell you all this by the Spirit. I love you so much.

Your friend always,
Rachel

Rachel was an eleven year old little girl who Elder Christopherson baptized when she was nine years old.

Continuing on this subject, this wise mission president continued:

Brother (Charles A.) Callis was converted over in Wales and was baptized as a small boy into the Church. As he was visiting a stake of Zion, he learned that an old man whom he had known in the mission field was ill. Brother Callis called on him. He found him cynical. Brother Callis tried to encourage him. The man seemed to be beyond encouragement. Then Brother Callis said, 'John, do you not remember your missionary labors in Wales? Do you not remember the good you did in the mission field?

'Oh, I didn't do any good,' he said.

'Didn't you ever baptize anyone?'

'No, not that I remember.'

Brother Callis then said, 'Are you sure?'

'Oh,' he said, 'I baptized a little urchin that used to bother us in our meetings.'

Then Brother Callis said,' Brother John, do you not know that I was that little urchin?'

Think of the importance of that one baptism! Think of the great work of Brother Callis during his thirty years of service in the Southern States Mission and then his great work as one of the Apostles of the Lord Jesus Christ. (Conference Report, April 1955, p.74.)

Yes, the worth of a single soul is great to the Lord. Why would any missionary or leader in the Church of Jesus Christ of Latter-day Saints ever want to prohibit a son or daughter of God from this or any ordinance?

Yet, there are those who understand, and who have done their part. President McKee brought home that message during a mission conference held in Kingman, Arizona when he talked to his missionaries about the importance of baptizing all of God's children, regardless of age. As I sat in the rear of the Relief Society Room, I heard some muffled sobbing coming from the front row where the Sister missionaries sat. Suddenly, a Sister missionary shyly raised her hand and asked if she could say something.

"Of course," President McKee responded.

With tears in her eyes, a valiant daughter of God stood and addressed her peers and related the following story.

My mother was raised in an area of northern Canada that rarely saw strangers. She was part of a large LDS family, but her father was an alcoholic and was very abusive. Because of this, the entire family was inactive.

One day, two Mormon missionaries came through the town and learned that there was a nine year old girl that had not been baptized. They went to my mother's home and she was that young girl. In one Saturday, they taught her, baptized her and then confirmed her.

Sunday they were gone, and after their leaving, my mother didn't go back to church. Time passed and life at home became unbearable.

At the age of twenty-one, she found herself in a large Canadian city, unmarried, pregnant, and deserted by her boyfriend. Discouraged and all alone, she remembered the feeling she had at the time of her baptism, a feeling she had never forgotten, but had not experienced again. Picking up a phonebook, she found the listing for the Mormon Church and called the first Bishop on the list.

As I sat and listened, sniffling could now be heard coming from the side of the room where the Elders sat. The Sister missionary continued.

A loving Bishop helped my mother. She put her life in order. She married my father and they have sent all of their children on missions. My father is a leader in the church in Canada and works for the Church Educational System. And I am now serving. All because two missionaries baptized a small, unknown, nine year old girl in a distant place many years ago.

The silence in the room was deafening, only occasionally broken by a sniffle that came not only from the Sister missionaries, but also Elders whose hearts had been touched.

Yes, the worth of a soul is great.

Their Countenance's Were Bright

I was conducting President's Exception Interviews in the Sunrise Stake, Hollywood and Stewart Building. I had a little over a year under my belt as a counselor and President McKee recently had replaced Ross McEachran as mission president.

One night Elders Cheney and Tidwell called and asked for an interview for a seventy-six year old female. We set the appointment and right on schedule, the Elders and their investigator arrived.

As I sat in President Wayne Anderson's office, I heard a timid knock on the door. When I opened the door, a trembling and frail woman supported by a cane stood before me. I invited her to have a seat. In a thick Scottish brogue, she thanked me.

She shared with me that during World War II, her husband was killed in combat leaving her with seven young children. During that time she committed a sin which had haunted her for many years.

This transgression fifty-six years earlier weighed heavily upon this dear woman all her adult life. Then, through the power of the Atonement, and after the process of repentance, this daughter of God received the knowledge that the Savior accepted her repentance and it now was over.

As I explained the ordinances of baptism and confirmation, tears flowed heavily down her cheeks. Minutes passed and once she had composed herself, I asked her how she learned about the church.

"Oh, President, I've known about the church for many years. The Elders have knocked on my door for the past forty years when I lived in San Diego, but I wouldn't ever let them in."

"Then what was different this time?"

With that question her sobs increased.

"Well, this time when I answered the door, these two Elders, Cheney and Tidwell, they just shone with bright countenances. They were smiling at me and it looked as though two angels were standing in front of me. I couldn't say no. I only could invite them in."

I concluded the interview, and another life was dramatically changed because two wonderful, young representatives of the Lord Jesus Christ radiated the light of Christ. And they smiled!

Twenty-Six Years Later

It was the night of December 20, 1997 and I had been serving in the Nevada Las Vegas Mission presidency for about two and one half years. On this night, I was using the office of President Wayne Anderson of the Sunrise Stake for the four President's Exception Interviews scheduled that evening.

The first interview, a single male, lasted about ninety minutes, and when it ended, another set of Elders brought in a couple. I spoke first with the wife and following her long and emotional interview, I interviewed the husband. Then I sat with them both. You need to understand how personal and confidential these interviews are. What the wife revealed was not discussed with the husband, nor was his interview discussed with his wife.

Then, they both sat in front of me. That was my opportunity to share in great detail The Atonement and the last week of the Savior's life. This included His entrance into Jerusalem up to and including The Resurrection. It was this descriptive dialogue that not only took the greatest amount of time, but also testified to the investigator in power and authority what was experienced by a God, individually for them. It was during that period of time, as I taught The Atonement, that if the investigator had a broken heart and contrite spirit, it was manifested. It also was during this time and immediately after that the great closure experience in their life occurred, for it was at this time and under the direction of the Spirit, they received the knowledge that the Savior accepted their repentance and it now was over.

When these two interviews ended, even though I had been interviewing for nearly four hours, there was one more interview yet to be conducted.

The interesting thing that I learned early in the interview process was that the Spirit renewed my body, and during the interviews I never was tired, however, when the interviews were over, exhaustion set in.

As I sat in the stake president's chair, I prayed for the physical, emotional and spiritual strength to continue. My petition was granted.

Then there was a knock on the door. I opened it and standing in front of me, visibly frightened, was a woman about forty years of age. I invited her in and asked her to have a seat. Very timidly, she sat down in the chair located directly across the desk.

The interview began and she shared with me her past. As we talked, the Spirit testified that she had a broken heart and a contrite spirit, and then suddenly, as happened on many occasions, the voice of the Lord came to my mind and I heard, *Richard, she is fine.* Considering the fact that I conducted many difficult interviews in that room, that confirmation always was a blessing. The Lord made the final decision. I only was His voice.

At the end of the interview, I asked the same question of her that I asked many investigators; "How did you hear about the church?"

This sweet woman, who had been crying softly throughout the interview, now broke down and began to sob. She then related the following story.

It was twenty-six years ago and I was a young girl of fourteen. I made a bad decision and became pregnant. I then had to make another decision; to have the baby or get an abortion. I decided to have the baby and give him up for adoption. When the baby was born, I immediately signed all papers and never saw him again.

Many years passed and about nine months ago, for some unknown reason, I felt prompted to complete the medical paperwork on myself and the biological father just in case anyone ever wanted it for that baby. I sent the papers to Carson City, and forgot about it.

About two months ago, I was at home and there was a knock on the door. I opened it, and there standing in front of me was the most handsome, clean-cut twenty-six year old young man I had ever seen. He introduced himself as my son and asked if he could come in. I couldn't believe it and was in a state of shock. I invited him in, and as we sat and talked, he thanked me for having the courage to give birth and place him up for adoption. By this time we were both in tears, but he continued.

'I was adopted by a wonderful family. They were members of the Church of Jesus Christ of Latter-day Saints. I was raised in the state of Washington, attended Primary and I was baptized at the age of eight. I earned my Eagle Scout, served an honorable mission for the Church and returned home to find my eternal companion and we were married in the temple. We have just had our first child, your grandson, and I will be blessing him soon. I am here to invite you and your family to that blessing.'

I was shocked. Yet I knew that I wanted to go to Washington for that blessing. So, that is what I did. I took my thirteen year old daughter and we traveled to Washington. The blessing was to take place the Sunday following our arrival. They told me that prior to attending church, the family was going to meet at the home of the adoptive parents and my daughter and I were invited.

On that special day, we gathered in the living room and this wonderful young man said to his father, 'Dad, this is the first time we have had all the family together. With your permission, could we kneel for family prayer and could I offer it?'

This wonderful woman then told me that she had never heard anyone pray like that, and she felt something in that home she never before had felt. She continued.

When it was over, the family went to the Sacrament meeting. I have never been in a meeting like that in my life. For the second time that day, I again felt what I felt in the home earlier that morning.

Following the blessing of the baby, we returned to Las Vegas. About two weeks passed and the UPS man knocked on the door and delivered a package. When I opened the package, I found a pictorial history of my son. In photographs were his early years as a baby and young child, his baptism, Eagle Court of Honor, his mission, marriage and even photographs of our visit which included pictures of me, my son and my grandson.

Another couple of days passed and my son called.

"With your permission I would like to send two young men, friends of mine, to your home to teach you more about the Gospel of Jesus Christ. Would that be all right with you?" To which I responded, "If they are anything like you, I would love to talk to them."

Within a few weeks, two representatives of the Lord Jesus Christ made that visit.

And now, in front of me sat the woman they had taught. With eyes red from tears she looked at me and said, "President, if I pass this interview, I am going to make a phone call and invite my son and his family to Las Vegas for my baptism and that of my daughter."

Well, I had long before known that she had passed and so it wasn't too many days later that this wonderful daughter of God made a phone call to a son, and shortly thereafter, both mother and daughter entered the waters of baptism.

The Lord blessed me to play a small part in that miracle and I knew that it was a very small part. I also knew that during that interview, the Spirit was so strong that we both were in tears, and I knew that we had not been alone in that sacred room.

Following her departure, I looked at my watch. For over five and one half hours, I had been interviewing, and now I was exhausted.

During my five years in the presidency and while I conducted over twenty-three hundred special President's Exception Interviews, I truly had learned what the Savior meant when he acknowledged that when a woman touched the hem of his robe, he felt virtue or power leave. That is what happens when the priesthood is righteously exercised. Power goes out.

A long, but wonderful night was over, or so I thought. Slowly, I walked over to the light in the office, turned it off and then as was my habit, walked back to the chair behind the desk and knelt down. I shed tears during that prayer as I thanked the Lord for the privilege of being a representative and instrument in the hands of Jesus Christ and having the opportunity to act as voice in that room that night.

I then got up, walked over to the light switch, turned it on and glanced back into the room, and there, standing in the back in brilliant white clothing were four brethren from the other side of the veil. I realized that they had been there for a specific reason and that they also had played a key role in the life of one young man, his adoptive parents and his biological mother.

Quietly, I spoke to the man closest to me, and said, "Thank you for your attendance this evening."

In a rather businesslike manner, this old High Priest turned to me and replied, "You're welcome, Brother Whitaker."

With that, I quickly turned off the light, quietly opened the door and slipped out of the room.

Trials Precede Our First Mission

I began my missionary service after my call as a Ward Mission Leader in June 1992. From that time on, I dedicated all of my time, means and talents to the building of the kingdom through my involvement in missionary work.

That effort included time spent as a Ward Mission Leader in the Morning Sun Ward, second counselor in the Sunrise Stake Mission Presidency serving with Don Nesbitt and Neil Dutson, and my five years in the Nevada Las Vegas Mission presidency as the first counselor to three mission presidents: Ross McEachran; Robert H. McKee and Warren G. Tate.

I was finishing my fifth year in the presidency and traveling with Warren Tate when he turned to me and said, "I received an interesting telephone call today. Elder Pinegar wants to know if you and Cheryle would submit your mission papers."

"I don't think there would be a problem," I answered.

"There are a couple of hitches."

"What are they?" I asked.

"First, he asked that the paperwork be completed in the next ten days, and secondly, that they be sent directly to his desk, attention to him and not to the Missionary Department."

So that is how it began. The year was 2000.

Miraculously, we completed the papers within the ten day period, which included the medical and dental appointments and sent them directly to Elder Pinegar. However, I failed to realize that one word on the back of my personal information sheet would dramatically impact the entire process; and what was the word? Spanish! On the back of the paperwork, I felt prompted to put my two years of high school Spanish, as well as the two years of Spanish at Los Angeles Valley College. That combined with the Spanish used on the streets of Los Angeles and during my five years in the Nevada Las Vegas Mission had a dramatic impact on our calling.

Whatever Elder Pinegar had in mind, it never materialized. Instead of an English speaking assignment, we were called to a Spanish speaking mission. Originally it was to the Employment Resource Center, Caracas, Venezuela. However, three weeks after receiving our call, we received an e-mail from Elder Cartmill, the Area Welfare Agent over the South America North Area advising us that the assignment had been changed from Caracas, Venezuela to Quito, Ecuador. This e-mail was later followed by a letter from President Hinckley making the change official.

So there it was. We were going to Quito, Ecuador to work in the Employment Resource Center. As I pondered the magnitude of the assignment, I felt comforted when the Spirit told me: *Richard, learn the language and love the people. You will be fine.* So that is what I did, and although we were both excited, the roller coaster ride had yet to begin.

Our mission farewell was the weekend before our leaving for the Mission Training Center (MTC). All the family attended, as did Bob and Venna McKee. Friday afternoon Bob and I sat in our kitchen talking about the experience Cheryle and I would soon have. When the topic of language came up, Bob said, "You don't need to spend any time in the MTC being taught Spanish. You know Spanish. You and Cheryle would do fine without that."

Then he picked up the telephone and while I sat and listened, he called Lloyd Owen in the Missionary Department. Before I knew it, McKee was telling Lloyd that, "The Whitakers don't need any Spanish classes in the MTC; just get them into the field."

McKee's telephone call and the recommendation by Lloyd Owen eliminated any Spanish language training in Provo and ensured our timely arrival in Ecuador. While I personally would have liked to have eliminated the entire Senior MTC experience, since it was far too lengthy, I was grateful that all we had to stay was thirteen days, not six weeks. So again, the Lord blessed me because of President Robert H. McKee.

Prior to the mission, Cheryle and I went to visit the McKee's in Houston. While at their home, I knew something was medically wrong, but said nothing.

On the plane flight back home, I suffered excruciating pain in my stomach, and I was vomiting blood. The day after we arrived home, I was unable to get out of bed. Then I heard a still small voice whisper, *Richard, you are dying. You must get to a doctor immediately.* I have learned always to listen, so when Cheryle returned home, I told her that I was immediately to get to the doctor. She didn't realize the severity of the illness at the time, but soon would.

Cheryle called Dr. Joe Hardy's office, and I went in on an emergency basis. Once there, Dr. Lisa Hayworth looked at me and realized that there was a severe problem. She recommended that I be admitted to the hospital where they discovered severe bleeding ulcers. During the next week they gave me four units of blood and some thought I would not make it due to the large amount of blood I already had lost.

Because of the number of transfusions, all the veins in my hands and arms collapsed which caused severe pain and difficulties. I remember the nurses putting the needles in and then moving them around as they tried to find a vein. While they watched, tears ran down my face because of the excruciating pain, but while they prodded and searched, I never said a word.

After a week, they released me from the hospital, and then came some outpatient surgery to close the bleeding ulcers. More discomfort. All this occurred six weeks before we left for Ecuador.

Few knew about this ordeal. Bob McKee and the Tate's knew. No one from the Missionary Department was advised, for as far as I was concerned, we had been called by the Lord to serve and we were going to fulfill that commitment. I had endured pain all my life. For me, it was not a new or unique experience.

Bob McKee in My Corner

On August 15, 2001, President Robert H. McKee sent me the following letter after a difficult time while serving in the Ecuador Quito, Employment Center.

Earlier, a Director of Temporal Affairs accused Daryl Nancollas and I of being dishonest and misusing church assets. The man later apologized to Daryl, but not to me.

Richard:

You have accomplished a great deal, just as the Lord wanted you to do. We live in difficult times. Getting things done is challenging and difficult. You have touched hundreds of lives, lives that are relatively unknown and unimportant to the world. But to the Savior, they are of the greatest value, and you have atoned in their behalf, patterning what the Savior has done for us.

Pres. Hinckley and Pres. Kimball would love telling you that you have done a great work and worthy of approval from those that understand. Joseph is grateful for your contribution to the strengthening of the Kingdom in a difficult setting.

Those that graduated from your classes will praise you throughout eternity as well as their families. Thank you for getting something to happen. I am proud to be your friend, your brother. My heart aches for you tonight because I know you have given everything you possess to do this work.

Peace will be your reward.

Love,

Your brother, Bob

Our Lives Spared

The Servicios de Recursos de Empleo, or employment office that I constructed in Quito, Ecuador was located directly below the Institute of Religion, Colon. We occupied the space in the right front corner of the basement in an office that was surrounded by the Area storage facility, or bodega.

The entire basement area sat at a level approximately fifteen feet below street level with the Institute of Religion sitting elevated about six feet above street level. The drainage for the basin-like area in which the building sat consisted of two drainage ducts, one located on each side of the facility. Unfortunately, the drainage pipes were rarely cleaned of debris or serviced, leaving them virtually inoperative.

Now with that background, I need to explain that when the office was built, it sat as a jewel and example for other employment centers not only in South America, but throughout the Church.

With our assignment completed and having been prompted by the Spirit to return to the United States, Cheryle and I left Ecuador in October, 2001. We completed what the Lord sent us to do and we were at peace with the decision to leave six weeks early.

On Wednesday, December 12, 2001, I received the following e-mail.

Dear Elder Whitaker:

Throughout Tuesday and Wednesday, December 11-12, the city of Quito endured the worst rain storm it had experienced in the past twenty years. Wednesday night, December 12, at 7:30 p.m. while Carlos Guerrero and another man sat in the employment office working, a wave of water nearly twelve feet high rolled down the long driveway and exploded through the front door of the employment center immediately filling the office to a height of nearly nine feet. With the impact of the water, all desks, chairs, tables, computers and equipment whether secured or not were violently washed to the rear of the office where the two men were seated. Both men struggled out the door of the Director's office and began to struggle and swim through the carnage. Amazingly they were able to struggle to the small glass front door which had been blown open by the force of the water and they escaped. Both, although losing their shoes and having their clothing torn, survived.

The pressure of the water caused the office walls to explode out causing a portion of the ceiling tiles to collapse. In minutes the office was totally destroyed. Everything was lost. All the computers, the telephones, the furniture, the copier and all paperwork, computer disks, reports and files were destroyed. Nothing remained. Additionally, the water caused a wall leading into the Institute to collapse.

With the implosion of the walls, a torrent of water rushed into the storage area where they stored the televisions, VCR's, all manuals, seminary supplies, Books of Mormon and equipment for five South American countries. Everything in the storage area was also destroyed. Water filled the entire basement to a depth of nearly eight feet.

When the water finally drained, nothing was salvageable. There was absolutely nothing left physically that would provide any evidence that an office once had occupied the area; only debris. It was as if Elder and Sister Whitaker had not even been there.

Danny Mino informed me that the sewers in Quito were so clogged that they literally stopped working. The water that normally would have flowed through the sewers was unable to do so, consequently building up until a wall of water similar to a tidal wave flowed down the Institute driveway gaining momentum as it moved downhill. The worst area impacted was the area of Colon where the Institute was located. Losses to the church exceeded one million dollars.

Not everyone was as fortunate as Carlos Guerrero and the other member of the church who were able to escape. In the apartment facility adjacent to the Institute the water trapped three people in an elevator as it sat in the basement area; all three drowned.

I am grateful that the life of Carlos Guerrero and the other man was spared. I am also grateful that Cheryle and I were not caught sitting in the office where we normally would have been. I am grateful that under the direction of the Spirit, the Lord sent us back to the United States six weeks earlier.

I later viewed a video tape of the carnage that Carlos Guerrero sent to me, and it was plain that Cheryle would have been killed when the wall of water swept through the front door and across her receptionist area. Additionally, when the surge struck the rear wall, it rebounded forward taking all the equipment with it and depositing everything in Cheryle's area.

I would have been seated in the Director's office instead of Carlos Guerrero.

I am grateful for the experience we had in Quito. We made a difference and fortunately the difference we made would be judged not by what remained of our once beautiful office, but in the lives that were impacted and changed.

The Old Guitar Maker

Our third mission assignment to South America found Cheryle and I assigned to the Perpetual Education Fund in Lima, Peru.

One weekend we had an assignment to accompany Elder Rene Loli, an Area Seventy, to assist with meetings held in Cusco, Peru. It was a Saturday afternoon and since we had some time before our meetings, Cheryle decided that she wanted to visit some of the small shops that lined the cobblestone streets which now had become familiar to us after our prior visits to Cusco. Stepping through the large front doors of our hotel, we made a hard left that led us down a cobblestone street no wider than a single car. As we walked down a slight hill, I noticed a small sign attached to one of the stone buildings that read: "Guitarras," or guitars.

Remembering that I needed to buy a capo, which is used to change the key signature on a guitar when you are playing, I told Cheryle to go ahead and I would catch up. With that, we separated and I stepped to the archway that led down a narrow street where I would find the guitar shop.

The arched doorway was no wider than four feet and was made from stone that once had been part of an ancient Inca building. Stepping through the doorway, I walked into a narrow, dimly lit passageway. Looking down the path, I saw a small sign attached to the rock that identified the location of the shop. I walked up to the entrance and looked in.

The shop was dark and very small. I stood in the doorway and watched as a hunched over elderly man worked meticulously at a scarred workbench where he placed small pegs in an instrument that resembled a Mandolin. With precision that only came from years of experience, he positioned each peg into the small hole and then lovingly tapped it into place with a small wooden mallet, the ends of which were covered with leather. Since his back was to me, I was able to stand silently for some time and watch this remarkable craftsman at work. Suddenly, he turned and saw me in the doorway. I noted that that he was about seventy-five years old, not over five foot six and slightly overweight. His gray trousers fit him tightly, his shirt was yellowed and he wore an old, sweat stained straw hat.

Seeing me, he said, "Bienvenido, Señor. Entre por favor."

I stepped down from the entrance onto the concrete floor and looked around. The shop was small and the walls were lined with the tools of his craft.

"How can I serve you?" he asked, bowing slightly.

"I am looking for a capo," I said, not believing that he would have one.

He turned to his left, shuffled slowly to a scarred wooden cabinet, opened a bottom drawer and pulled out a new capo.

"That is perfect," I said. "How much?"

"Twenty-four soles, Señor" (Eight US dollars)

"Demasiado," I responded. "Fifteen soles."

"Oh Señor, I cannot sell this for less than eighteen. It is new, and you might not find another in Cusco."

"You are right by dear friend," I said as I pulled out my wallet, "Eighteen it is." (Six US dollars.)

As he placed the capo in a small plastic bag, he looked up and read my missionary tag. Immediately, his countenance changed.

"What kind of work do you do?" he asked, a tone of reverence surrounding his words.

"I am a representative of the Lord Jesus Christ, my dear friend, a servant of God."

As soon as I finished my last word, the Spirit flooded that small room to the point that both the guitar maker and I recognized it. Immediately, his hand went to his head and he pulled off the crumpled old hat and held it gently against his chest with both hands.

As he looked into my face, tears filled his eyes and then they began to flow gently down the cheeks of his weathered face. At this moment, the power of the Spirit increased and flooded the room that by now was occupied not only by us, but also unseen others. I knew that we were not alone.

I looked into his eyes and saw a face that not only had seen a lifetime of pain and hardship, but also carried in its features a brightness of hope brought about by one who had exercised great faith in the Savior over many hard and difficult years.

Bowing his head slightly and with trembling hands, he said, "Oh Father, would you give me a blessing?"

His reference to "Father," as used in South America for a religious leader did not offend, but magnified the solemnity of the occasion.

With those words, the noises of the street disappeared and it was as though the wooden door to the small shop had been closed by unseen hands, leaving us alone, standing in reverent silence.

"Of course I will, my dear friend," I answered, "but first, let us talk."

With head bowed and tears flowing, he explained the physical demands of his craft and the pain he endured. He silently sobbed, not for himself, but for his beloved wife of many years who was also in poor health.

"Oh Father...will you please include my wife in your blessing?"

"Of course," I answered, remembering the story of the woman who touched the hem of the Saviors cloak and was healed; her faith had made her whole. So now I stood before one with such faith, a man of many years and great faith. One who felt and recognized the Spirit and knew the miracles wrought under the hands of a servant of the Lord Jesus Christ.

Slowly, he pulled a small battered wooden stool into the middle of the room and as he stood meekly, I asked him to have a seat. I then asked for his full name, placed my hands lightly on his head, and waited. Silently, I requested that the heavens be opened and the Spirit rest upon me to ensure that I would speak the words the Savior would speak if He were physically standing in that small room.

What I said in the blessing I do not remember, but as the words flowed, I felt a humble man tremble as the Spirit touched the depth of his soul.

When I ended, the old guitar maker slowly stood and in words choked with emotion, said, "Oh Father, God bless you and thank you. You are truly a man of God."

With those sweet words, we hugged, said our goodbyes and I left, walking back up the narrow cobblestone street knowing that I had just had an experience I never would forget.

Upon our return to Lima, I submitted a missionary referral and missionaries from Cusco were assigned to follow-up with the old guitar maker.

Well Done My Good and Faithful Servant

It was January 2011, and our final week in Lima, Peru. I felt I had accomplished what the Brethren had requested by developing a Perpetual Education Fund (PEF) program that would see the priesthood leaders more fully use priesthood correlation not only to move the PEF programs forward, but also to rescue those who had fallen away or forgotten the criticality of their sacred temple covenants. When we completed the program, the Brethren told me it would be used throughout the Church. Now we were readying ourselves to leave.

During the eighteen month assignment, I had become very close to Elder Marcus Nash, our Area President and a member of The First Quorum of the Seventy.

We spoke quite often and it was apparent that he was pleased with what we had accomplished.

On our last Tuesday, Cheryle and I went to the Nash home to say goodbye. Before going, I had asked in my prayers for a confirmation that the Savior accepted my sacrifice which I placed upon the alter, and I would hear the sweet words, "Well done my good and faithful servant."

Sister Nash met us at the door and said her husband was upstairs working out. Soon, Elder Nash came downstairs and met us in the hallway. As Cheryle and Sister Nash walked into another room to visit, Elder Nash and I talked.

He thanked me for our service and the completion of a difficult assignment. He then stepped closer, and became very serious. He explained that in the Church there are many that will tell you they will do something, but very few complete the task requested.

"Elder Whitaker, you are in the one percent of those who actually will complete what you have committed to do."

He then told me about the time when he was ready to leave his mission. He had been an Assistant to the President and when they had their final supper prior to leaving for home, the other departing missionaries asked if he was ready to leave. Elder Nash told me that he had not even thought about leaving, and was not even packed.

Pondering the past two years, he said that he moved into a solitary place in the backyard. As he sat, the mission president approached him. The president said little, but handed him a small picture of his family. On the back of the photograph were printed in Spanish the words, "Bien hecho mi bueno y fiel servidor" or as translated in English, "Well done my good and faithful servant."

Elder Nash went on to explain that to him, those were the most important words one could hear when completing an assignment.

Then, with tears in his eyes, he took me by the shoulders and in Spanish said, "Bien hecho mi bueno y fiel servidor."

I received the confirmation I requested, and knew that what I had been sent to do had been accomplished.

PRESIDENT'S
INTERVIEWS

Evil Attends an Interview

I had not served long in the Nevada Las Vegas Mission presidency and was conducting President's Exception Interviews at the Hollywood and Stewart building in the Sunrise Stake. I used the unused stake president's office and felt blessed to have use of the facility.

It was a weekday evening, and I just had finished two interviews when a missionary companionship brought in a large man who stood at least six feet six inches and weighed a hefty four hundred and fifty pounds.

When he approached me in the hallway, I had the impression that the man would not pass the interview and it was my responsibility to determine why and help him put his life in order so a further interview could be scheduled.

The man entered the room and took a seat directly across the desk from me. About two minutes into the process, he became very belligerent. As the interview progressed, his belligerence increased.

During the interview, it surfaced that he was homosexual, had homicidal tendencies and in the past when a set of missionaries were teaching him, he became violent and attempted to harm them as they hurriedly left the apartment. He readily admitted this to me.

During my interview, as he became more and more belligerent, the Spirit became more firm. Soon he was yelling, and in one quick motion, he jumped out of his chair and started across the desk in my direction. As I sat behind the large stake president's desk, I didn't move, or even flinch, yet I knew I was in danger.

Without moving, I silently prayed, *Father, in the name of Jesus Christ, I now request Thy holy angels to surround me.* No sooner had I completed my request, I knew they were present.

I watched as the irate man immediately began to move back. It was obvious that the evil in him knew and recognized that others also were present in that room. The interview abruptly ended, and I told the man to leave. He did so, still yelling and calling me names.

Parents Attend a Special Interview

I want to share how sacred the offices are in which sit the Lord's anointed servants. Members far too often fail to realize that in the office of a bishop, a stake president, or a mission president, the Spirit of the Lord is present and angels do, on many occasions, attend. It is in these special rooms that revelation is received, the veil is parted and lives are changed.

So the next time you enter one of these offices, remember how sacred these rooms are. And remember that although we love and honor our leaders, it is not the messenger, but the message that is of the greatest import.

They, who occupy those offices for whatever time allocated by the Lord, do so to serve and not to bring upon their own heads the praise of men. As they magnify their respective callings, the Lord blesses them and others who might use these rooms with wonderful experiences designed to build the kingdom and glorify God.

A President's Exception Interview had been scheduled by Elder Call. He was from the Colonies in Mexico, spoke fluent English and Spanish and was as obedient a missionary as I had ever seen. Were it not so, he would not have been invited to sit with me and translate. For when the salvation of another rested in my hands and was dependent on that special interview, I would not allow someone to sit in that room who, in any way, would offend the Spirit and hamper the flow of revelation.

The investigator was one taught by Elder Call. Normally, I would have had someone other than the teaching Elder translate, but considering his level of spirituality, I perceived no problem in using him.

I began the interview with questions that this investigator clearly answered. As the interview progressed, I was aware that the Spirit in the room was greater than usual, and I knew that Elder Call, his investigator and I were not alone.

Sitting behind the stake president's desk, I watched Elder Call and the young investigator who were seated on the opposite side of the desk. As the interview progressed, the Spirit in the room increased. Soon all in the room had tears streaming down their cheeks. Then I looked behind the young man. Against the far wall was seated an elderly Hispanic couple. I immediately knew that they were his parents.

"Are your parents still alive?" I asked.

"No, they died in Cuba many years ago," he answered.

Yet they now attended this special interview and listened as their son expressed his love for them and his gratefulness for their many sacrifices while they lived in Cuba. He told of their love for the Lord and their desire to worship God, which was very difficult since they lived in a country that banned religion. They sat quietly through a portion of the interview, each with unrestrained tears flowing down their cheeks. During this entire experience, I had a difficult time speaking and continuing.

Elder Call saw the emotion that had overcome me, and toward the end of the interview, he casually turned his head and looked back in the direction of the empty seats. Suddenly, he snapped his head around and with astonishment in his eyes, looked at me as if he had seen something he shouldn't. With that, the interview ended and as quickly as they appeared, the couple left. But the Spirit that had filled the room remained.

I dismissed the investigator and asked Elder Call what he had learned. As I asked this question, emotionally he said, "We weren't alone in the room tonight, were we President?"

"No Elder Call, we weren't."

"I didn't think so," he answered. "When I turned my head to look behind us I saw someone sitting in the chairs. That's when I quickly turned my head and looked at you."

"The Lord allowed the parents of your investigator to attend a portion of the interview, Elder. That's who was seated in the two chairs."

It was another wonderful experience that testified to the thinness of the veil and the love the Lord has for not only those on this side, but also those who have passed on.

Again, I testify that angels attend and revelation is received in this marvelous work. And I testify to the sacredness of those wonderful rooms wherein great things occur, unknown to the world and most members of the church.

But the story does not end here.

After the Lord called Cheryle and I to fill our second assignment in Quito, Ecuador, we found ourselves sitting in the Los Angeles Airport waiting because mechanical problems developed with our plane. Repeatedly, we experienced gate changes. On the final change, when the new gate was announced, we both got up and started to move down the concourse to our next destination.

As we began the trek to the new gate, the air was pierced by a shout, "President Whitaker, wait!" Both Cheryle and I stopped and turned around. Running in our direction was Elder Call!

"What are you doing here? I asked.

"I am traveling on business and because of some changes in flights, I ended up here. I was supposed to be in another concourse, but I was sent here instead."

I asked him about his family, work and if he was still active.

"Of course I am, President!

"Do you still remember that special interview we had?" I asked.

"I think of it often," he said. "Indeed, it truly was a special experience!"

Righteous Indignation

In all of the President's Exception Interviews I conducted, only once did I feel the full indignation of an angry God. Only once did the voice of the Lord become so intense that the office shook because a man tried to destroy that which was precious in the eyes of the Lord.

The interview began as all did. The Elders introduced me to the investigator and in their eagerness, told me that he was "Golden," had a testimony of the gospel and was ready for baptism. As I looked deep into his eyes, I saw a darkness that assured me something was wrong and that today this man would not be approved to enter the waters of baptism. With this inspiration, it now became my responsibility to determine why.

As the interview began, I asked the investigator a question that I had never before asked: "Have you ever seduced and had sexual relations with a member of the Church of Jesus Christ of Latter-day Saints?"

Smiling, he arrogantly replied, "Yes."

He then proceeded to explain the circumstances.

He told me that the woman was a young married sister who held a leadership position in the church and had a temple recommend. As he shared the knowledge of the temple recommend, he smiled. He continued by sharing that she had children, and within a short period of time she succumbed to his advances.

After a very long and thorough interview, I detailed the process of repentance and at the conclusion, I counseled him not to have any relationship, whether professional or otherwise with any female member of the Church of Jesus Christ of Latter-day Saints.

After giving the admonition, I asked, "Do you understand what I have said?"

He acknowledged that he did and repeated the counsel.

Three months passed and during that time the husband of the young woman heard that this man was attempting to be baptized. The husband, heartbroken and confused, called President McKee to plead that this not be allowed to happen.

President McKee explained to the distraught husband that I was conducting the interviews, no one would slip by, and that a baptism would not be conducted unless the Lord approved.

At the end of the three month period, much to my astonishment, the man returned for his second interview.

As I looked into his face, and then into his eyes, it was apparent that the darkness remained. My first question was, "Since our last meeting, have you again seduced and had sexual relations with a member of the Church of Jesus Christ of Latter-day Saints?"

His answer was an arrogant, "Yes."

When asked about the circumstances, he explained that it was a different sister, older, who lived in Southern California and was a wealthy widow. He was pleased that she also held a current temple recommend.

With that response, the entire climate in the room dramatically changed, and the words that I uttered was not mine, nor was it my voice. I stood and faced one of the most evil men I had ever interviewed. The Spirit rebuked him and condemned his actions. As I spoke the words, the room shook and the man's eyes widened. God would not be mocked, and through his deceitfulness, through his lies, the truth surfaced and one who was a predator and evil in the eyes of God would be refused entrance into the Kingdom of God. The intensity of the Spirit and the great displeasure the Savior felt for this man were staggering.

When it was over, everything in the room had vanished except that man and me. Never had I experienced such a powerful condemnation of any human being as I heard and felt that day.

After admonishing him as to the grievous nature of his actions and the Lord's displeasure, he leaned forward and shouted, "By what authority do you speak to me in that manner?"

Calmly, and softly, I said, "By the authority of the Melchizedek Priesthood which I hold and in the sacred name of Jesus Christ."

His face emanated evil and though he wanted to do so, he could not speak.

"Now, I command you leave," I said.

I walked over, opened the door and he bolted from the room. As he left the building, the Elders who had taught the man stood in the reception area with astonished looks on their faces.

One finally spoke.

"President, I don't know what happened in that office because the words were more like a rumbling, but we could feel the room shake."

Later, I was told that because of this man's actions, both sisters lost their membership in the Church.

Shark Infested Waters

I just had finished a Spanish speaking President's Exception Interview and asked a Cuban man how he got to the United States? He told me that he and six other men had fashioned themselves a raft using old truck inner tubes and wood. They then set off from the Cuban coast at night toward the shores of Florida.

About five days out, things went terribly wrong. His companions began to die, and they saw sharks circling the flimsy raft. As each man slipped into the water, the sharks devoured them. Seeing this gave him greater resolve to stay alive.

By the time the United States Coast Guard arrived, he was the sole survivor. He was imprisoned in Florida and spent over a year in jail. Then remarkably, he was released and granted political asylum.

As I concluded the interview, the Spirit testified to me that this man had been spared and was in the United States and Las Vegas for the purpose of finding the gospel.

PERSONAL REVELATION

Warned of Danger in a Dream

It was April 1970. I was serving as the Elder's Quorum president in the North Hollywood I Ward when a ward member, also a LAPD cop, asked if I wanted to attend General Conference. I told him of course. He said we would stay at his parent's home and then attend the Priesthood Session. We planned to leave Los Angeles late in the afternoon, drive to St. George and spend the night, then drive straight to his parent's home the next day.

I had a 1967, blue Volkswagen Bug and we decided to take it because of the gas mileage. The drive to St. George was uneventful. We checked into our motel, ate and went back to our room to get a good night's rest. The next morning we had breakfast and at about 8:00 a.m. started for Salt Lake. Steve told me that he wouldn't mind driving since he had driven the road many times and knew it well. I asked him if he was sure, for he looked somewhat tired. He said that he was fine, and so I handed him the keys and off we went.

About fifteen minutes out of St. George, I asked him if he was all right. He said that he was fine so I put my head against the passenger window and fell asleep. It wasn't long before I had a dream.

In the dream, I saw the road upon which we were traveling. I watched as telephone poles whipped past and then suddenly, as I looked out the passenger window, I saw the

Volkswagen angle off the road towards a deep ditch. Glancing up, I watched as the car slid toward the ravine and in the direction of a telephone pole. The shock of the scene and the rapidity at which we were traveling toward our destruction awakened me.

Startled, I looked out the window and there in front of me was the exact scene depicted in the dream. We were traveling at the same speed, approaching the same ditch and looming in front of the small car was the same telephone pole. Turning to Steve, terror gripped my heart. He was slumped over the steering wheel. Asleep! And at over seventy miles an hour we were speeding to imminent destruction and our deaths.

Without hesitating, I screamed at him and then grabbed the steering wheel and snapped it to the left as violently as I could. I was aware that we could be killed if the car rolled, but that was a chance I was going to take. I also realized that we would never survive the head on collision with the telephone pole after traveling air borne across the ditch.

Incredibly we didn't roll. The instant I snapped the steering wheel, an unseen power literally lifted the car from the soft shoulder and in the twinkling of an eye placed it on the asphalt where we continued to speed down the highway. Regaining his composure, Steve applied the brakes, pulled off to the side and stopped the car. Angered, I told him his driving on this trip was over. He tried to apologize, but I will admit that it took a few hours before I calmed down.

Bob Sturgis Will be Your Secretary

It was 1971. I recently had been called as the Elders Quorum president in the North Hollywood I Ward. I now needed to call two counselors and a secretary. After much prayer, the Spirit directed me to two men who were less active. These were to be my counselors.

I remember going to the home of each to introduce myself. First, I went to the home of Rob Watts, a returned missionary. He was less active and unmarried. Since he had not yet attended the ward, we hadn't had the opportunity to meet, but the Spirit confirmed that he should serve as my first counselor.

Then, I visited the home of Richard Rashi. Again, the Spirit confirmed to me that he should serve as my second counselor. Well, I knew that I had my counselors, but a secretary was the difficult position. Day after day I reviewed the ward list concentrating on younger, active men. While I pondered and prayed about the names on the list, no inspiration came. Then, when I returned to the less active, I received the answer. *Richard, Bob Sturgis will be your secretary.*

I had never met Brother Sturgis, although I was the Home Teacher to the Sturgis/Stiefvater family. I knew that his brother, Steven, had served a mission and from personal experience, knew that his mother, Barbara Stiefvater, was a less active member of the church who often would say things to me just for shock value. Eventually, this ended when she realized that because of my being a tough street cop from the ghetto of Los Angeles, nothing shocked me.

During one of my home teaching visits, Barbara, with a great deal of delight in her voice, shared with me that she was an aunt to D. Todd Christofferson, who was very active in the church. Elder Christofferson would later be called as a General Authority and serve in The First Quorum of the Seventy and then as a member of the Quorum of the Twelve Apostles.

With marching orders in hand, I went to visit Bob Sturgis. Although I had no keys to issue a call, I did have the authority to ask some questions. When I asked Bob about his weekends, he told me that every Sunday he rode motorcycles and that nothing was going to take him away from that activity. *Nothing but the Lord*, I thought.

"Well, Brother Sturgis, if you happen to change your mind, give President Pratt or me a call. Here are our telephone numbers."

"Don't worry, President," he said with a large grin on his face, "I won't be changing my mind!"

I submitted the names of all three brethren to the stake presidency and waited. The Stake Presidency immediately approved and interviewed the two counselors, each of whom accepted the assignment.

But I still did not have a secretary. One week passed and then another. Then I received a telephone call advising me that the stake presidency interviewed Brother Sturgis and he had accepted the calling. I was more curious than shocked at his acceptance and asked Brother Sturgis to meet with me. He was eager to do so, and in that meeting he related the following.

"The Sunday after you came and visited me, I went out to get my dirt bike ready to go riding, but found that I had a flat tire. That killed that day. I fixed the tire and decided that I would go the next Sunday. Well, the following Sunday, I again went out to get my bike and guess what? I had another flat tire. I then decided that something was going on and I knew that I was to accept the calling. So I did. But I will swear that it was you, President Whitaker that let the air out of my tires, because there was absolutely nothing wrong with them. Each time I checked them, they were fine…. they just had no air!"

I tried to tell Brother Sturgis that I had nothing to do with the air disappearing, but to this day, I am confident that he still believes I was responsible.

Bob went on to marry Kathy Barton, the stake president's daughter and has remained active these many years. Barbara also turned things around and during a conversation with Elder Christofferson during his visit to the South America Northwest Area, he told me that before Barbara passed away, she had become active and served as a temple worker. I always felt that this would happen since inside the rough exterior, Barbara was one of the kindest, most generous people I have known.

Kirk Alger Will Be Your Secretary

In the past, I have shared the inspiration received in the calling of counselors and a secretary in the Elders Quorum Presidency. The calling of a secretary in the Saugus Second Ward High Priests group was no different.

After two years in the Saugus Second Ward, the stake president called me to the Santa Clarita Stake High council. That lasted about a year and ended suddenly when a counselor in the stake presidency walked up to me and told me that I made the Stake President very uncomfortable. "Brother Whitaker, in nine years, no one has made the president as uncomfortable as you do. So you are being released."

"Fine," I said. "His High Council, his call."

They released me the next Sunday.

About three months later, I was called as the High Priest Group Leader in the Saugus Second Ward. Bishop Bob Smith and I became very close friends and had a wonderful working relationship. Mike Padovich was Bob's first counselor. Mike followed Bob as the Bishop and eventually served as a mission president in Africa. Bob, after his move to Pennsylvania, served as a Stake President and an Area Seventy.

As High Priest Group Leader, I had little difficulty in the calling of Assistant's, but the identification of a secretary was far more challenging.

My first assistant was Karl Moody and Second Assistant, David Walker. Both would later serve as Bishops. And while serving as my assistants, each was excellent.

But I needed a secretary. As I pondered the remaining priesthood holders in the ward, I literally was stymied as to who the Lord desired to have in the position. Over and over I pondered the list doing everything necessary to receive confirmation, but the answer never came, so I decided to go to the Los Angeles Temple and approach the matter in a different way.

In the temple, I walked into the Endowment Room and sat down on the second row. Following a long and pleading prayer, I asked who it was that the Lord wanted to serve in that position. I explained that I had presented every name I knew, everyone in the High Priest group, and I was at a loss.

Then as plainly as if someone were standing directly in front of me and speaking, I heard in my mind, *Richard, call Kirk Alger to be your secretary.*

But I don't know him and he is inactive.

Again, the still small voice. *Richard, call Kirk Alger to be your secretary.*

But he smokes.

A third time, *Richard, call Kirk Alger to be your secretary.* And with that, the conversation ended.

I didn't know Brother Alger. I had never met or even talked to him. I knew that he was a coach and administrator at Saugus High School where Shannyn and Cindy attended, but other than that, to me he was a total stranger. However, this isn't my church, so I knew what must be done.

The next day was Sunday. After my meetings, I walked into the small Melchizedek Priesthood room located in the Saugus Ward building and picked up the telephone. I dialed the Alger residence.

When Brother Alger picked up the telephone, I told him who I was and asked to meet with him the following Wednesday. I then listened to his excuses, but I finally prevailed and scheduled an interview. On Wednesday evening, Brother Alger and I met in the small priesthood room. After a prayer and the usual greetings, I cut to the chase.

"Brother Alger, the Lord is extending to you the opportunity to serve as secretary to the High Priests group in the Saugus Second Ward. Will you accept the calling?"

"But I smoke."

"The Lord knows that."

"But I'm inactive, Brother Whitaker."

"The Lord knows that also. You need to understand Brother Alger that I don't know you from Adam, but the Lord does. And as I sat in the temple the other day pleading with the Lord to direct me to whom it was He wanted to serve in the position, He counseled that it was you. If you accept, it won't be easy. I am a very hard task master. When someone commits to the Lord and me that they will serve, I expect them to do just that. Will you accept the call?"

With that, Brother Alger broke into tears. "I can't believe it," he sobbed. "My wife and I had been praying for the past two weeks about what we needed to do to change our lives, and we decided that we needed to go back to church, and now this."

Brother Alger accepted the call and over a period of time, his life and that of his family changed. Within a year, he and his wife received the sealing ordinances in the Los Angeles Temple. A son returned to activity and served an honorable mission; and a daughter put her life in order.

As I watched the miracle unfold, I was grateful that the will of the Lord had been accomplished and I was a tool in His hands. The years have passed, and the Alger's since have moved to Utah, but I am confident that the Alger's never will forget how their prayers were answered when the Lord issued a call and it was accepted.

REBECCA ANN
WHITAKER

Rebecca Ann Whitaker

It was Mother's Day, Sunday, May 10, 1992. As a family we had spent a great morning at church. In the afternoon while we all were resting, there was a knock at the door. When I answered it, there stood an older gentleman dressed in a brown uniform. He identified himself as a representative from the Clark County Coroner's Office and asked if he could speak to Cheryle Whitaker. In his hand was a piece of paper. As he stood at a slight angle, I saw that on the paper were the words, "Rebecca Ann Whitaker, deceased."

I had spent too many years in law enforcement not to know the meaning of the visit. He entered the home and the first thing Cheryle did was offer him a seat and ask if he would like something to drink. He politely refused and then advised us that our daughter, Rebecca had been killed earlier that morning in a traffic accident just south of Nephi, Utah.

Following his notification and departure, a feeling of great loss permeated our home. However, I knew that much needed to be accomplished, so I made the first of many phone calls. This was to our Home Teacher, President Gordon Bergquist. I did not call the Bishop, nor did I call the Stake President. I called the one person who was the second father to my family; my Home Teacher. From there, the ball started rolling.

I then moved into the mode of a policeman and took care of the necessary details surrounding the death of a loved one. I called the doctor in Nephi who had pronounced her dead. After explaining that Becky was my daughter and my professional background, he shared with me the details of the accident. It was a single car rollover. Becky, who was not wearing a seatbelt, was thrown head first into the windshield and as the car rolled, she was thrown from the car and down an embankment. The car then rolled over her. She died instantly from the impact into the windshield.

I contacted the mortuary in Nephi and knowing that she had purchased a new dress for Mother's Day, asked that she be dressed in that dress.

When Becky was brought back to Las Vegas, I asked Bishop Burns and Jim Biehahn, my son-in-law, to accompany me to the mortuary.

At the mortuary, we entered the viewing room. Becky was in the beautiful blue casket that Cheryle and I had picked out earlier. The room was cold, and after Jim and Bishop Burns looked at her, they left the room leaving me alone. When they shut the door, the room suddenly began to warm. I found myself surrounded by this warmth and as I looked down at Becky, I could not help but saying out loud, "Sweetheart, I have seen you looking better."

The warmth increased, and then from behind me came a sweet voice that I recognized. *Thanks Dad, I needed that!*

There was laughter in her voice and happiness filled the room. We spoke for about ten minutes. She told me that she never felt a thing when the accident occurred and shared with me her experience on how Grandpa Don met her and took her through the veil and into the spirit world.

We spoke about our love for each other and I asked her if it would be all right to take the silver bracelet from her wrist so I could wear it. She said, *Sure Dad.* I also asked if she minded if I removed the earrings so I could give them to her mother, and we laughed when she said she had no need for them now.

After Becky departed, spiritually and emotionally exhausted, I left the room and Bishop Burns, Jim and I returned to the house.

During the next year when I took my walks and prayed, often the Lord allowed Becky to visit with me. During these talks she constantly expressed her desire to receive her endowment. She was anxious to serve as a missionary, but could not go with her Aunt Doni until she had been endowed. I explained to her that Richard Jr. was preparing for his mission and when he went for his endowment, her mother, acting as proxy, would complete her work.

More than once, she told me that if for any reason Richard did not receive his endowment as planned, she expected her mother to complete the work. I promised her it would be done.

We scheduled Richard's Missionary Farewell ten days prior to his endowment session. That was a special Sacrament meeting, because when Shannyn, Cindy, Tracy and Jamie stood at the pulpit to sing, five voices, not four could be heard. Becky, standing with her sisters, was not going to be left out. Many heard her and later testified to that marvelous manifestation of the Spirit.

The day came for me to accompany Richard to the Nevada Las Vegas Temple for his endowment and Cheryle to act as proxy for Becky's endowment.

After I took Richard in for his initiatory ordinance, I excused myself, went outside and prayed. I prayed for Richard. I prayed for Cheryle and me, and I prayed that Becky would be granted permission to join us. While I was outside and Richard was involved in the initiatory portion, Cheryle also was busy.

As she stood in the small washing and anointing room, the sister conducting soon realized that Cheryle was the mother of the son who was receiving his endowment and also the mother of the young lady who had passed away over a year prior. As the temple worker performed the ordinances, she asked Cheryle if she knew that Rebecca was present in the room. Cheryle, thinking that the sister meant in spirit, answered, "Yes, I thought that she would be here."

"No, you don't understand," said the sister, "She is here and is standing right there!" And so it was, Becky was in the room.

As we entered the small room for Richard's talk by a member of the temple presidency, we sat on the couch with the president standing in front of us. I do not know if he was aware of it or not, but before he closed the door, Becky entered and took a seat in the chair to our right. As he spoke, she listened carefully. After he finished, we all walked out but Richard asked to remain behind. About five minutes passed when he exited the room, and said, "Dad, Becky and I are now fine." In that small room, they resolved their issues, forgave each other and again enjoyed a loving relationship.

In the endowment room, I watched as it filled. Cheryle walked in with Shannyn, Cindy and Jamie and took their seats on the second row on the sister's side. The girls sat to Cheryle's left saving the aisle seat for Tracy. When I turned and looked to the rear doors, I watched as Tracy stepped into the room, stopped and then stepped back outside. She had become faint, and was forced to sit down outside.

As they began to close the doors, suddenly, Tracy stepped into the room and took a seat in a folding chair next to the door. This left the seat next to Cheryle vacant.

As the doors closed, I watched Becky step through the open door and walk to the only vacant seat in the room. She was in a long white dress and her hair was pulled back in a ponytail. She was as beautiful as ever and said, *Hi, Dad*, as she passed my seat. Reaching the vacant seat next to her mother, she sat down. Although the session was crowded and additional folding chairs set up, no one physically came forward and took the empty seat next to Cheryle.

After sitting down, I saw Becky turn, look to the rear of the men's seats, and smile at someone.

The session then began. During the session, Becky followed all of the instructions. When Cheryle went to the front, Becky went also, stood behind her mother and listened.

Becky and I were able to speak during the session, but only on occasion in that she was intent on listening and learning. Toward the end, I wanted to help explain something, but as I started, she turned and said, *Dad, please, I am trying to listen.* Getting the hint, I became quiet.

The session ended and we, as well as many family members from the other side, met in the Celestial Room. That was the last I saw of her that day.

On Tuesday night at my Sunrise Stake Mission Presidency meeting, President Don Nesbitt appeared to have something on his mind, so when our meeting ended, he asked me if he could ask a question about the session. I knew that during the session, he and our secretary, Brother Joe Woods were in the back on the right hand side. As we sat around the table, President Nesbitt asked me if anyone ever came in and sat next to Cheryle. I paused, and told him for all intents and purposes no one sat in the seat. He looked at me and smiled. "Oh yes they did. A young, very pretty woman with brown hair walked in as the doors were shutting and sat next to Sister Whitaker. After sitting down, Becky turned in my direction, smiled and then turned to the front."

Then President Nesbitt stopped and tears formed in his eyes. "I had another experience with Becky that I have not shared. One day as I walked to the mailbox, I was surrounded by a flood of spirit. It was so powerful and overwhelming that I had to stop as tears formed and I began to cry. Then from within its warm embrace, I heard a sweet, soft voice say, *Thank you President Nesbitt for calling my dad into the mission presidency.* Overwhelmed, I could only whisper, 'You're welcome.'"

It was another testimony to the special events of that day.

Since her endowment, I have had the opportunity to speak with Becky about many things. She told me that Grandpa Don, Aunt Doni, Grandpa James Clement Moran and many others attended the temple on that special day.

Often, I ask in my prayers if Becky could find and visit some of my friends and former partners who had died. She has told me about many of her experiences while doing this and how appreciative they are for my concern.

Bishop Burns also had some unique experiences with Becky before she passed. Here is one.

After being called as a young Bishop, he was on his knees in the office one night and was praying as to what he should do and who he should talk to. The Spirit told him to call in Becky Whitaker. This was the beginning of Becky's transformation. From the age of thirteen to eighteen, Becky was inactive. However, under the direction of the Spirit and with the help of a wonderful Bishop, she returned to activity.

On May 3, 1992, on the last Sunday that she was with us, she stood and bore her testimony to the Relief Society. She told the sisters that she had not borne her testimony in years, but wanted to do so today. This would be her first and last time attending Relief Society. After a beautiful testimony, she looked across the room and said, "Sisters, don't ever give up on your children. We will be back. I am back."

A week later she was gone.

On Tuesday, May 5, she had her last interview with Bishop Burns. He later referred to it as her exit interview. The Bishop has since told me that he has never known anyone more prepared and ready to go home than Becky.

Later that week and just before she traveled to Utah, Becky asked me for a father's blessing. I never heard the request. Saturday, May 9, I spoke to her on the phone and I asked why she had not asked for a blessing. She told me that she had asked three times and I never responded.

Never before had I not heard a child's request for a blessing. I firmly believe that the blessing was not meant to be given. For nothing was to stop the call home from being issued.

Since her death, my testimony of the Gospel has increased greatly. Many loving and well-meaning friends expressed concern to Cheryle about the affect Becky's death could have on me. They were concerned that because of my stroke, the pressure and grief of the situation would drive me over the edge, and to be truthful, there was a time that it very well may have. I am so grateful that my faith in Father in Heaven and my Savior, Jesus Christ has grown to such a proportion as to sustain me through this very difficult and grievous time in my life, and I pray that the strength I have been given can stand as a witness to others, so they likewise may be sustained through the difficulties they encounter.

Becky Returns and Reports

One afternoon as I was reading a talk by Elder Gene R. Cook on missionary work, I felt moved to take a break and sit down at the old piano. With Jamie in Colorado visiting Warren and Tracy and Cheryle driving some girls to camp, I was alone in the house. Or so I thought.

As I sat and started to play, I caught a glimpse of movement to my left, near the wall where the paintings hang. Suddenly, before I had a chance to turn or say a word, the room filled with a tremendous flood of spirit and Becky was there.

Toodels, Dad.

I could not contain myself and with the intensity of the spirit in the room, I started to cry like a baby. I was not only crying, but sobbing. I thought, *Come on, get control of yourself,* but the spirit was so overwhelming that I just could not contain the tears.

Then Becky, in a very loving way said, *It's all right, Dad. It's all right.*

She told me of the great love so many had for me on her side. She said that I could not fathom the number that loved and appreciated me for the work that I was performing. She told me that she had an opportunity to see Bruce Handwerker quite often and that he had accepted the gospel and was waiting for his temple work to be completed. She also said that Carl Porter always mentions how much he admires me, but then she added, pertaining to the gospel, *He has a long way to go, Dad.* This I knew.

She saw Russ Custer who Carl Porter and I trained as a new recruit in Wilshire Division and they talked about the experiences he remembered with her dad. She was, as she always is, in a hurry, but I was so very grateful to have spoken to her.

I cannot remember when the power of the Spirit has ever been stronger. Her sweet spirit completely filled the room. After she left, I continued to cry until there were no more tears.

A Special Missionary Discussion

While I served in the Sunrise Stake Mission Presidency, the full-time missionaries had scheduled Dennis Archer, a member of the Morning Sun Ward, to receive his first missionary discussion. Dennis was the stepfather to Jim Ashment who was serving a mission in Southern California and who was a dear friend of Becky's.

Prior to the discussion, the Ward Mission Leader asked if I would attend. I told him I would be pleased to do so.

I met the Sister missionaries at the Archer home and along with Sister Joan Archer, sat in the front room for the discussion. Before we began, Dennis asked me to offer the invocation. As I did, the Spirit flooded the room and I had a very difficult time finishing the prayer.

As the discussion began, Becky, and my little sister Doni, who died after only six hours in mortality, entered the room. In the presence of angels the flood of Spirit was overwhelming. As the tears fell, I barely could see.

When they entered, Doni, who was a beautiful young woman looked at me and said, *Hello, my brother Richard.*

Throughout the discussion, I had the opportunity to speak to each of these wonderful missionaries from the other side and what a great testimony this was to me of the role that those spirits play in the work. As the discussion progressed, the Spirit grew in magnitude, and at one time during our conversation Becky stopped and said, *Dad, I just want you to know how very proud I am of you.*

I did not say anything to the Archers about the experience, but at the conclusion of the discussion, Dennis testified to all in the room as to the great impact that Becky had on their family. It was interesting that even he felt Becky's influence that night, but at the time, did not know why.

We scheduled a Second Discussion for the next Wednesday. As I left the house, I shed more tears. There is not a greater experience on this earth than to be involved in sharing the gospel and having missionaries from both sides of the veil attend.

Cheryle and I arrived early for the Second Discussion. After visiting with the Archers, we took our seats and waited for the opening prayer and the discussion to begin.

Becky and Doni again appeared, however their stay was brief, for just before the missionaries asked Dennis to make a baptismal commitment, Becky turned to me and said, *Dad, Brother Archer is not going to commit to baptism and we are busy, so we need to leave.*

With that, she and Doni departed.

When Dennis was asked to make a commitment, he looked at the missionaries and said, "I need to talk to Bishop Burns, first."

Bishop Burns later told me that Dennis did not make the commitment because he wanted either to travel to Anaheim, California, where his stepson Elder Jim Ashment was serving, and be baptized in that mission, or wait until Elder Ashment finished his mission and have Jim baptize him in Las Vegas.

Bishop Burns explained to Brother Archer the impossibility of the first request and told him that one never should put off the Ordinances of Salvation. Dennis agreed and was baptized the next week.

I forever will be grateful for the thinness of the veil and the missionary effort that is correlated on both sides.

MEMORIAL SERVICES

George Frederick Veit

Memorial Service
for
George Frederick Veit, Jr.
October 1, 1955
to
February 3, 1998

Talk Delivered on February 7, 1998
By: President Richard B. Whitaker, First Counselor, Nevada
Las Vegas Mission

"I am a child of God. / Rich blessings are in store; / If I but learn to do his will / I'll live with him once more. / Lead me, guide me, / walk beside me, help me find the way. / Teach me all that I must do / to live with Him some day."

These are simple words to a sweet song, but a song loved and doctrinally understood by Brother George Veit.

As we gathered today in the Relief Society Room preparatory to this service, I stood with close friends and members of the family while they shed tears and expressed feelings of love and sadness. Yet, as I stood there, the Spirit bore witness to me that even with the deep feelings of loss experienced, the level of rejoicing on the other side of the veil was a thousand times greater for one noble and great who had returned home honorably.

I also reflected on an experience I had Wednesday night after visiting Sheral and the children. It was late when I left their home, and as I walked out of the house into the crisp night air, suddenly from out of the silence came a very familiar voice that simply said: Thank you, President.

You're welcome, George.

I zipped up my jacket and headed for home.

Many years ago when I was a very young man, I was asked to serve as a pall bearer for one of my closest friends, a fifteen year old boy named Steven Arthur Smith. Steven, like George Veit, was a faithful member of the church, was loved by many and would be greatly missed. The weight and impact of that solemn occasion has remained with me for these many years and again, today, I feel that responsibility as I address family and friends who are gathered at this memorial service for our dear friend and loved one, Brother George Frederick Veit, Jr.

At this time I ask for your prayers, and I request that the Spirit of the Lord rest upon me so that those things said might be of comfort, not only to those who sit today in this vast congregation, but also to those who have been permitted to join with us and attend in the spirit.

Following Tuesday's tragic events, I went to the Wray home to meet with Sister Sheral Veit and other members of the family. At that time, Sheral related to me a comment made by their daughter, Rachael, when someone mentioned her daddy. "Oh my

daddy's not coming home," she said, "he's with Heavenly Father."
Out of the mouths of babes, those so pure and close to the Lord,
often comes wisdom and understanding far beyond their
capabilities. This little one in particular, so young in mortal
years, yet for whom the veil is still thin, understands one of the
most important doctrines of eternity.

The death of a beloved husband, father and righteous son of
God changes the lives of many. The passing of George Veit has
done just that. Although not on this earth the biblical three score
and ten years, his work has been completed, and I have a firm
testimony that a call was issued, accepted and one noble and great
was needed on the other side of the veil even more than he was
needed on this side by friends and family. And because of this
call, Brother Veit will be recognized throughout all eternity as a
very special, righteous son of God and servant of the Lord Jesus
Christ.

Long before Brother Veit came to this earth to reside in
mortality, as a spirit son of God he was raised in a heavenly
home. He walked with, talked to and was nurtured by a loving
Father in Heaven. Also there was one who would have an eternal
influence on him: the Lord and Savior, Jesus Christ; First Born
of the Father in the preexistence; He who would be the Only
Begotten of the Father in the flesh.

Brother Veit knew his Savior well and loved him deeply.
This is evident in the life he lived and the Christ-like example he
always set. In the preexistence, he was taught the Plan of
Salvation, that Great Plan of Happiness presented by God the

Eternal Father to all His spirit children, the plan that outlined the course required in mortality if they were to return to Father's presence and again live with Him, that wonderful plan that outlined the Creation, the Fall, the Atonement of the Lord Jesus Christ, and the Resurrection. As Brother Veit was taught that wonderful plan, so were we all, and it was accepted by each of us.

For some time, I had the privilege of serving with George in various callings in the church. As we served together, I marveled at the childlike faith he exhibited no matter what the calling or how difficult the assignment. I recall on one occasion receiving a call from Bishop Burns.

"President," he said, "I have a problem and the Spirit has directed me to call you. I cannot go to the individual's home because of a work conflict. Will you go?"

"Yes Bishop," I said, "but what is the problem?"

"I don't know," he responded, "but you need to go to the following address and under the direction of the Lord, you will know what to do."

Under the direction of the Spirit, I called Brother Veit who was serving as the Ward Mission Leader in the Morning Sun Ward.

"Brother Veit, we have an assignment from the Bishop. I don't know what it is. I don't know who it is with, nor do I

know what we will find when we get there. I would like you to dress and meet me at the church as soon as possible."

"I'm on my way, President!" Brother Veit didn't hesitate a moment.

We met at the church, found a vacant room and knelt in prayer. After pleading to the Lord for direction, we were on our way. As we drove, I reflected on how grateful I was to be upon my Father's business and on my Lord's errand with one so humble and obedient. Upon our arrival at the home, the Spirit assisted us in knowing what direction to take.

Because of my other responsibilities, the follow up was left to Brother Veit. He organized the ensuing work with the family and full-time missionaries. With the combined efforts of a loving ward and capable Bishop, a daughter of God, who had left church activity thirty years earlier, returned to activity. Her nonmember husband eventually was baptized, and one year later, they were sealed in the House of the Lord for time and all eternity. The worth of souls is great in the sight of God. George Veit knew this only too well.

As we served together, I constantly marveled at the love he had for the Savior and his deep appreciation for what I consider to be the greatest event that ever will transpire on this earth or any other; the Atonement of our Lord and Savior Jesus Christ. Allow me to share with you some of the doctrines that so deeply impacted the thoughts, speech and actions of Brother George Veit.

(Briefly describe the Atonement beginning with the last Thursday of the Saviors life…then:

1. *The Last Supper*
2. *The Betrayal of Christ by Judas Iscariot*
3. *The Ordeal of Gethsemane*
4. *The Arrest*
5. *The Three Illegal Trials before the Jews*
    a. *Before Annas*
    b. *Before Caiaphas and members of the Sanhedrin*
    c. *Being taken to the small guard room in the Hall of Judgment and beaten and spit upon*
    d. *Before the Sanhedrin*
6. *Before Pilate*
7. *Before Herod Antipas*
8. *Again to Pilate*
9. *The Scourging*
10. *Crucify Him! Crucify Him! Cried the Jews*
11. *The Crucifixion*
    a. *The Seven Utterances*
    b. *His death*
12. *His glorious resurrection and the jubilant call that went forth: "He is risen…He is risen."*

Brother Veit understood that for the fullness of the Atonement to be in place in one's life, it required that they exercise Faith in the Lord Jesus Christ, truly repent of all their sins, be baptized by immersion for the remission of sins, and receive the Gift of the Holy Ghost by the laying on of hands.

He further understood the requirement that when all this had been accomplished, it was necessary to endure to the end, always remembering the commandment: "Thou shalt love the Lord thy God with all thy heart, might, mind and strength, and love thy neighbor as thyself."

I never have known any man who understood that doctrine better or lived it more fully than Brother Veit.

George loved missionary work, and he loved the missionaries. Many sister missionaries called Bro. Veit for help and were met with a simple, "What do you need, Sister?" They would then go on to explain that they had run out of gas, had a flat tire, the brakes were bad, or they had locked the keys in the mission vehicle. Whenever requested, Brother Veit responded to assist the Lord's anointed. He also understood the statement by the Savior when He said, "...the thing which will be of the most worth unto you will be to declare repentance unto this people, that you may bring souls unto me, that you may rest with them in the kingdom of my Father."

Together, Brother Veit and I visited many homes, and in each he shared his beautiful testimony of the divinity of this great and marvelous latter-day work.

Although he never had the opportunity to serve a full-time mission in his youth, the opportunity now has been provided, for we are told that, "...the faithful elders of this dispensation, when they depart from mortal life, continue their labors in the preaching of the gospel of repentance and redemption through the sacrifice of the Only begotten Son of God, among those who are in darkness and under the bondage of sin in the great world of the spirits of the dead."

To those on the other side to whom he is sent, Brother George Veit now will be known as Elder Veit, and throughout eternity, he will stand as a savior on Mount Zion to the many he visits who did not have the wonderful opportunity to hear the Gospel of Jesus Christ while they lived in mortality.

Yes, a very special son of God was sent to this earth, accepted the Gospel of Jesus Christ, was obedient to the commandments, served his fellowmen and set such an example that his Savior issued to him a new call and change of assignment.

Yes, the Lord issued a call for one to serve in another area of the vineyard. We must remember that God is no respecter of persons. Our Father in Heaven wants all of his children to have the opportunity to hear the Gospel of Jesus Christ, and for this to happen, it must be preached by his servants not only in mortality, but also in the spirit world.

Has not the Lord told us in reference to both sides of the veil that, "Behold the field is white already to harvest, and lo, he that thrusteth in his sickle with his might, the same layeth up in store that he perisheth not but bringeth salvation to his soul." The Savior knew that the call would, without hesitation, be accepted, for Brother Veit took great delight in being obedient with exactness.

For Sheral, his eternal companion, the children, friends and loved ones, the gateway we call death is not a passage of dark despair and gloom, but rather it is a gateway that has opened within each of us a greater understanding of the Plan of Salvation. It answered the eternal questions of Who am I? Where did I come from? And where am I going? And it has planted within each of us a greater resolve to live as the Savior has directed so that we too can be together as eternal families.

Although to some it would appear that the life of Brother Veit prematurely was cut short, we always must remember that the Savior has told us that, "...thy days are known, and thy years shall not be numbered less; Therefore, fear not what man can do, for God shall be with you forever and ever."

George understood that in this life we were to be tested and tried to see if we would do all things the Lord commanded. He knew that this often required that we as families and individuals, would be called upon to suffer the pain and endure the grief associated with the loss of a dear friend and loved one.

Repeatedly, as I have served in the Kingdom, I have seen this occur. As a change of assignment came suddenly to Brother Veit and will have an eternal impact on his family, so it happened to our family when a daughter was called home to serve her mission in the spirit world rather than remain in mortality.

It occurred on Sunday, May 10th, 1992, Mother's Day. A day when we as a family would receive a knock on our door and be informed that our nineteen year old daughter Rebecca had been killed that morning in a traffic accident just outside of Nephi, Utah. As a family, we understand the pain and grief associated with the loss of a loved one. We also as parents, like Brother and Sister Veit and others in this room, understand that death is but an event that is required if we are to continue on our eternal journey back to the presence of our Father in Heaven.

With the loss of one as special as George, we must grieve. We must feel the pain of loss and the afflictions associated with this separation. Tears must be shed, for tears not only reflect the deep feelings of loss, but also reveal the closeness of the Spirit of the Lord and act as a healing agent as they soothe our soul and allow us to express our deepest feelings of grief.

Orson F. Whitney wrote of the instructional value of affliction when he said, "No pain that we suffer, no trial that we experience is wasted. It ministers to our education, to the development of such qualities as patience, faith, fortitude and humility. All that we suffer and all that we endure, especially when we endure it patiently, builds our characters, purifies our hearts, expands our souls, makes us more tender and charitable, more worthy to be called the children of God…and it is through sorrow and suffering, toil and tribulation, that we gain the education that we came here to acquire which will make us more like our Father in Heaven."

While it is important to remember that spiritually mature and valiant men of God often are called by their Creator to return home at a time we consider to be premature, we also must remember that they often have proven to the Lord their worthiness and level of obedience and have accomplished all He sent them here to do. Is it not true that His time is not our time, and His ways are not our ways, and His thoughts are not our thoughts? For Brother Veit and other extraordinary men like him, we learn that there is no premature death for a righteous individual. Death only can be premature if the person is not prepared to meet his or her maker.

We are taught by the scriptures and by our holy prophets that the family is the most important unit in eternity. George and Sheral each have a deep understanding of that sacred truth, although we each feel a deep loss today, and we should, for we have surrendered a noble redwood in the forest of mortality, we each must also place our trust in a loving Father in Heaven.

Our Father in Heaven has promised a special reward for those who endure these losses and suffer in silence, who spend long days and longer nights shedding tears of bereavement. The Lord has promised, "For after much tribulation, come the blessings. Wherefore the day cometh that ye shall be crowned with much glory; the hour is not yet, but is nigh at hand." For are we not also told that we "receive no witness until after the trial of our Faith."

This promised glory includes the blessing of reunion of a loving husband and father with each family member.

So now the responsibility rests with each of us to review our standing with our Savior and if necessary, place our lives in order so that we too, might receive our heritage with the Lord.

We also must remember that the veil of death is thin. To each of us, our loved ones who have passed may be just as close as the room nearby, separated only by the gateway to immortality and eternal life.

As Children of God, we have not been placed on this earth to tread life's pathways alone. True, we must be tested, tried and proven worthy. Yes, we will feel the loss when one as noble and great as Brother George Veit is called home, but we can be soothed by the Savior's love, and His words, "Peace I leave with you. My peace I give unto you, not as the world giveth, give I unto you. Let not your heart be troubled, neither let it be afraid." And He further has promised, "I will not leave you comfortless." This wonderful family that sits before me today understands this eternal principle, for in their life, the Holy Ghost not only bears witness of truth, but also provides comfort in this, their great hour of need.

As a servant of God, I leave upon each of you a blessing. Upon Sheral and the children, I bless you with the comfort that comes through faith in our Lord and Savior Jesus Christ, faith that bears witness to the soul of the truth that, "...and should we die / before our journey's through/ Happy day!/ all is well!/ We then are free /from toil and sorrow too/ With the just we shall dwell...."

As a representative of the Lord Jesus Christ, I testify that "All is well!"

I further testify that if Brother Veit were allowed to speak to us today, I am confident that his final words would be, "I have gone to the place of my rest, which is with my Redeemer; for I know that in him I shall rest. And I rejoice in the day when my mortal shall put on immortality, and shall stand before him; then shall I see his face with pleasure, and he will say unto me: Come unto me, ye blessed, there is a place prepared for you in the mansions of my Father."

Of these things I humbly testify, in the name of Jesus Christ, Amen.

Valeri Elizabeth Patton

Valeri Elizabeth Patton
January 9, 1996
To
March 9, 1997

Delivered on March 13, 1997
By: President Richard B. Whitaker, First Counselor, Nevada
Las Vegas Mission

"Oh, My Father, are words that bring comfort to my soul and joy to my heart.

As I was standing in the hallway just before the service began, a wonderful little boy by the name of Nathaniel Patton stopped me, looked into my eyes and said, "My sister is gone up to heaven!" Out of the mouths of babes....

Many years ago as a small boy, I was asked to offer a prayer at the graveside of my little sister who passed away just after birth. I still remember the impact of that occasion and the special request. With the simple humility and sincerity of a young child, and oblivious to those gathered around, I knelt at that grave and with all of my heart, called upon my Father in Heaven to bless my sister, Doni. The weight and impact of that solemn occasion has remained with me over the years and again, today, I feel the responsibility I have as I address family and friends gathered at this memorial service for Valeri Elizabeth Patton.

I would ask you for your prayers and request that the Spirit of the Lord rest upon me so that those things said might be of comfort, not only to those who are here with us today, but also to those who are here in spirit.

The death of a small one moves and changes the lives of many, and Valeri Patton has done just that. Although only on this earth for a very brief period of time, her work here has been completed. She was, and continues to be a very special, righteous, daughter of God.

Long before she came to this earth to reside in mortality, as a spirit daughter of God, Valeri walked and talked with her Father in Heaven. He taught her; He nurtured her; He loved her. She also knew well and loved deeply her Savior, Jesus Christ. She was taught the Plan of Salvation; that great plan presented by God our Eternal Father who outlined the course required in mortality that His children must follow if they were to return to His presence; that wonderful plan which outlined the Creation, the Fall, The Atonement and the Resurrection. And, as Valeri was taught this wonderful plan, so were each of us.

Although this precious little girl was not with us long, she has had a great impact on many lives, and her passing has brought her earthly parents face to face with life, death and our Father in Heaven's Plan of Salvation.

A number of months ago, in the capacity of serving in the mission presidency, I had the opportunity to sit with Brother Patton as he prepared himself for baptism. His spirit was sweet and humble. He expressed to me the love that he had for his beloved wife and children, and especially how grateful he was for the time given to him and Sister Patton to have Valeri in their home. He never complained, but only expressed thanks to his Father in Heaven and the Savior for allowing this wonderful spirit to leave their presence and reside in his home. He told me of the great sacrifices required, but especially, those made by his wife. He talked about how she endured many long hours without sleep or rest, but never complained. He also told me how this experience had brought them closer as a family, closer to each other and closer to their Savior. During our time together, with tears in his eyes, referred to Valeri as his, "Gift from God."

As we sat and talked, knowing the nature of Valeri's illness, I had the opportunity to share with Brother Patton what I consider to be the greatest event that ever will transpire on this or any other earth: the Atonement of our Lord and Savior Jesus Christ. Allow me now to share with you some of what we discussed.

(Briefly describe the Atonement).

1. *The Last Supper*
2. *The Betrayal of Christ by Judas Iscariot*
3. *The Ordeal of Gethsemane*
4. *The Arrest*
5. *The Three Illegal Trials before the Jews*
   a. *Before Annas*
   b. *Before Caiaphas and members of the Sanhedrin*
   c. *Being taken to the small guard room in the Hall of Judgment and beaten and spit upon*

   d. *Before the Sanhedrin*
6. *Before Pilate*
7. *Before Herod Antipas*
8. *Again to Pilate*
9. *The Scourging*
10. *Crucify Him! Crucify Him! Cried the Jews*
11. *The Crucifixion*
   a. *The Seven Utterances*
   b. *His death*
12. *His glorious resurrection and the jubilant call that went forth: "He is risen…He is risen."*

The Atonement of Christ fully covers those children who die and have not arrived at the years of accountability, as was Valeri, and all such will be raised in immortality and eternal life.

The illness that eventually claimed the life of Valeri influenced many individuals for good, both directly and indirectly. In her brief stay on this earth, she strengthened our faith in Jesus Christ; she expanded our Hope in the Atonement of the Savior and our hope in a glorious resurrection. And in her own special way, she testified of Charity-the pure love of Christ, exhibited by many as they responded to her needs and the needs of her family. This special little spirit blessed the lives of many, for as they were able to provide service, the Lord opened the windows of heaven, and in turn, they were blessed.

For Brother and Sister Patton, the gateway we call death is not a passage of dark despair and gloom. Rather, it is a gateway that has opened within them a greater understanding of the Plan of Salvation and a resolve to live as the Savior has directed so they can be together as an eternal family.

Yes, a special daughter of God came to this earth, received a small, frail, mortal body, was tested to that degree required by her Father in Heaven and then returned home.

The Prophet Joseph Smith taught that, "The Lord takes these special spirits home to Him early, as if to spare them some of the weighty trials that mortality would have brought."

Repeatedly, as I have served in the Kingdom, I have seen this happen. As it happened to Tony and Mayla, so it happened to our family, when a daughter was called home to serve her mission in the spirit world rather than mortality.

It occurred on Sunday, May 10th, 1992, Mother's Day. A day when we as a family would receive a knock on our door and be informed that our nineteen year old daughter Rebecca had been killed that morning in a traffic accident just outside of Nephi, Utah. As parents and as a family, we understand the pain and grief associated with the loss of a child. We also as parents, like the Patton's, the Burns and others in this room, understand that death is but an event that is required if we are to continue on our eternal journey back to the presence of our Father in Heaven.

With the loss of one so special, we must grieve. Tears must be shed, for tears not only reflect the deep feelings of loss, but also reveal the closeness of the Spirit of the Lord, and they act as a healing agent as they soothe our soul and allow us to express our deepest feelings of grief

It is important to remember that spiritually mature and sensitive children often are called home prematurely by their Creator, (that is according to human criteria) to pass through the gateway to immortality and eternal life.

The Prophet Joseph Smith expressed himself on this subject when he said: "The Lord takes many away, even in infancy, that they may escape the envy of man, and the sorrows and evils of the present world. They were too pure, too lovely, to live on earth; therefore, if rightly considered, instead of mourning, we have every reason to rejoice as they are delivered from evil, and soon shall have them again." He further explained, "All children are redeemed by the blood of Christ. The only difference between the old and young dying is, one lives longer in heaven and eternal light and glory than the other."

For Valeri and other extraordinary children like her, we learn that there is no premature death for a righteous individual. Death only can be premature if the person is not prepared to meet his or her Maker.

How deep the love is that our Father has for these little ones. He expressed this when he said, "Little children are redeemed from the foundation of the world through mine Only Begotten; wherefore, they cannot sin, for power is not given unto Satan to tempt little children, until they begin to become accountable before me; for it is given unto them even as I will, according to mine own pleasure."

Elder Bruce R. McConkie, an Apostle of the Lord Jesus Christ further stated: "Little children shall be saved. They are alive in Christ and shall have eternal life. For them the family unit will continue, and the fullness of exaltation is theirs. No blessing is withheld. They shall rise in immortal glory, to grow to full maturity, and live forever in the highest heaven of the Celestial Kingdom."

Although I for one know of the grief endured with the loss of a child, I also know that, "the mother who laid down her little child, being deprived of the privilege, the joy, and the satisfaction of bringing it up to manhood or womanhood in this world, would after the resurrection, have all the joy, satisfaction and pleasure, and even more than it would have been possible to have had in mortality, in seeing her child grow to the full measure of the stature of its spirit."

And so we are taught by the scriptures and by our holy prophets that the family is the most important unit in eternity. Brother and Sister Patton understand this sacred truth, and although they, with other family members and friends feel a deep loss today, and they should, for they have surrendered the sweetest and smallest flower from the family's garden, they also have placed their trust in a loving Father in Heaven.

Our Father in Heaven has promised a special reward for those who endure these losses and suffer in silence, who spend long days and longer nights shedding tears of bereavement. The Lord has promised, "For after much tribulation, come the blessings. Wherefore the day cometh that ye shall be crowned with much glory; the hour is not yet, but is nigh at hand."

This promised glory includes the blessing of reunion with each little child who has left the family circle early. Those small children still live and are an heritage of the Lord, so now the responsibility rests with each of us to review our standing with our Savior and if necessary, place our lives in order so that we too, might receive our heritage with the Lord.

The veil of death is thin. To each of us, our loved ones who have passed may be just as close as the room nearby, separated only by the gateway to immortality and eternal life.

As children of God, we have not been placed on this earth to tread life's pathways alone. True, we must be tested, tried and proven worthy. Yes, we will feel the loss when one so young and dear is called home, but we can be soothed by the Savior's love: "Peace I leave with you." He said. "My peace I give unto you, not as the world giveth, give I unto you. Let not your heart be troubled, neither let it be afraid." And He further has promised: "I will not leave you comfortless."

Brother and Sister Patton understand this wonderful truth, for in their lives, the Holy Ghost not only bears witness of truth, but also provides comfort in this, their great hour of need.

As a servant of God, I leave upon each of you a blessing. Upon Brother and Sister Patton, I bless you with the comfort that comes through faith in Jesus Christ; a Faith that bears witness to the soul that "all is well." Again, Brother and Sister Patton, "All is well."

Of these things I humbly testify, in the name of Jesus Christ, Amen.

WHITAKERISM'S

Whitakerism's

During my five years in the Nevada Las Vegas Mission presidency, I was known to toss out a morsel or two of homespun wisdom, often even surprising myself. Here are a few I used.

"Preparation is the key to proper implementation!"

"All it takes is a phone call, Elder!"

"Talk's cheap, and small change rides the bus!"

"Brethren, let's all get on the same page of the hymn book!"

"Don't dance with me, Elder!"

"Excuses don't alter performance!"

"If the kitchen gets too hot, get out!"

"When you play, you pay!"

"Let's get with the program, brethren!"

"Cut me some slack!"

"I'm just a soldier in this army!"

"I know that they do things differently in other stakes....and I don't care!"

"Stay in your own lane, brethren!"

"Play between the lines."

"Teach the people; train the leaders."

"Speak little, listen much, smile, and make every word count!"

"We don't ask for volunteers, we make assignments."

"When the time comes for delivery, the time for preparation is past."

"Don't procrastinate the Ordinances of Salvation."

"Be obedient with exactness."

"I won't poison the well, but I will prime the pump."

"Now Elder, where am I, and where are you?"

"Pray often, listen much and work hard."

"I learn from listening to the Spirit and the Brethren, not by listening to myself talk."

"When expectations are diluted, the sharpest saw soon becomes dull."

"Opposition provides opportunities to perform."

"My opinion on that subject is the same as my president."

"It only takes one and a half seconds!"

"For me, confrontation is the deadliest form of conflict resolution."

"Silence is a deadly sword."

"NO is a complete sentence."

"As a counselor, you are in attendance to be taught, not to teach."

"Counselors in a full-time mission presidency are cannon fodder. They can be replaced in a heartbeat!"

"Remember…in silence there is exhibited a command presence that is not identified with verboseness."

"To volunteer is an act of sacrifice. To accept an assignment and successfully complete it is an act of obedience. And obedience is greater than sacrifice."

"We should rivet ourselves to the doctrines of Jesus Christ."

"Develop a oneness of mind with your Mission President."

"Always stay in character."

"We tend to look for excuses to justify poor performance."

"Your investigators should be either in the water, or out of the teaching pool."

"I don't care if you love me or like me, just respect me. If you do this, the others will come."

"It is far better to say nothing at all, than to say something stupid."

"Las Vegas is hot, but Hell is hotter. So let's go to work!"

"As the frequency in our voice increases, the persuasiveness of our words decreases."

"Play the tape through to the end."

"Prior preparation prevents poor performance."

"He who doesn't count, doesn't care."

"As your physical appetites decrease—and your self-control increases—your level of spirituality will accelerate."

"When performance is measured, performance improves. When performance is measured and reported, the rate of improvement accelerates." Thomas S. Monson

Richard B. Whitaker

To be continued...

Made in the USA
San Bernardino, CA
13 August 2017